TREATING
COMPLEX TRAUMA
in Adolescents
and Young Adults

TREATING COMPLEX TRAUMA
in Adolescents
and Young Adults

John N. Briere
University of Southern California,
Keck School of Medicine, Los Angeles

Cheryl B. Lanktree
Private Practice

Los Angeles | London | New Delhi
Singapore | Washington DC

Los Angeles | London | New Delhi
Singapore | Washington DC

FOR INFORMATION:

SAGE Publications, Inc.
2455 Teller Road
Thousand Oaks, California 91320
E-mail: order@sagepub.com

SAGE Publications Ltd.
1 Oliver's Yard
55 City Road
London EC1Y 1SP
United Kingdom

SAGE Publications India Pvt. Ltd.
B 1/I 1 Mohan Cooperative Industrial Area
Mathura Road, New Delhi 110 044
India

SAGE Publications Asia-Pacific Pte. Ltd.
33 Pekin Street #02-01
Far East Square
Singapore 048763

Acquisitions Editor: Kassie Graves
Editorial Assistant: Courtney Munz
Production Editor: Kelle Schillaci
Copy Editor: Mark Bast
Typesetter: C&M Digitals (P) Ltd.
Proofreader: Joyce Li
Indexer: Maria Sosnowski
Cover Designer: Candice Harman
Marketing Manager: Katharine Winter
Permissions Editor: Adele Hutchinson

Copyright © 2012 by SAGE Publications, Inc.

Printed in the United States of America

Library of Congress Cataloging-in-Publication Data

Briere, John.

Treating complex trauma in adolescents and young adults / John N. Briere, Cheryl B. Lanktree.

p. cm.
Includes bibliographical references and index.

ISBN 978-1-4129-8144-6 (pbk.: alk. paper)

1. Post-traumatic stress disorder in adolescence—Treatment. 2. Family therapy. I. Lanktree, Cheryl. II. Title.
[DNLM: 1. Stress Disorders, Post-Traumatic— therapy. 2. Adolescent. 3. Family Therapy. 4. Psychotherapy, Group. 5. Young Adult. WM 172]

RJ506.P55B746 2012
618.92'8521—dc22   2011009800

This book is printed on acid-free paper.

11 12 13 14 15 10 9 8 7 6 5 4 3 2 1

Contents

Acknowledgments

We would like to acknowledge and thank the many individuals who were involved in the development of the ITCT-A treatment model or worked as ITCT-A therapists. These include former MCAVIC staff (Barbara Adams, Psy.D.; Juan Carlos Aguila, Ph.D.; Lorraine Al-Jamie, M.F.T.; Tracey Burrell, Ph.D.; Laura Benson; Karianne Chen, M.F.T.; Nicole Farrell, M.S.W.; Susana Flores, M.S.; Sara Hernandez, Psy.D.; Jeff McFarland, M.S.; Stephen Neal, Ph.D.; Maria Pannell, Ph.D.; Eric Rainey-Gibson, Ph.D.; Andrea Sward, M.A.; Laurie Trimm, B.S.; and Kathleen Watkins, Ph.D.), the MCAVIC-USC program evaluator and consultant (Carl Maida, Ph.D.), USC Psychological Trauma Program staff and fellows based at MCAVIC (Wendy Freed, M.D.; Natacha Godbout, Ph.D.; and Monica Hodges, Ph.D.), William Saltzman, Ph.D., Patricia Lester, M.D., and the many psychology interns, externs, and volunteers who supported the mission at MCAVIC. We also express appreciation to the MCAVIC-USC Expert Panel on Cultural Issues, including Veronica Abney, Ph.D., L.C.S.W.; Meghan Berthold, Ph.D., L.C.S.W.; Thema Bryant-Davis, Ph.D.; Renda Dion, Ph.D.; and Russell Jones, Ph.D., who provided feedback on the appropriateness of ITCT for different cultural and demographic groups. (Any remaining errors are our own.)

We are further indebted to those clinicians, researchers, and friends who provided support and input on this book at various points in its development. This includes many of the people just thanked, as well as Colleen Friend, Ph.D., L.C.S.W.; Anne Galbraith, M.F.T.; David Kim, M.F.A.; Barbara Maida, Ph.D.; Sebastien Malette, Ph.D.; and Sage Publications reviewers Eric J. Green, Ph.D.; Victoria White Kress, Ph.D.; and Anna Mercedes Caro, Psy.D. We also thank our colleagues at the National Child Traumatic Stress Network, in particular John Fairbank, Ph.D.; Mandy Habib, Psy.D.; Victor LaBruna, Ph.D.; Jenifer Maze, Ph.D.; Robert Pynoos, M.D.; and Alan Steinberg, Ph.D., as well as members of the ITCT Learning Community, for their support.

Special appreciation is due Malcolm Gordon, Ph.D., for his support and feedback as the project officer on our second Substance Abuse and Mental

Health Service Administration (SAMHSA) grant, as well as those governmental and private entities who funded the development, assessment, and application of ITCT-C and ITCT-A, including SAMHSA, U.S. Department of Health and Human Services; Office of Criminal Justice Planning, State of California; UniHealth Foundation; Long Beach Memorial Medical Foundation; In-and-Out Burger Foundation; Mark McGwire Foundation for Children; Ralph M. Parsons Foundation; and the California Community Foundation.

Finally, we thank our various family members, who provided so much caring and support, especially the Brieres (Adelle, Danny, and Eugene), Lanktrees (Beryl, Bruce, Jean, and Roy), and Mansons (Harald and Lynda), as well as the next generation and their partners (Andrew, Allison, Dave, Ethan, James, Tayler, Matt, Laura, Mike, Ellen, Sarah, and Jason).

1

Introduction

This guide has been developed to help clinicians evaluate and treat adolescents and young adults who have experienced repeated, extended, and/or severe traumatization. We take the clinician through the process of assessment, target prioritization, selection of appropriate treatment components, and the actual conduct of therapy. The approach described in this book, *Integrative Treatment of Complex Trauma for Adolescents* (ITCT-A), is inherently customizable: its various treatment components are meant to be adapted to the specific history, symptoms, and problems experienced by each given client. Yet, although it does not assume that "one size fits all," it provides a specific, organized approach to the treatment of complex trauma, regardless of which components are ultimately applied. In the appendices of this book are various forms, handouts, and group treatment examples that will assist the clinician in using ITCT-A with his or her clients. Some of these materials are also available at no charge at *johnbriere.com* in a slightly larger format.

Background

Complex trauma usually involves a combination of early and late-onset, sometimes highly invasive traumatic events, usually of an ongoing, interpersonal nature, frequently including exposure to repetitive childhood sexual, physical, and/or psychological abuse (Briere & Scott, 2006; Cook et al., 2005). As described in Chapter 2, the impacts of complex trauma are substantial, ranging from anxiety and depression to posttraumatic stress, interpersonal problems, and dysfunctional or self-endangering behaviors.

1

Especially as they present themselves in mental health clinics, schools, hospitals, and residential treatment contexts, complex trauma effects are often complicated by adverse social circumstances. Social and economic deprivation—as well as racism, sexism, homophobia, and homelessness—not only produce their own negative effects on children and adults (e.g., Bassuk et al., 2003; Carter, 2007), but also increase the likelihood of trauma exposure and often intensify the effects of such victimization (e.g., Breslau, Wilcox, Storr, Lucia, & Anthony, 2004; Chen, Keith, Airriess, Wei, & Leong, 2007). Social marginalization also means that many traumatized youth have reduced access to appropriate mental health services (e.g., McKay, Lynn, & Bannon, 2005; Perez & Fortuna, 2005; Rayburn et al., 2005).

It is a general finding of the clinical literature that people with lesser social status are more likely than others to be victimized (Briere & Scott, 2006). Among the traumas more common among those with lower socioeconomic status, in addition to child abuse, neglect, and witnessing domestic violence, are sexual and physical assaults by peers, gang or community violence, "drive-by" shootings, robbery, sexual exploitation through prostitution, trauma associated with refugee status, and loss associated with the murder of a family member or friend (e.g., Berthold, 2000; Breslau, Davis, & Andreski, 1991; Farley, 2003; Giaconia et al., 1995; Macbeth, Sugar, & Pataki, 2009; Schwab-Stone et al., 1995; Singer, Anglin, Song, & Lunghofer, 1995; Sugar & Ford, in progress).

However, despite the prevalence of complex trauma in economically deprived and socially marginalized youth, it is also true that higher-socioeconomic-status adolescents are not protected from abuse and neglect by parents and other caretakers, nor are more-advantaged schools and social environments free of interpersonal violence by adults or other young people. Noteworthy is the prevalence of sexual and physical abuse among those of higher socioeconomic status (e.g., Smikle, Satin, Dellinger, & Hankins, 1995) and the substantial risk of sexual victimization for girls and young women in university or college (Fisher, Cullen, & Turner, 2000). Even in economically less-impacted neighborhoods, adolescents run significant risk of physical assault, threats of harm, and gang activity (Singer et al., 1995). The potential presence of violence and maltreatment at all socioeconomic levels and in all cultural or ethnic groups highlights a point we will make multiple times in this book: child abuse, peer assaults, and other forms of trauma are broadly prevalent in North America and elsewhere; no child, adolescent, or young adult is necessarily exempt from such experiences, and the effects of such maltreatment permeate our entire society.

Unfortunately, although complex trauma and its effects are common, there are few empirically informed treatments specifically developed for multiply traumatized children or adolescents. This is partially due to the challenging nature of the problem—the range of these impacts often requires a multimodal, multicomponent treatment strategy. Treatment approaches that are limited to a single modality (e.g., exposure therapy, cognitive therapy, or psychiatric medication) can sometimes be insufficient—especially if the intervention approach is not adapted to the specific experiences, psychological needs, and cultural matrix of the affected youth.

The MCAVIC-USC Experiment

This book describes an integrated, multicomponent approach to the psychological and social issues faced by young people exposed to complex trauma. It is an adaptation and expansion of a treatment model developed by a joint project of the Miller Children's Abuse and Violence Intervention Center (MCAVIC) at Miller Children's Hospital, Long Beach, California, and the Psychological Trauma Program of the University of Southern California, Department of Psychiatry and the Behavioral Sciences—hereafter referred to as the MCAVIC-USC Child and Adolescent Trauma Program. This four-year (2005–2009) experiment in providing culturally relevant, multidisciplinary outreach and treatment services to multiply traumatized, socially marginalized youth, was supported by the U.S. Substance Abuse and Mental Health Administration, who funded MCAVIC-USC as a Category II Center of the National Child Traumatic Stress Network (NCTSN). The resultant treatment model, Integrative Treatment of Complex Trauma, has been adapted for two different age groups: *ITCT for Adolescents (ITCT-A)* and *ITCT for Children (ITCT-C)*, the first of which is the focus of this book. Both ITCT-C and ITCT-A guides were adapted and revised over the lifetime of this project, with input from MCAVIC and USC staff, members of MCAVIC-USC's Expert Panel of Cultural Issues, members of the community, and attendees from a nationwide NCTSN Learning Community on ITCT. Recent analyses of treatment outcome data indicate the efficacy of both ITCT-C and ITCT-A, as presented in Chapter 21 and Lanktree et al. (2010).

Overview of ITCT-A

The core components of the adolescent version of ITCT include the following:

- *Assessment-driven treatment*, using an interview-based symptom review measure (the Assessment-Treatment Flowchart [ATF; see Chapter 4]) and, when possible, trauma-specific tests, administered at three-month intervals

- *Attention to complex trauma issues*, including posttraumatic stress, behavioral and affect dysregulation, and interpersonal difficulties
- *Customization*, involving application of different treatment components for each client, based on his or her own particular history, needs, symptoms, and cultural context
- *Multiple treatment modalities*, including cognitive therapy, exposure therapy, affect regulation training, and relational treatment in individual, group, and caretaker therapy
- *Focus on a positive working relationship with the therapist*, deemed crucial to the success of therapy for complex trauma
- *Attention to attachment difficulties* associated with early, developmental trauma
- *Cultural adaptations* of treatment components to maximize their relevance to clients from different social and ethnocultural groups
- *Early focus on immediate issues* such as acute crisis and self-endangering behaviors
- *Skills development,* in terms of building emotional regulation and problem-solving capacities
- *Titrated therapeutic exposure and exploration of trauma* within a developmentally appropriate and safe context, balanced with attention to the client's existing affect regulation capacities
- *Advocacy and interventions at the system level* to establish healthier functioning and to address safety concerns
- A *flexible time frame* for treatment, since the multiproblem nature of complex trauma sometimes precludes short-term therapy

Because this multimodal treatment takes into account a range of psychological, social, and cultural issues, its effectiveness rests on the therapist's previous training, skill, sensitivity, creativity, and openness to the client. Although specific interventions and activities are described here, this is not a "how-to" manual. Instead, we offer a semistructured approach that can be adapted on a case-by-case basis by the therapist in order to meet the youth or young adult's specific developmental level, psychological functioning, and cultural/ethnic background.

SECTION I

Complex Trauma Outcomes and Assessment

2

Complex Trauma in Adolescence and Young Adulthood

I n this chapter, we provide a brief overview of the social context and psychological outcomes associated with complex trauma in adolescents and young adults. Most traumatized youth will not experience all of the difficulties described here; many, nevertheless, will encounter a significant combination of adverse effects. More detailed discussions of the psychosocial contexts and effects of complex trauma relevant to adolescents and others can be found in Briere and Spinazzola (2005), Cook et al. (2005), and Courtois and Ford (2009).

Risk and Endangerment

Although many of the effects of trauma exposure are chronic in nature, and may not require rapid intervention, others are more severe and potentially endanger the client's immediate well-being, if not his or her life. Some of these issues reflect the youth's environment; his or her victimization may be ongoing, as opposed to solely in the past, and his or her social context may continue to be invalidating or dangerous. Other issues may involve the impact of trauma on the client's personality, internal experience, and relationships with others: he or she may be suicidal, abusing major substances, or involved in various forms of risky behavior.

Environmental Risks

When complex trauma has occurred within the context of socioeconomic deprivation or social marginalization, it is unlikely that conditions will have changed substantially at the time of treatment. The adolescent who was abused in the context of caretaker neglect or nonsupport, or who was assaulted as a result of gang activity—and who lives with poverty, inadequate schools, social discrimination, and/or hard-to-access medical and psychological resources—is often struggling not only with a trauma history and social deprivation, but also with the likelihood of future adversities. The fact that negative economic and social conditions increase the risk of interpersonal victimization has direct implications for treatment: as we will discuss later in this guide, optimal assistance to such youth often requires not only effective therapy, but also advocacy, collaboration, and systems intervention (e.g., Saxe, Ellis, & Kaplow, 2007).

The traumatized adolescent's environment also may be noteworthy for the continued presence of those involved in his or her victimization. If the client was sexually or physically victimized by an adult or peer, there is often little reason to assume that the danger from such individuals has passed. Hate crimes such as assaults on minorities, the homeless, and gay, lesbian, or transgendered youth may not stop merely because law enforcement has been notified. As is true for adverse social conditions, the continued presence of perpetrators in the adolescent's environment may require the clinician to do more than render treatment—ultimately, the primary concern is the client's immediate safety.

Self-Endangerment

In addition to dangers present in the social and physical environment, the adolescent may engage in behaviors that threaten his or her own safety. Although the youth may appear to be "acting out," "self-destructive," "borderline," or "conduct-disordered," these behaviors often represent adaptations to, or effects of, prior victimization (Runtz & Briere, 1986; Singer et al., 1995).

The primary self-endangering behaviors seen in youth suffering from complex trauma exposure are suicidal behavior, intentional (but nonsuicidal) self-injury, major substance abuse, eating disorders, dysfunctional sexual behavior, excessive risk-taking, and involvement in physical altercations (Briere & Spinazzola, 2005; Cook et al., 2005). The traumatized adolescent or young adult may not only seek out violent ways to externalize distress, but also may be further traumatized when others fight back (e.g., the aggression-retaliation cycle associated with gang activity) or may become involved in the juvenile justice system, with its own potential negative effects. He or she also may experience less obviously endangering relational difficulties, such as poor sexual-romantic choices and inadequate self-protection—including passivity or dissociation —in the face of dangerous others.

Some of these difficulties involve what is referred to in the literature as *revictimization*: those who were severely maltreated as children have an elevated risk of also being assaulted later in life (Classen, Palesh, & Aggarwal, 2005). This phenomenon can result in a scenario well known to clinicians who work with traumatized youth: the abused and/or neglected child may, as he or she matures, engage in various activities and defenses (e.g., substance abuse, dysfunctional sexual behavior, or aggression) as a way to reduce posttraumatic distress, only to have such coping strategies ultimately lead to even more victimization and, perhaps, even more self-endangering behavior (e.g., Koenig, Doll, O'Leary, & Pequegnat, 2004). In this regard, self-endangerment—as well as dangerous environments—requires the clinician to focus on safety as much as symptom remission and increased capacities.

Longer-Term Trauma Outcomes

In addition to immediate endangerment, many adolescent trauma survivors suffer the chronic, ongoing psychological effects of previous adverse experiences. Arising from traumas that may have begun in early childhood (e.g., abuse) and continued into adolescence (e.g., victimization by peers or adults), such impacts may emerge as relatively chronic psychological symptoms, sometimes presenting as one or more psychiatric disorders.

In some cases, symptomatic or "acting out" behaviors may represent coping responses to trauma, in which case they are referred to as *tension reduction behaviors* (Briere, 1996a, 2002). Such activities, which include nonsuicidal self-injury and problematic sexual behavior, may serve, in part, as a way for the adolescent to distract, soothe, avoid, or otherwise reduce ongoing or triggered trauma-related dysphoria.

Summary of Lasting Outcomes of Complex Trauma in Adolescents

Whether symptomatology, skill deficits, or maladaptive coping strategies, there are a number of longer-term impacts of childhood and adolescent trauma. The most common and significant of these are the following:

- *Anxiety and depression*, which may range from brief symptom states (e.g., panic attacks or depressed mood) to full-blown disorders

- *Cognitive distortions*, such as extreme helplessness, hopelessness, and low self-esteem

- *Posttraumatic stress*, including reexperiencing symptoms (e.g., flashbacks and nightmares), avoidance behaviors (e.g., avoiding people or situations reminiscent of the trauma) and numbing (reduced emotional reactivity or responsiveness), and autonomic hyperarousal (e.g., hypervigilance, sleep disturbance, and irritability)

- *Dissociation*, including depersonalization, derealization, and disengagement (e.g., "spacing out")

- *Identity disturbance*, including impaired self-awareness, boundary problems, and excessive susceptibility to influence by others

- *Affect dysregulation*, involving a relative inability to tolerate and regulate painful internal states, leading to overwhelming affective experiences

- *Interpersonal problems*, ranging from difficulties in forming positive, stable relationships to repetitive involvement in relationships that are psychologically or physically harmful

- *Substance abuse*, often serving as a way to "self-medicate" or anesthetize trauma-related distress or to induce momentary positive states that briefly reduce underlying dysphoria

- *Self-mutilation*, generally involving nonsuicidal, intentional self-harming behavior (e.g., cutting on the arms or legs, burning self, piercing body parts), as a way to reduce awareness of psychological pain through the distraction of physical pain

- *Bingeing and purging*, either as discrete symptoms (i.e., excessive eating, purging through laxatives, or induced vomiting) or in the context of an eating disorder such as bulimia

- *Unsafe or dysfunctional sexual behavior*, including indiscriminate involvement with multiple sex partners, unsafe sexual behaviors, and the use of sexual activities in the service of emotional avoidance (e.g., self-soothing, distraction from posttraumatic dysphoria)

- *Somatization*, involving excessive preoccupations with bodily dysfunction, in some cases resulting in self-reported somatic symptoms that cannot be explained fully by any medical condition

- *Aggression*, which may arise secondary to trauma-associated anger or that may serve as a way to externalize negative feelings

- *Suicidality*, involving thoughts of killing oneself or actual suicidal behavior

- *Dysfunctional personality traits*, especially involving "conduct disorder," "borderline," or "antisocial" symptoms or behaviors (including many of the problems and issues just listed), which may or may not be diagnosable as a formal personality disorder in older adolescents.

We refer the reader to the following literature reviews for detailed information on these trauma-symptom relationships: Briere, 2004; Briere & Spinazzola, 2009; Cole & Putnam, 1992; Cook et al., 2005; Courtois & Ford, 2009; Herman, Perry, & van der Kolk, 1989; Janoff-Bulman, 1992; Myers et al., 2002; Putnam, 2003; van der Kolk, Roth, Pelcovitz, Sunday, & Spinazzola, 2005.

These various symptoms and coping strategies are sometimes referred to as "complex PTSD" (Herman, 1992), "disorders of extreme stress" (DESNOS; van der Kolk et al., 2005), or as evidence of a "developmental trauma disorder" (van der Kolk, 2005). The breadth and extent of such outcomes generally requires a therapeutic approach that includes multiple treatment modalities and interventions, as opposed to solely, for example, cognitive therapy or therapeutic exposure (Courtois & Ford, 2009). ITCT-A allows the clinician to address these various difficulties in a relatively structured way that is—nevertheless—responsive to the specific clinical presentation and needs of the individual adolescent client.

3

Assessment

As outlined in the last chapter, abused or otherwise traumatized adolescents and young adults may experience a wide range of symptoms and problematic behaviors. The type and extent of these difficulties often vary as a function of the types of trauma the youth has experienced, when in the developmental process they occurred, and their frequency and duration, as well as other biological, psychological, and social variables that might intensify or otherwise moderate the clinical presentation (Briere & Spinazzola, 2005). For this reason, it will rarely be true that any given adolescent or young adult presents with exactly the same clinical picture as any other one. This variability means that the treatment of complex posttraumatic disturbance can only occur after some form of psychological assessment is performed.

In ITCT-A, assessment typically involves collecting information from a number of sources, including the client's self-report, caretaker reports of his or her functioning, collateral reports from caregivers, teachers, and other providers, and psychometric testing. The primary focus of assessment is the adolescent's trauma exposure history and his or her current psychological symptoms or problems. Other types of information may also be collected, however, as needed. This may include the youth's developmental history, primary attachment relationships, child protective services involvement and placement history, current school functioning, history of losses, medical status, coping skills, and environmental stressors such as community violence. It may also be important to assess the psychological functioning of caretakers and other family members.

Evaluation of Current Safety

Most obviously, the first focus of assessment is whether the client is in imminent danger or at risk of hurting others. In cases of ongoing interpersonal violence, it is also very important to determine whether the client is in danger of victimization from others in the immediate future. Most generally, the hierarchy of assessment is as follows:

- Is there danger of imminent injury or death?
- Is the client incapacitated (e.g., through intoxication, illness, brain injury, or psychosis) to the extent that he or she cannot attend to his or her own safety (e.g., wandering into streets or unable to access available food or shelter)?
- Is the client acutely suicidal or a danger to others (e.g., homicidal or making credible threats to harm someone)?
- Is the client's immediate psychosocial environment unsafe (e.g., is he or she immediately vulnerable to maltreatment or exploitation by others)?

The first goal of trauma intervention, when any of these issues is present, is to ensure the physical safety of the client or others, often through referral or triage to emergency medical or psychiatric services, law enforcement, child protection, or social services. It is also important, whenever possible, to involve supportive and less-affected family members, friends, or others who can assist the client in this process.

At a less acute level, questions include the following:

- Does the client have a place to stay tonight?
- When did he or she last eat?
- When did he or she last get a medical examination?
- Does he or she have a serious or life-threatening medical condition? If so, is he or she reliably taking any required medication?
- Is he or she engaged in unsafe sex, IV drug abuse, or other risky behaviors?
- Does he or she report self-injurious behavior (e.g., self-cutting, self-burning)?
- Is there evidence of a severe eating disorder?
- Is he or she being exploited sexually or otherwise by another person? Is he or she engaged in prostitution?
- Is he or she involved in a gang? If so, how dangerous is the situation, both to the client and to others?

Evaluation of Trauma Exposure History

After evaluating immediate safety risks, typically next considered is the client's trauma history. Common types of trauma are the following:

- Child abuse (physical, sexual, and psychological)
- Emotional neglect and/or abandonment
- Assaults by peers (both physical and sexual)
- Community violence
- Events associated with homelessness and/or prostitution
- Witnessing violence done to others
- Traumatic loss
- Exposure to serious accidents (e.g., motor vehicle accidents) and disasters
- Serious medical illness or injury

Assessment typically involves determining not only the nature of these various traumas, but also their number, type, and time of onset.

The adolescent or young adult may not report all significant trauma exposures during the initial assessment session or early in treatment. In some cases, important historical events may be disclosed only later in therapy, as the client engages more fully with the clinician and experiences a greater sense of trust and safety. The manner in which adolescents, as well as caretakers, are directly questioned regarding trauma exposures may also determine the extent to which a complete account is provided (Lanktree & Briere, 2008a).

The environmental context in which the assessment is conducted also can affect the extent of trauma information that is disclosed by the adolescent and/or family, whether by interview or on psychological tests. For example, in school settings, the youth may not feel as free to divulge information due to concerns about confidentiality, including fear that his or her trauma history or symptoms will be shared with school personnel or other students. In hospital settings, where an adolescent may be assessed for psychological trauma following serious medical illness or condition (e.g., HIV infection, cancer, surgeries) or traumatic injury (e.g., the results of an assault or accident), the client and family's need to cope with urgent or chronic medical issues may lead them to overlook or suppress information regarding prior (or even current) abuse or violence. In forensic contexts, such as a child abuse investigation, the adolescent may be reticent to disclose information that could lead to separation from the family or incarceration of an alleged perpetrator.

Initial Trauma Review for Adolescents (ITR-A)

Because clients may interpret trauma labels in different ways, evaluation of trauma exposure is often more effective when it employs behavioral descriptions of the event(s), as opposed to merely asking about "rape" or "abuse." This is often best accomplished by using some sort of structured measure or interview that assesses exposure to the major types of traumatic events in a standardized way. The reader will find in Appendix I of this book a version of the Initial Trauma Review (Briere, 2004)—hereafter referred to as the ITR-A—adapted for adolescent and young adult clients. We recommend that this trauma exposure measure be used in ITCT-A, since it covers most of the major traumatic experiences likely to be encountered by adolescents and young adults.

Information From Caretakers

Discussions with caretakers can reveal significant information on the adolescent's developmental, family, mental health, trauma, and substance abuse history, as well as ongoing psychological and social functioning that might not otherwise be available from the client, treating professionals, child protection, or the schools. Assessment is also crucial in determining background family factors, the readiness of family members for therapy, current caretaker and family functioning, intergenerational abuse and other traumatic exposures, and losses, separation, or abandonment by caretakers. Finally, family stressors such as poverty, homelessness, and caretaker unemployment must be taken into account.

Some of this information can be garnered in parent interviews, during the process of caretaker or family therapy, or through the administration of relevant psychological tests. On the other hand, such information may be biased or compromised by caretaker issues, including their own psychological problems, trauma histories, level of investment in the youth, and emotional responses to the adolescent's difficulties, both positive and negative (Friedrich, 2002; Gil, 1996; Pearce & Pezzot-Pearce, 2007).

Because complex trauma often includes insecure attachment associated with inconsistent or emotionally neglectful parenting (Blaustein & Kinniburgh, 2010; Cook et al., 2005), the caretaker may provide a sketchy or incomplete developmental history for the adolescent. The caretaker may also have difficulty disclosing background information on themselves or the family. There also may be limited developmental information from the current caretaker because the youth had multiple caretakers, was in foster care, or early parenting was provided by a person who is no longer available and had minimal communication with the current caretaker.

As a result, we advise the clinician to gather information and test data from a variety of sources, including, but not limited to, caretakers and to "triangulate" these data to come to a more accurate set of conclusions about the youth and his or her social, familial, and psychological matrix (Lanktree et al., 2008; Nader, 2007).

Evaluation of Trauma-Relevant Symptoms

An optimal assessment of traumatized adolescents and young adults generally includes a detailed estimation of current psychological functioning in all pertinent areas. The results of such assessment, in turn, determine whether an immediate clinical response is indicated, as well as what specific treatment modalities (e.g., cognitive interventions, therapeutic exposure, family therapy, psychiatric medication) might be most helpful. Further, when the same tests are administered on multiple occasions (e.g., every three months), the ongoing effects of clinical intervention can be evaluated, allowing the clinician to make midcourse corrections in strategy or focus when specific symptoms are seen to decrease or exacerbate (Briere, 2001).

For some clients, abuse, neglect, family and community violence, major losses, and injuries or illnesses may have occurred more-or-less concomitantly, resulting in a more complex clinical picture. In addition, gender-related, developmental, and cultural factors may affect how any given symptom or psychosocial problem manifests. For this reason, when possible, it is preferable to administer multiple psychological tests, tapping a variety of different symptoms, or to make sure that interview-based assessment covers the full range of complex posttraumatic outcomes. Further, whether interview-based or psychometric, such assessment should take mediating demographic, social, and cultural issues into account.

Interview-Based Assessment

When formal psychological testing is unavailable or inappropriate, the clinician may have to assess various potential trauma impacts during the course of the interview, ideally touching on all the potential outcomes described earlier. Although interview-based symptom reviews can be quite helpful, they are by nature relatively subjective, and it is quite easy for the assessor to overlook certain symptoms or problems and/or to be unclear about whether the level of symptomatology or difficulties disclosed by the individual reaches clinically meaningful levels. On the other hand, assessment questions that are integrated within the clinical interview may be less disruptive and more acceptable to those traumatized youth who find psychological testing intimidating or not relevant to their experience. As noted later, ITCT-A provides a specific symptom assessment template, the Assessment-Treatment Flowchart, that guides the interview process, whether or not it is augmented with psychological testing.

Psychological Testing

Trauma symptom assessment using psychological tests has several advantages. It is more objective and structured, in that it does not rely on the clinician to articulate the full range of possible trauma outcomes and accurately interpret the client's responses to questions. Further, when tests are standardized and normed (a basic requirement of modern psychometric instruments), the youth's self-report of symptomatology can be compared to a reference group of other youths in the general population, so that his or her symptomatology can be evaluated for its severity relative to "normal" respondents. As well, in some cases traumatized youth will respond more honestly and with less avoidance when they are endorsing symptoms on a pencil-and-paper measure, as opposed to a face-to-face inquiry by the therapist. Finally, some young clients find it validating that an independent, standardized test inquires about specific experiences and symptoms they have undergone, with the implication that such issues are relatively commonplace and not necessarily "about them," per se.

Rapport and safety. As noted in the trauma assessment literature, psychological testing is best conducted in the context of safety and good clinical rapport (Briere & Spinazzola, 2005; Lanktree & Briere, 2008a). Especially for very traumatized or alienated youth, this may require that the clinician specifically demonstrate by his or her behaviors, demeanor, and words the fact that

(a) the assessment will be helpful to the client, in terms of allowing the clinician to understand the client and his or her difficulties, and thus provide better, more targeted, treatment;

(b) the assessor and the testing environment are not dangerous to the client, either physically (e.g., through physical assaults, sexual exploitation, or punishment) or psychologically (e.g., through criticism, judgment, or rejection); and

(c) the client has the right to discontinue testing at any point.

Also discussed should be the possibility of some (typically small and temporary) exacerbation of distress when traumas or symptoms are being evaluated, and any possible uses of the test data in legal contexts, if relevant.

It is our clinical experience that traumatized youth are much more forthcoming and less defensive in their test responses if they feel safe and supported, are allowed to ask questions and, to some extent, control their participation in the testing process, and if they believe that the testing has an actual helpful purpose, as opposed to just being an institutional requirement.

Immediate information. Unlike other contexts in which psychological testing may occur, there is sometimes a need to determine the client's emergent psychological status immediately after psychological testing. Most typically, this occurs when the client discloses a danger to himself or herself, a danger to other people, or severe psychological disturbance that requires immediate attention. Much of this potential danger can also be assessed during the clinical interview. However, some clients will deny danger to self or others in an interview, yet endorse it in psychological testing. For this reason, we recommend that—whenever possible—test data be scored as soon as possible after it is collected and that the clinician review specific test items before the client leaves the session. It might be important that the therapist knows, for example, that items # 20 and 52 on the Trauma Symptom Checklist for Children (Briere, 1996b) ask about suicidality, and that other items, e.g., # 21 and 50, inquire about potential for aggression and fear of being killed, so that he or she can rapidly examine these specific items before the client is no longer immediately accessible.

Choice of tests. Standardized trauma assessment measures are almost always preferable to those without norms or validation studies. Such tests may involve either caretaker reports of the adolescent's symptoms and behaviors or self-reports of their own distress and/or behavioral disturbance. In addition, such measures may be either generic or trauma-specific; we recommend that at least one test of each type be included in the assessment battery.

The choice of whether to use self- or caretaker-reports of adolescent symptoms can be difficult, since each approach has its own potential benefits and weaknesses. Self-report measures allow the client to directly disclose his or her internal experience or problems, as opposed to the clinician relying on "secondhand" reports of a parent or caretaker. However, the youth's self-report may be affected by his or her fears of disclosure or denial of emotional distress (Elliott & Briere, 1994). Similarly, a caretaker report of the youth's symptomatology has the potential benefit of providing a more objective report of the client's symptoms and behaviors, yet may be compromised by parental denial, guilt, trauma history, or reactivity to the adolescent's trauma (Friedrich, 2002). Caretakers also may have difficulties accurately assessing the adolescent's internal experience, especially if the adolescent, for whatever reason, avoids describing those experiences to the caretaker (Lanktree et al., 2008). For these reasons, and assuming the caretaker has ongoing contact with the child,[1] it is recommended that the assessment of traumatized adolescents uses *both* self- and caretaker-report measures whenever possible, so that the advantages of each methodology can be maximized, and the child's actual clinical status can be triangulated by virtue of multiple sources of information (Lanktree et al., 2008; Nader, 2007). Caretaker-report will not be appropriate, of course, when the client is an emancipated youth or when the caretakers are abusive, neglectful, or unavailable.

Specific Psychological Tests

Generic (non-trauma-specific) measures. Perhaps the most commonly used generic test in the assessment of traumatized youth is the Child Behavior Checklist (CBCL; Achenbach, 2002), which has separate Parent Report, Teacher Report, and Youth or Young Adult Self-Report versions. Other good indices of general functioning for adolescents are the Behavioral Assessment System for Children (BASC-2; Reynolds & Kamphaus, 2006), adolescent versions of the Psychological Assessment Inventory (PAI-A; Morey, 2008), and the Minnesota Multiphasic Personality Inventory (MMPI-A; Butcher et al., 1992). Standardized tests for specific symptoms or disorders include the Child Depression Inventory (CDI; Kovacs, 1992), Suicidal Ideation Questionnaire (SIQ; Reynolds, 1988), and Tennessee Self-Concept Scale (TSCS; Roid & Fitts, 1994). Projective tests like the Rorschach (Exner, 1974) and Robert's Apperception Test (RATC; McArthur & Roberts, 1982) also may be helpful in some instances (Briere & Spinazzola, 2009). Although these various instruments often do not enquire about posttraumatic symptoms (e.g., flashbacks, dissociation, hyperarousal) in particular, they do examine other issues that are very relevant to the traumatized client, such as depression, anxiety, suicidality, externalization, and low self-esteem. For this reason, we recommend that at least one generic test be administered in addition to one or more trauma-specific tests. In the MCAVIC-USC project, for example, the CBCL and CDI were administered to almost all clients.

Trauma-specific tests. Standardized, trauma-specific self-report measures for adolescents can be divided into those for youth ages 12–17, those for adolescents aged 18–21, and those for all adolescents (aged 12–21). Some of these trauma-specific measures are briefly described here.

Trauma Symptom Checklist for Children (Briere, 1996b). Normed on over 3,000 children and adolescents across a range of sociodemographic strata, the 54-item TSCC evaluates self-reported trauma symptoms in children ages 8–16, with minor normative adjustments for 17-year-olds. It has two validity scales and six clinical scales: *Anxiety, Depression, Anger, Posttraumatic Stress, Sexual Concerns* (containing two subscales: *Distress* and *Preoccupation*), and

Dissociation (containing two subscales: *Overt* and *Fantasy*). There is an alternate form (the TSCC-A) that does not include any sexual items.

UCLA PTSD Index for DSM-IV (Pynoos, Rodriguez, Steinberg, Stuber, & Frederick, 1998). An updated version of what was formerly described as the Reaction Index, the UPID is a 48-item interview that can be administered to children and adolescents aged 7–18 years. It evaluates exposure to a variety of traumatic events and provides a PTSD diagnosis, as well as containing additional items that assess associated features such as guilt, aggression, and dissociation.

Trauma Symptom Inventory (Briere, 1995) and *Trauma Symptom Inventory-2* (Briere, 2011). The TSI taps the overall level of posttraumatic symptomatology experienced by an individual in the prior six months and can be used in the current context with older adolescents and young adults, ages 18 to 21. It has three validity scales and 10 clinical scales (*Anxious Arousal, Depression, Anger/Irritability, Intrusive Experiences, Defensive Avoidance, Dissociation, Sexual Concerns, Dysfunctional Sexual Behavior, Impaired Self-Reference,* and *Tension Reduction Behavior*). The new TSI-2 evaluates all of these areas but additionally includes *Attachment Insecurity, Suicidality,* and *Somatization* scales, the first of which may be especially helpful in assessing complex trauma issues.

Inventory of Altered Self-Capacities (Briere, 2000). The IASC is a standardized test of difficulties in the areas of relatedness, identity, and affect regulation. As such, it is especially relevant to the concerns and presentations of older adolescents (i.e., those aged 18 to 21) presenting with more complex posttraumatic outcomes. IASC scales are *Interpersonal Conflicts, Idealization-Disillusionment, Abandonment Concerns, Identity Impairment, Susceptibility to Influence, Affect Dysregulation,* and *Tension Reduction Activities.*

Trauma Symptom Scales for Adolescents (TSSA: Briere, in progress). An adaption and extension of the unpublished *Trauma Symptom Review for Adolescents* (TSRA: Briere, 2007), the TSSA was developed specifically to tap the major issues of traumatized adolescents aged 12 to 21. It has scales measuring, among other constructs, posttraumatic stress, attachment issues, dissociation, dysfunctional sexual behavior, social isolation, tension-reduction (acting-out) behaviors, and substance abuse. It is currently undergoing standardization trials and is expected to be published in 2013. Prior to that point, scores on the TSSA cannot be used to determine norm-referenced levels of clinical disturbance.

Assessing the Caretaker

Of course, it is not only the youth who should be assessed. Also important are factors impinging on the caretaker's capacity to parent their child. These include his or her

- own attachment history, especially the extent to which he or she felt support and emotional attunement from his or her primary caretaker(s);

- cultural background, as well those of his or her children (they may not be the same);

- history of trauma and loss;

- issues and symptoms that may be associated with trauma, such as depression, anxiety, anger, lack of empathy for others, posttraumatic stress, dissociation, impaired self-functioning (including affect regulation problems), substance abuse, and tension reduction behaviors;

- history of previous therapy and whether it was experienced as helpful;

- current emotional resources and coping capacities;

- psychiatric status, including whether he or she is suffering from schizophrenia, bipolar disorder, or a severe personality disorder; and

- other stressors, including those related to single parenting, domestic violence, poverty, unemployment, homelessness, cultural or religious pressures to not seek help from others or permit governmental intervention, substance abuse in the family, and other children in the home requiring parenting.

In addition, Gil and Drewes (2005) suggest that assessment of the client's and family's culture(s) should include information on family values, spirituality, child-rearing principles, and culture-specific ways that families resolve conflict, express anger, and deal with aggression.

Overall Assessment Sequence for ITCT-A

Although there is a variety of approaches to the assessment component of ITCT-A, we suggest that it occur in the following stepwise fashion:

1. Conduct one or more clinical interviews, as outlined in this chapter, accessing as many sources of information (e.g., from the client, caretakers, the school, child welfare system, etc.) as possible, in combination with any

relevant medical, psychological, or forensic records. Based on this assessment process, consider additional psychological testing.

2. If psychological testing is possible, employ assessment instruments known to be reliable and valid indicators of issues identified by the interview(s). In order to facilitate this process, refer to the ITCT-A Assessment Locator, presented here and also found in Appendix II. Acronyms are explained in the table, or refer to the tests described earlier in this chapter. The column *ATF-A Item* refers to clinical issues potentially relevant to adolescents and young adults with complex trauma exposure. Detailed coverage of the ATF-A is found in Chapter 4.

3. Based on the interview, record and (if possible) test data and complete the ATF-A, as outlined in Chapter 4.

ITCT-A Assessment Locator

ATF-A Item	Assessment (Tests applicable only for relevant age ranges)
1. Safety—environmental	Adolescent self-report in session (A-S), parent/caretaker-report in session (C-R)
2. Caretaker support issues	A-S, C-R, and clinical impressions during parent interview
3. Anxiety	A-S, C-R, CBCL, BASC-2, PAI-A, MMPI-A, TSCC, TSSA, TSI, TSI-2
4. Depression	A-S, C-R, CBCL, CDI, BDI-II, BASC-2, TSCC, TSSA, TSI, TSI-2
5. Anger/aggression	A-S, C-R, BASC-2 (parent report), CBCL, PAI-A, TSCC, TSSA, TSI, TSI-2
6. Low self-esteem	A-S, C-R, BASC-2, TSCS, TSSA
7. Posttraumatic stress	A-S, C-R, PAI-A, MMPI-A, TSCC, TSSA, TSI, TSI-2, DAPS, UPID
8. Attachment insecurity	A-S, C-R, BASC-2, TSI-2, TSSA
9. Identity issues	A-S, C-R, IASC, TSI, TSI-2
10. Relationship problems	A-S, C-R, BASC-2, CBCL, TSSA

(Continued)

(Continued)

ATF-A Item	Assessment (Tests applicable only for relevant age ranges)
11. Suicidality	A-S, C-R, TSCC, PAI-A, TSI-2, TSSA, DAPS, SIQ
12. Safety—risky behaviors	A-S, C-R, BASC-2, TSI, TSI-2
13. Dissociation	A-S, C-R, TSCC, TSSA, TSI, TSI-2, DAPS
14. Substance abuse	A-S, C-R, BASC-2, PAI-A, TSI, TSI-2, DAPS
15. Grief	A-S, C-R
16. Sexual concerns and/or dysfunctional behaviors	A-S, C-R, TSCC, TSSA, TSI, TSI-2
17. Self-mutilation	A-S, C-R

Note

1. It is sometimes the case that the caretaker has only occasional visits with the youth, is uninvolved with his or her care, or is a new foster parent. In such instances, caretaker report may be inaccurate or even misleading (Briere, 2005).

4

Completing and Using the Assessment-Treatment Flowchart for Adolescents (ATF-A)

A carefully selected psychological test battery and/or detailed interview-based assessment—in combination with other types of information—is often critical in determining the client's current symptomatology and psychosocial difficulties. Information on the youth's psychological and behavioral functioning informs the clinician's treatment plan, allowing customization of interventions based on the client's specific clinical presentation and needs. When assessment is repeated over time, it can also indicate the need to change or augment the treatment focus. For example, ongoing evaluation may suggest a shift in therapeutic focus when posttraumatic stress symptoms begin to respond to treatment but other symptoms continue unabated or even exacerbate.

Assessment-Treatment Flowchart

In ITCT-A, the actual transformation of test data, interview-based data, collateral information, and clinical impressions into a specific treatment plan occurs through the use of the Assessment-Treatment Flowchart, adolescent form (ATF-A), found in Appendix III. An example of a completed ATF-A is presented later in this chapter.

This form not only helps guide the initial treatment plan, but also provides a serial reassessment of symptoms and possible interventions on a regular basis thereafter. Unfortunately, because the development of standardized measures for posttraumatic outcomes in adolescents is in its relative infancy, not all problems listed in the ATF-A have corresponding psychological tests that aid in their evaluation. As well, some clinicians choose not to conduct psychological testing. In either of these instances, the clinician must rely on the youth's self-report, his or her behavior and responses in the intake session and in therapy, parent report, data from other systems (e.g., legal, academic, child welfare), and generalized clinical impressions to complete the ATF-A. In nontesting situations, each ATF-A item should be used as a prompt to ask about the relevant domain. For example, item # 6 ("Low self-esteem") would involve interview questions about not liking self, feeling that one is bad or unacceptable, etc.

Completion of the ATF-A thus proceeds in two steps:

(1)   At intake: Review all assessment data and/or the adolescent's interview-based report of symptoms and problems, parent or caretaker interview-based report of the adolescent's symptoms and problems, collateral data such as school reports, other caregiver (e.g., health care professionals, other therapists) feedback, juvenile justice reports, information from social workers (if abuse or neglect has prompted assignment to the child protection system), etc. Consents for communication with various professionals should be obtained from whomever is the holder of the privilege, i.e., the young-adult client, the caretaker if the client is a minor, or the relevant child protection worker or other professional if the client has been placed in a foster home or residential treatment and is in the custody of the court.

(2)   Proceed through each of the 19 items of the ATF-A (the 17 items just described, plus two additional "other" items when additional issues are identified) in the "Intake" column, rating the treatment priority (ranging from *1* ["Not currently a problem, do not treat"] to *4* ["Most problematic, requires immediate attention"]) for each item based on the data collected at step 1. In many cases, ATF-A treatment priority ratings, and thus associated treatment goals and treatment approaches, can be discussed with the client, with his or her input solicited. Such discussions emphasize the therapist-client partnership and may be quite beneficial in empowering the client and facilitating the therapeutic relationship.

At each following assessment period (typically every three months, unless indicated more frequently), review the last prioritization of symptoms and problems and, based on repeat assessment, *reprioritize* the focus of treatment based on the client's current clinical and social status. In some cases, reassessment and treatment reconfiguration will occur prior to a three-month assessment period, generally when some new event intercedes (e.g., a crisis or life event) or a significant treatment event (e.g., a breakthrough or newly uncovered information) alters the therapy trajectory. In such cases, ATF-A ratings (completed columns) might occur more frequently than every three months. When ATF-A assessments occur in addition to the usual three-month periods, it is especially important to indicate the date at the top of the column for that assessment.

An Example of an ATF-A

Presented shortly is an ATF-A from a 17-year-old client, who was assessed at intake and three months later.

Based on the TSCC, UPID, and other tests, as well as his verbal self-report in the evaluation session, his parents' feedback, and the therapist's clinical impression, three symptom clusters, *Anxiety*, *Depression*, and *Posttraumatic stress*, are prioritized as 4s ("Most problematic, requires immediate attention"). Two additional problems (*Anger/aggression* and *Dissociation*) are prioritized as 3s ("Problematic, a current treatment priority"), and the remainder of ATF-A items are rated as 2s ("Problematic, but not an immediate treatment priority") or 1s ("Not currently a problem, do not treat").

At the next ATF-A assessment period (three months into treatment), the client shows clinical improvement in *Anxiety*, *Depression*, and *Dissociation*, leading the clinician to prioritize these problems as, respectively, "3," "2," and "2" (see the following ATF-A example). Further, one problem (*Identity issues*) is downgraded from a "2" to a "1." However, additional stressors in the client's life, and other undetermined factors, have resulted in an increased score for *Safety—Risky behaviors* (specifically, staying out late at night and reported reckless driving) and an increase in seemingly indiscriminant sexual activities (*Sexual concerns and/or dysfunctional behaviors*), resulting in new ratings of "3" for each domain. Thus, at intake, the highest level of treatment attention was on anxiety, depression, and posttraumatic stress, whereas at the next assessment period the focus continues to be on posttraumatic stress but is now followed by anger/aggression, risky behaviors, and dysfunctional sexual behaviors.

Priority ranking (circle one for each symptom):

1 = Not currently a problem, do not treat

2 = Problematic, but not an immediate treatment priority: treat at lower intensity

3 = Problematic, a current treatment priority: treat at higher intensity

4 = Most problematic, requires immediate attention

(S) = Suspected, requires further investigation

Assessment Period

	Intake			
Date:	*5/10/10*	*8/11/10*		
Problem Area	*Tx Priority*	*Tx Priority*	*Tx Priority*	*Tx Priority*
1. Safety—environmental	1 ②3 4 (S)	1 ②3 4 (S)	1 2 3 4 (S)	1 2 3 4 (S)
2. Caretaker support issues	①2 3 4 (S)	①2 3 4 (S)	1 2 3 4 (S)	1 2 3 4 (S)
3. Anxiety	1 2 3 ④(S)	1 2 ③4 (S)	1 2 3 4 (S)	1 2 3 4 (S)
4. Depression	1 2 3 ④(S)	1 ②3 4 (S)	1 2 3 4 (S)	1 2 3 4 (S)
5. Anger/aggression	1 2 ③4 (S)	1 2 ③4 (S)	1 2 3 4 (S)	1 2 3 4 (S)
6. Low self-esteem	1 ②3 4 (S)	1 ②3 4 (S)	1 2 3 4 (S)	1 2 3 4 (S)
7. Posttraumatic stress	1 2 3 ④(S)	1 2 3 ④(S)	1 2 3 4 (S)	1 2 3 4 (S)
8. Attachment insecurity	1 ②3 4 (S)	1 ②3 4 (S)	1 2 3 4 (S)	1 2 3 4 (S)
9. Identity issues	1 ②3 4 (S)	①2 3 4 (S)	1 2 3 4 (S)	1 2 3 4 (S)
10. Relationship problems	1 ②3 4 (S)	1 ②3 4 (S)	1 2 3 4 (S)	1 2 3 4 (S)
11. Suicidality	①2 3 4 (S)	①2 3 4 (S)	1 2 3 4 (S)	1 2 3 4 (S)
12. Safety—risky behaviors	1 ②3 4 (S)	1 2 ③4 (S)	1 2 3 4 (S)	1 2 3 4 (S)
13. Dissociation	1 2 ③4 (S)	1 ②3 4 (S)	1 2 3 4 (S)	1 2 3 4 (S)
14. Substance abuse	①2 3 4 (S)	①2 3 4 (S)	1 2 3 4 (S)	1 2 3 4 (S)

	Intake			
Date:	5/10/10	8/11/10		
Problem Area	Tx Priority	Tx Priority	Tx Priority	Tx Priority
15. Grief	①2 3 4 (S)	①2 3 4 (S)	1 2 3 4 (S)	1 2 3 4 (S)
16. Sexual concerns and/or dysfunctional behaviors	①2 3 4 (S)	1 2③4 (S)	1 2 3 4 (S)	1 2 3 4 (S)
17. Self-mutilation	①2 3 4 (S)	①2 3 4 (S)	1 2 3 4 (S)	1 2 3 4 (S)
18. Other: _____	1 2 3 4 (S)	1 2 3 4 (S)	1 2 3 4 (S)	1 2 3 4 (S)
19. Other: _____	1 2 3 4 (S)	1 2 3 4 (S)	1 2 3 4 (S)	1 2 3 4 (S)

Moving from ATF-A to treatment plan. As will be discussed in Chapter 6, upon completion of any ATR-A assessment, the clinician then consults the second ITCT-A tool, the *Problems-to-Components Grid* (PCG) (see also Appendix IV). Through use of the PCG, the various problems and symptoms described in the previous chapters are linked to specific intervention approaches (e.g., cognitive processing, therapeutic exposure, psycho-education) outlined in the following chapters. In this way, assessment and treatment—followed by repeat assessment and further treatment—are directly linked. Treatment of a specific issue only occurs if it is assessed to be a problem (i.e., has a higher ranking on the ATF-A), and only continues as long as assessment indicates it is still problematic. As a result, treatment for two different clients may differ significantly as a function of initial test data, collateral input, and response to treatment or external circumstance.

Response to emergent issues. An implicit but important aspect of this approach is that the clinician is directly encouraged to view each treatment session as a new assessment opportunity and to shift the focus of treatment according to what is happening with the client at any given point in time. Especially for youth embedded in chaotic, disruptive, or marginalizing environments, there easily may be new traumas, crises, or adversities at school or in the home since the last session. The client's anger, posttraumatic stress, suicidality, or acting-out potential may have escalated dramatically, such that attention to "old" (previous sessions') issues may not be the appropriate use of the therapist's time at present. These life or symptom changes may be significant enough to warrant an additional ATF-A assessment (i.e., prior to the next scheduled assessment point) and, thus, potentially new treatment components.

In this regard, an adolescent may be in treatment for childhood sexual abuse that occurred in the past but may experience a new assault by a peer, witness new community violence, or may report that his or her caretaker has been incarcerated. Or, the child may only now feel safe enough in treatment to disclose a prior trauma that has major implications for his or her current functioning. In such instances, the clinician is encouraged to not see this as just another "crisis of the week," but rather as an important aspect of the client's life that deserves clinical attention, if not acute intervention. When the clinician takes the client's ongoing life experiences—and potentially chaotic environment—seriously, the therapeutic relationship is typically reinforced and deepened, since the youth feels "heard" and understood. Given the dynamic and potentially dangerous nature of many traumatizing environments, let alone the complexity of many affected youths' clinical presentations, support for changes in treatment targets as a function of emergent issues (as opposed to a relentlessly structured treatment algorithm) is an important feature of ITCT-A.

SECTION II

Overview of Treatment

5

Central Aspects of ITCT-A

This chapter briefly outlines the primary foci of ITCT as it is applied to adolescents and young adults, above and beyond the specific components of therapy described in later chapters.

The Primacy of the Therapeutic Relationship

Although modern trauma treatment is characterized by a number of specific techniques—many of which are presented in the Problems-to-Components Grid (PCG) described in Chapter 6—research and clinical experience suggest that a positive therapeutic relationship is one of the most important components of successful therapy (Cloitre, Stovall-McClough, Miranda, & Chemtob, 2004; Lambert & Barley, 2001; Martin, Garske, & Davis, 2000). This is probably especially true for multiply traumatized youth, whose life experiences have taught them to mistrust authority and to expect maltreatment in relationships. This dynamic can be further intensified for youth who live in deprived and marginalized social environments and/or have experienced racism or other discrimination on a regular basis.

In this complex psychosocial matrix, client trust and openness becomes less likely at the very time it is especially needed. Some level of vulnerability and trust is necessary before the traumatized adolescent or young adult can meaningfully revisit and process painful memories. If the therapist maintains a consistently positive, caring demeanor, and indicates by his or her behavior that he or she will not maltreat, disrespect, discriminate against, exploit, or otherwise harm the client, the multiply besieged youth may slowly come to realize that there is no immediate danger associated with treatment, gradually reducing his or her defenses and avoidance behaviors and eventually entering into a more therapeutic connection with the clinician.

For some especially traumatized and maltreated adolescents, this process may take time, requiring considerable patience on the part of the therapist. The client may test the clinician in various ways regarding his or her actual feelings and intentions for the client. There may be an expressed attitude of disinterest, or even disdain, even though the adolescent may actually be hungry for connection and validation. For example, a client may appear withdrawn and angry and complain about therapy, yet continue to make a concerted effort to attend sessions.

The client may challenge or, conversely, attempt to pacify the therapist in various ways that have proved helpful with powerful others in the past. Only when the therapist does not "take the bait" and become angry, dangerous, exploitive, seductive, or rejecting may the client begin to perceive the therapist, and the therapeutic relationship, as benign.

Beyond the need for the client to participate in treatment, and thus lower his or her defenses against expectations of maltreatment, the experience of a safe and caring client-therapist relationship is often a technical requirement of trauma therapy (Briere & Scott, 2006). Almost inevitably, the therapeutic relationship will trigger memories, feelings, and thoughts associated with prior relational traumas, as well as, in some cases, more recent social maltreatment (e.g., experiences of racism, sexism, or homophobia). As noted in Chapters 8 and 15, when these activations and expectations can be processed in the context of a safe, supportive relationship, their power over the adolescent survivor often diminishes. In this regard, as the client experiences reactivated rejection, abandonment fears, misperception of danger, or authority issues at the same time that he or she perceives respect, caring, and empathy from the therapist, such intrusions may gradually lose their generalizability to current relationships and become counterconditioned by current, positive relational feelings. In this sense, a good therapeutic relationship is not only supportive of effective treatment; it is technically integral to the resolution of major relational traumas.

Customization

In actual clinical practice, clients vary significantly with regard to their sociocultural background, presenting issues, comorbid symptoms, and the extent to which they can utilize and tolerate psychological interventions.

For this reason, therapy is likely to be most effective when it is tailored to the specific characteristics and concerns of the individual person. Above and beyond the differing symptomatic needs of one client relative to another, treatment may require adjustment based on a number of other relevant variables. Presented here are several factors that should be taken into account when providing trauma therapy to adolescent and young-adult trauma survivors.

Age

Although it is often implied that adolescence through young adulthood is a single developmental stage, in actuality the usually cited age range for this category (ages 12 to 21) comprises several smaller developmental periods. In addition, any given adolescent may be "a young" X-year-old or "an old" one, psychologically and/or physically. Further, childhood abuse may delay some individuals psychological or physical development and accelerate others, and some environments may demand "older" psychosocial functioning than others.

A common error made by clinicians working with traumatized youth is to intervene as if the adolescent is older or younger than his or her actual psychological age. The older adolescent may feel that "my counselor treats me like a baby," whereas the younger (or more cognitively impaired) adolescent may not fully understand the clinician's statements or may feel insufficient emotional connection with the therapist because the clinician is interacting with him or her in a way that is too intellectualized. Such potential problems highlight the need to provide developmentally sensitive and appropriate treatment to adolescents with trauma histories.

Gender

Although adolescent males and females experience many of the same traumatic events and suffer in many of the same ways, it is also clear that some traumas are more common in one sex than the other, and that sex-role socialization often affects how such injuries are experienced and expressed. These differences have significant impacts on the content and process of trauma-focused therapy for adolescents.

Research indicates that girls and women are more at risk for victimization in close relationships than are boys and men and are especially more likely to be sexually victimized, whereas boys and men are at greater risk than girls and women of physical abuse and assault (Kessler, Sonnega, Bromet, Hughes, & Nelson, 1995; Yehuda, 2004). In addition to trauma exposure differences, young men and women tend to experience, communicate, and process the distress associated with traumatic events in somewhat different ways. For example,

- boys and men may be more reluctant than girls and women to seek out therapy following trauma;
- certain traumas (e.g., sexual assault) may be even more stigmatizing for males than females;
- female clients may be willing to express sadness and fear but more reluctant to verbalize angry feelings, whereas the reverse may be true for male clients; and
- given their socialization to externalize distress, male youth may be more prone to "act out" emotional pain through aggression. (See Briere & Scott, 2006; Cochrane, 2005; and Renzetti & Curran, 2002, for a more-detailed discussion of gender-related issues.)

These sex-role related differences in symptom expression and behavioral response often manifest themselves during trauma-focused psychotherapy. As a result, the therapist should be alert to ways in which traumatized youth express or inhibit their emotional reactions based on sex-role-related expectations. Not only should the clinician avoid treating clients in a sex-role stereotypic manner, he or she should be sensitive to how gender-related socialization impacts the client and respond accordingly.

Sociocultural Matrix

Although many North American therapists are firmly rooted in the middle class, with the assumptions and perspectives that go along with that context, a significant proportion of mental health service consumers, including many adolescent and young-adult trauma survivors, are embedded in a different psychosocial environment—one that includes a range of cultural or subcultural experiences, expectations, and rules of interpersonal engagement and that is often characterized by marginalization due to poverty, race, culture, gender, or sexual orientation (see, e.g., Bryant-Davis, 2005). As a result, the traumatized adolescent may present with a variety of issues beyond his or her specific trauma history; not only will he or she have been hurt by physical or sexual violence, he or she may have experienced the direct and indirect effects of social maltreatment and may view the world from a cultural lens that differs substantially from that of the therapist (Abney, 2002; Cohen, Deblinger, Mannarino, & De Arellano, 2001; Jones, Hadder, Carvajal, Chapman, & Alexander, 2006).

Sociocultural and experiential differences between clients and therapists may easily extend to inherent disagreements regarding the requirements and process of therapy. Although the therapist may assume that the client feels safe, understood, and supported in treatment with him or her, these beliefs may not always be accurate. Further, the client may not subscribe to the clinician's perspective on what constitutes therapy. There may be differing expectations about how private issues are discussed during treatment, the extent to which therapy is focused on practical (as opposed to more psychological) issues in the client's life, the importance of regularly scheduled weekly sessions, or even the role of eye contact or therapist self-disclosure (e.g., Abney, 2002; Ford, 2007; Marsella, Friedman, Gerrity, & Scurfield, 1996). Differences in client-versus-therapist class or culture may result in clinician errors, such as the treatment provider's belief that the adolescent female client's late or missed sessions represent "resistance" or "acting out," when, in fact, the client may have multiple impinging concerns (e.g., child-care issues, a changing work schedule, or difficulties in arranging transportation) and/or a different perspective on the relative importance of being "on time." Similarly, the client may assume that the therapist is uninvolved or uncaring, when, in fact, the therapist is quite concerned about the client, but his or her culture (or training) dictates less emotional expression or visible interpersonal closeness.

The impacts of social discrimination and cultural differences are not things that the clinician can overlook when working with many traumatized adolescent and young adults. Minimally, the therapist should take into account (1) the adverse conditions and additional trauma exposure that the client may have experienced, (2) the anger and/or anxiety that he or she may feel when in contact with a therapist whose social characteristics are more representative of the dominant (i.e., White, middle class) culture, and (3) differences in worldviews and experiences often associated with different socioeconomic strata or cultural/subcultural membership. In some cases, the therapist will be of the same background, race, or ethnicity as the client and will place the intervention in the context of the client's cultural and/or socioeconomic experience (e.g., Dionne, Davis, Sheeber, & Madrigal, 2009). In many other cases, however, the best approximation will be a culturally competent clinician who is sensitive and responsive to these issues, irrespective of his or her personal demographics.

Affect Regulation Capacity

Not only should treatment be customized based on the youth's symptomatic presentation and sociodemographic/cultural characteristics, there is an important psychological variable that frequently affects how therapy is delivered: the client's level of affect regulation—his or her relative capacity to tolerate and internally reduce painful emotional states. Adolescents with limited affect regulation abilities are more likely to be overwhelmed and destabilized by negative emotional experiences—both those associated with current negative events and those triggered by painful memories. Since trauma therapy often involves activating and processing traumatic memories, those with less ability to internally regulate painful states are more likely to become highly distressed, if not emotionally overwhelmed, during treatment and may respond with increased avoidance, including "resistance" and/or dissociation (Briere & Scott, 2006; Cloitre, Koenen, Cohen, & Han, 2002). Such responses, in turn, reduce the adolescent's exposure to traumatic material and to the healing aspects of the therapeutic relationship. As described in Chapters 11 and 14, treatment of those with impaired affect regulation capacities should proceed carefully, so that traumatic memories are activated and processed in smaller increments than otherwise might be necessary. Often described as *titrated exposure* or "working within the therapeutic window" (Briere, 2002), this involves (1) adjusting treatment so that trauma processing that occurs within a given session does not exceed the capacities of the survivor to tolerate that level of distress and, at the same time, (2) providing as much processing as can reasonably occur.

Advocacy and System Intervention

Traumatized youth often have issues that extend beyond psychological symptomatology, per se. Some of these concerns are associated with a lack of financial and/or social resources. Others arise from ways in which the adolescent's trauma history, family difficulties, and living environment have affected his or her interactions with external systems, such as schools, law enforcement, juvenile justice, child protection, and social welfare agencies. The client may be involved in gang activity, prostitution, significant substance abuse, theft, revictimization, or violence against others. Other, older clients, who have no family support and desire to have a more functional lifestyle, will benefit from the therapist's support and problem-solving about independent housing, employment, and/or further education/training.

In such situations, psychotherapy—by itself—may not be of sufficient assistance. For this reason, ITCT-A and other approaches to multiproblem youth typically include a social advocacy/systems intervention component. This may involve the clinician dealing with "red tape" in health or social welfare bureaucracies so that the client can receive needed services or funding (e.g., through victim-witness compensation programs), advocating for the client in a judicial hearing, providing advocacy regarding placement issues or obtaining emancipated minor status, helping the client to apply for U.S. resident status, or working with school personnel to keep the client in the educational system. It may include filling out forms, writing letters, making phone calls, or completing reports.

In addition, for clients who are economically disadvantaged and have limited resources, ITCT providers (i.e., agencies) with sufficient resources or funding may offer a range of extratherapeutic services, including the following:

• Transportation to therapy sessions through taxi vouchers, bus passes, or an agency van

• Food and clothing

• Advocacy and referrals for legal support and housing. In some cases, such assistance can significantly change the survivor's life by ending his or her homelessness or moving him or her to a safer neighborhood.

• Emergency financial assistance for youth and families when starting back to school and for holidays

• Access to community afterschool programs and participation in neighborhood organizations, such as Big Brothers, Big Sisters, the Boys and Girls Club, mentoring programs, and other more young-adult-oriented community organizations that can help the client transition from school to, for example, a trade. Clients and their caretakers may not be aware of free services in their community, and these resources can supplement the advantages of ongoing therapy.

• Collaborations with child protection and school social workers, as well as school counselors and medical practitioners, so that the client can more fully access the resources just listed

These various activities provide real-world support to the young trauma survivor in the most basic and important ways, involving food, shelter, financial support, social integration, and physical/social protection; conditions that typically must be met before meaningful progress on psychological issues can be made. Extending such support to the client may also enhance his or her sense of trust and significantly strengthen the therapeutic relationship.

6

From Assessment to Intervention

The Problems-to-Components Grid (PCG)

As described briefly in earlier chapters, an important part of ITCT-A is the use of specific treatment components, matched to specific problems or symptom clusters. Following assessment with the ATF-A, the clinician consults the Problems-to-Components Grid (PCG) to determine which interventions are most relevant to the problems or symptoms that have been identified. In this way, each adolescent or young adult receiving ITCT-A actually undergoes a different regimen of treatment, according to his or her needs and difficulties—much as a medical patient will receive specific treatments according to what physical disorders or symptoms he or she has.

The PCG is a compendium of treatment modules that have been reported in the clinical literature as efficacious for the issues identified by the ATF-A. In most cases, these modules have been empirically validated in treatment outcome studies. In a few cases, although discussed widely in the literature, the intervention in question (e.g., *Relational processing*, Chapter 15) has research and clinical support but not at the level of specificity present for other modules. Once ATF-A identified problems are linked to appropriate interventions in the PGC, the clinician can access chapters in Section III of this book to further explore how that specific module can be applied for adolescent or young-adult trauma survivors. The PCG is presented here, as well in Appendix IV. Chapters discussing each intervention are indicated in parentheses following each component name, with the exception of psychiatric medication, which is not addressed in this book (see Stamatakos & Campo [2010] for information on this intervention).

Problems-to-Components Grid (PCG)	
Problem (from ATF-A)	Treatment components that may be useful (relevant chapters are bolded and in parentheses)
1. Safety— environmental	Safety training (9), system interventions (5), psychoeducation (10)
2. Caretaker support	Family therapy (17), intervention with caretakers (18)
3. Anxiety	Distress reduction/affect regulation training (11), titrated exposure (14), cognitive processing (12), medication
4. Depression	Relationship building and support (8), cognitive processing (12), group therapy (19), medication
5. Anger/aggression	Distress reduction/affect regulation training (11), trigger identification/intervention (13), cognitive processing (12)
6. Low self-esteem	Cognitive processing (12), relational processing (15), group therapy (19), relationship building and support (8)
7. Posttraumatic stress	Distress reduction/affect regulation training (11), titrated exposure (14), cognitive processing (12), psychoeducation (10), relationship building and support (8), trigger identification/intervention (13), medication
8. Attachment insecurity	Relationship building and support (8), relational processing (15), group therapy (19), family therapy (17)
9. Identity issues	Relationship building and support (8), relational processing (15)
10. Relationship problems	Relationship building and support (8), relational processing (15), cognitive processing (12), group therapy (19)
11. Suicidality	Safety training (9), distress reduction/affect regulation training (11), cognitive processing (12), systems intervention (5), medication

Problem (from ATF-A)	Treatment components that may be useful (relevant chapters are bolded and in parentheses)
12. Safety—risky behaviors	Psychoeducation (**10**), safety training (**9**), distress reduction/affect regulation training (**11**), cognitive processing (**12**), titrated exposure (**14**), trigger identification/intervention (**13**)
13. Dissociation	Distress reduction/affect regulation training (**11**), titrated exposure (**14**), trigger identification/intervention (**13**)
14. Substance abuse	Psychoeducation (**10**), trigger identification/intervention (**13**), distress reduction/affect regulation training (**11**), medication
15. Grief	Psychoeducation (**10**), cognitive processing (**12**), relationship building and support (**8**)
16. Sexual concerns and/or dysfunctional behaviors	Distress reduction/affect regulation training (**11**), cognitive processing (**12**), titrated exposure (**14**), psychoeducation (**10**), safety training (**9**), cognitive processing (**12**), trigger identification/intervention (**13**)
17. Self-mutilation	Distress reduction/affect regulation training (**11**), cognitive processing (**12**), titrated exposure (**14**), trigger identification/intervention (**13**)

Part of what makes components-based treatments such as ITCT-A potentially complex is that, in the presence of multiple problems or symptoms clusters, several different interventions or approaches may have to be used in the same session. As well, for complex trauma survivors, certain components (e.g., *Relationship building and support*) must be present in all sessions, yet may be insufficient in and of themselves to provide full resolution of trauma-related suffering. This means that the clinician must become skilled at interweaving different components while, at the same time, making sure that the most important interventions are sufficiently present to be maximally helpful.

In general, the guiding principle underlying the successful interweaving of ITCT-A components is one of balance. If an adolescent is currently suffering from flashbacks and intrusive thoughts associated with a particular trauma, yet also has significant abandonment and attunement issues associated with early neglect, the therapist may provide titrated exposure to painful memories while, at the same time, working to communicate caring, support, and empathic attention. He or she may focus on cognitive processing or psycho-education or switch to an affect regulation intervention, depending on what is most relevant or necessary at any given point in the session.

In this way, the ATF-A and PCG are advisory; signposts to what are the most important interventions for the client's immediately presenting symptoms and concerns. Most complex trauma survivors will have ATF-A priority ratings between 2 (*Problematic, but not an immediate treatment priority*) and 4 (*Most problematic, requires immediate attention*) for a number of different issues. Although the PCG will allow overall prioritization of treatment modalities, it will not be definitive as to what specific approach or intervention is most indicated during any specific session. For this reason, ITCT-A calls upon the therapist's clinical experience—in general, and specifically with ITCT-A—to use the appropriate interventions at the appropriate times.

7

Sequence and Session-Level Structure of ITCT-A

In the following chapters, information will be provided on various techniques and components of ITCT-A. At the outset, however, we include this chapter in order to outline the general sequence of interventions or activities that typically occur within a given ITCT session.

Based on initial and ongoing assessment with the Assessment-Treatment Flowchart (ATF-A), and applying the Problems-to-Components Grid (PTC), the clinician customizes the type and extent of intervention for any given adolescent or young adult, so that his or her specific difficulties can be addressed in a systematized manner using relevant components. At the same time, an overbridging philosophy of ITCT-A is the focus on the therapeutic relationship: both as a necessary support for the hard work of trauma processing, as well as a technical requirement for the resolution of the relational/interpersonal difficulties of many young trauma survivors.

Although the actual processing and desensitization of traumatic material typically varies in degree from session to session, and certain general aspects of treatment transcend technique, it is also true that therapy for trauma survivors often works best when it conforms to a basic structure. Such a framework allows the therapist to assess the client's current needs, provide relevant processing activities as needed, reassess the client's current state, de-escalate emotional responses, if needed, and provide end-of-session closure.

In general, we suggest that therapy for traumatized adolescents involve one 50–60 minute individual session per week, as well as group and/or family sessions that may occur on a weekly to monthly basis. In a minority of cases, more than one individual session per week may be indicated, and, in some cases, family or group therapy may be completely absent. Some version of the following is usually appropriate for the individual ITCT-A session:

- Presession: The ATF-A should be reviewed and principle targets for the session ascertained. These targets may change as the session unfolds, but they should not be abandoned unless necessary. If targets have changed, the clinician should consult the PTC grid to plan out which components may be used. (Note: As the session unfolds, the therapist may abandon or change planned components to address issues that newly emerge.)

- Opening (5–15 minutes):

  1. Spend a few minutes making contact with the client. Authentic caring and interest should be expressed early in the session and repeated thereafter as appropriate (Chapter 8).

  2. Inquire about any changes in the youth's life since the last session.

     - Have there been any new traumas or victimization?
     - Has the client engaged in any dysfunctional, self-destructive, or risky behaviors?
     - If any of the foregoing is of concern, work to assure or increase the client's ongoing physical safety. Do this before (or instead of) formal trauma processing.

  3. Check with the adolescent regarding his or her symptoms since the last session. Have intrusive or avoidance symptoms increased significantly between sessions? If yes, normalize the experience and validate symptoms as internal trauma processing. If the intrusions or avoidance responses are substantial, consider decreasing the intensity of exposure and activation in the current session.

  4. Based on information from the opening part of the session, revise—if necessary—the goals of treatment for the session.

  5. If the client is especially anxious or hyperaroused, or if the therapist chooses to begin each session this way, spend five minutes or so doing a relaxation or breathing exercise, or brief mediation (see Chapter 11 for information on these options), in

order to begin the session at a lower level of activation and to encourage more mindful (here-and-now) attention.

- Midsession (20–30 minutes):

  1. Provide emotional and cognitive memory processing, as needed, staying within the therapeutic window (Chapters 12 and 14). Facilitate the youth's discussion of his or her trauma history and support identification and expression of emotions when possible. Communicate caring and support.

  2. If significant processing turns out to be contraindicated (i.e., because it is potentially overwhelming or new safety issues emerge), revert to safety/stabilization interventions (Chapter 9), or engage in psychoeducation (Chapter 10), affect regulation skill building (Chapter 11), or less activating cognitive interventions (Chapter 12).

  3. Avoid therapist-centered activities, extensive interpretation, or lecturing. Maintain and communicate a nonjudgmental, caring, and accepting attitude.

- Later in session (15–25 minutes):

  1. Debrief, normalize, and validate any material (cognitive or emotional) or client responses that emerged during the session.

  2. Inquire about the client's experience during emotional or cognitive processing, as well as any other thoughts or feelings he or she had during the session.

  3. Provide cognitive reconsideration, as needed (Chapter 12), for additional cognitive distortions that emerged during debriefing.

  4. If the client's level of activation remains high, work to de-escalate his or her emotional arousal. This may include identifying and resolving conflicts or emotional responses left over from earlier in the session; a reduced focus on—or redirection from—further emotional processing; further cognitive processing; or breathing/relaxation and/or grounding (see Chapter 11).

- Ending (Last 5–15 minutes):

  1. Remind the client (if necessary) of the potential delayed effects of trauma processing, including possibly increased flashbacks, nightmares, and—for some clients—a desire to engage in avoidance activities such as substance abuse or tension-reduction behaviors.

Do this in a noncatastrophizing/nonpathologizing way, and omit this step if it does not appear necessary.

2. If relevant, acknowledge and validate any relational activation and/or processing that occurred in the session. Reframe and/or normalize any conflict or relational distortions that occurred as potential evidence of good therapeutic interaction. This is not a time to engage in further relational processing, only to acknowledge and reassure.

3. Provide safety planning (if necessary) regarding dangers identified in the session or any possible self- (or other) destructive behavior that may emerge between sessions (Chapter 9).

4. Provide closure statements (e.g., summing up the session) and encouragement.

5. If indicated, spend three to five minutes doing a breathing or relaxation exercise, in order to allow the session to end in a relatively calm state.

6. Explicitly refer to the time and date of the next session.

7. End with some communication of caring, appreciation, and hope.

SECTION III

Treatment Components

8

Relationship Building
and Support

As noted earlier, a positive therapeutic relationship is of major importance in the treatment of multiply abused or traumatized individuals. Because of its crucial nature, the relationship between client and therapist should be directly addressed in the same way as are other clinical phenomena. It may not be sufficient to merely wait for a positive relationship to build on its own accord. Traumatized youth may experience significant ambivalence—if not outright distrust—regarding any sort of enduring attachment to an older, more powerful figure. Others appear to attach very quickly, but their connection may remain insecure, based primarily on relational hunger or neediness associated with early attachment deprivation rather than a true belief in safety. In either instance, therapy may be slowed or compromised by insufficient trust and, as a result, reduced openness to the healing aspects of therapy. This chapter outlines ways in which the clinician can encourage, if not accelerate, a positive therapeutic relationship.

Safety

Because danger is such a part of many trauma survivor's lives, the therapist's ability to communicate and demonstrate safety is a central component to relationship building. The adolescent is more likely to "let his or her guard down" and open himself or herself to a relationship if, repeatedly over time, there is little evidence of danger in the therapy process. Conversely, if the client perceives or believes that some form of danger (whether it be physical, sexual, or associated with criticism or judgment) is potentially present, this experience may become a trigger for memories of prior instances of victimization, betrayal, exploitation, or abandonment, that—when reexperienced in the session—may reinforce the client's mistrust and hypervigilance.

Therapist behaviors and responses that increase the client's sense of safety are likely to include the following:

• *Nonintrusiveness*: The clinician is careful to avoid questions or behaviors that push the youth beyond where he or she is willing to go, that activate feelings of shame, or that violate his or her personal/cultural boundaries.

• *Visible positive regard*: The therapist is able to access and communicate positive feelings about the client and to respond to the client in ways that reinforce the client's entitlements and intrinsic value.

• *Reliability and stability*: The clinician behaves in such a manner that he or she is perceived as someone the client can count on—to be on time for sessions, to keep therapy safe, to be available at times of need, and to be an "anchor" in terms of consistent emotional caring.

• *Transparency*: The therapist is as honest and open as possible and does not appear to be operating with hidden agendas—including covert alliances with parents or social institutions—over the youth's own needs. Obviously, in some cases, the clinician must be responsive to systems beyond the client, but when this must occur, the therapist discloses this to the client so that he or she does not appear to be operating from duplicity.

• *Demarking the limits of confidentiality*: In some ways similar to transparency, confidentiality issues are highly relevant to the client's overall perception of the therapist as predictable and straightforward. This means that the clinician should always be clear with the adolescent regarding his or her responsibility to report child or elder abuse, some instances of domestic violence, and client danger to self or others, or to otherwise intervene without the client's permission when certain events occur or are likely to occur. Although such initial discussions are sometimes difficult, and the client may view them as evidence of clinician authoritarianism or dominance, in reality, the message is the reverse—that the client can count on the therapist to try to keep him or her safe and to clearly demarcate the rules and boundaries of therapeutic interaction so that there are few surprises.

- *Careful attention to countertransference issues*: As described later in this chapter, the clinician must strive to avoid responding in ways that reflect his or her history or concerns, as opposed to the client's needs. Minimally, of course, this means avoiding aggressive, seductive, or exploitive behaviors. More subtly, the therapist must be on guard against voyeurism, attention-seeking, excessive self-disclosure, or self-preoccupation that might suggest to the client that he or she is not the primary focus of therapy and, thus, not entirely psychologically safe.

Visible Willingness to Understand and Accept

A major effect of traumatization is often the sense that one is alone, isolated from others, and, in some sense, unknowable. Having the opportunity to interact regularly with someone who listens, and who seems to care and understand, can be a powerfully positive experience—one that tends to strengthen the bond between client and therapist. Therapist behaviors that may increase this dynamic include the following:

- *Attunement*: The clinician is demonstrably aware of the client's moment-to-moment emotional state during treatment, such that the adolescent feels that he or she is attended to and (by implication) worthy of such attention. In this way, the client feels "heard" by someone he or she views as important: a phenomenon that otherwise may be rare in the young person's life.

- *Empathy*: The therapist feels for the client, in the sense that he or she has compassion for the client's predicament or circumstance, and truly wants to help. This is to be discriminated from pity, which implies client weakness or incapacity, and therapist superiority. It should be noted that even true therapist empathy can be problematic if it is expressed too intrusively or couched in a manner that appears artificial or as merely what would be expected of a therapist (Briere, in press).

- *Acceptance*: The clinician is nonjudgmental of the client and accepts the client as he or she is. This does not always mean that the therapist supports the adolescent's behavior, for example, when he or she is involved in self-destructive or hurtful behavior. Instead, the acceptance is of the client, himself or herself—of his or her internal experience, inherent validity, and rights to happiness. When the client feels accepted, he or she has the opportunity to experience relational input that directly contradicts the rejection, criticism, and invalidation he or she may have experienced from harsh family members, peers, or society. This balance between acceptance of the client and, yet, nonsupport of his or her injurious behaviors is sometimes hard to accomplish—especially with acting-out adolescents. Examples would include these:

- o How to accept and support a traumatized, hurt, and angry adolescent without endorsing or reinforcing his aggression toward others
- o How to support a multiply abused and exploited young woman without also supporting her negative views of herself or her suicidal behavior

- *Understanding*: The therapist, partially as a result of his or her attunement and empathy toward the client, and partly due to his or her training, communicates that he or she "gets" the client—that the young person's internal experience and behavior makes sense. Feeling understood by one's therapist generally fosters a sense of shared experience and intensifies the importance and positive nature of the therapeutic relationship.

- *Curiosity about the client's perspective and internal experience*: The therapist communicates an active interest in the client (as opposed to solely support and caring), with respect to his or her perspective on life, the details of his or her interactions with the world, and, most importantly, the specifics of his or her thoughts, feelings, and other internal experiences. This curiosity should not be intrusive, nor should it reflect clinician voyeurism, but rather should communicate the notion that the client's process and experience is interesting, worthy of attention, and reflective of his or her inherent worth.

Active Relatedness (Including Emotional Connection)

ITCT-A encourages the therapist to be an active (as opposed to a passive or neutral) agent in therapy. The therapist makes direct statements about the wrongness of the adolescent/young adult's victimization and shows his or her emotional responses to the extent that they are helpful, i.e., neither extreme nor therapist-focused. The clinician does not give extensive unsolicited advice, but he or she actively assists the client in problem identification and problem-solving, supports and encourages him or her, emphasizes his or her strengths, and generally is psychologically available to the youth within the boundaries of the therapeutic relationship. This approach to therapy encourages connection, because the clinician emerges as an active, caring, and involved participant in the client-therapist relationship.

Patience

Psychotherapy for complex trauma effects rarely proceeds rapidly. Yet, the adolescent (and sometimes the therapist) understandably wants rapid improvement. The client may become frustrated that, for example, cognitive insights do not always result in immediate behavior change or that an instance of talking about a trauma does not immediately desensitize emotional distress to it. Such experiences may lead to helplessness and self-criticism, as the youth interprets a lack of relatively immediate distress reduction, or continued involvement in unhelpful behaviors, as evidence of personal failings. He or she may also feel that he or she is letting the therapist down or in some way being a "bad" or unintelligent client. As the therapist counsels patience and a longer-term perspective, and remains constant and invested in the therapeutic process, he or she communicates acceptance of the client and trust in the value of the therapeutic relationship.

This process requires, of course, therapist patience as well. Despite the prevalence of short-term interventions for traumatized youth in the treatment literature, effective interventions with multiply and chronically traumatized adolescents often take time (see, for example, the treatment outcome data for ITCT-A in Chapter 21, and a study by Lanktree and Briere [1995], wherein longer time in therapy was associated with greater clinical improvement). The development of a trusting relationship with a repeatedly sexually and physically abused 14-year-old, for example, may require a relatively long therapeutic "track record" of safety and support, especially if he or she is also dealing with ongoing community violence, poverty, and lack of family support. There may be distrust of the therapist based on the latter's race, ethnicity, or social status. The client's attention to the therapeutic process may be adversely affected by hunger, lack of sleep (a common issue for youth raised in the context of community violence, chronic maltreatment, or a need to work long hours to support the family), or worry about other compelling, real-life issues, such as impending homelessness or the traumatic loss of a friend. In addition, multiply traumatized adolescents, as noted earlier, frequently suffer from a range of different psychological symptoms or disorders and may be involved in substance abuse—all of which are significant impediments to psychological processing of traumatic stress. As a result, the clinician must be patient in the face of what may appear to be minimal clinical progress within the first months of treatment and should be careful to note and comment upon any signs of progress or emerging psychological strengths. Although the client's problems may be chronic and complex, and his or her current circumstances less than optimal, in many cases socially marginalized and traumatized youth can show real improvement and significant symptom remission in the context of therapies such as ITCT (Lanktree, 2008).

In some cases it may seem that the adolescent or young adult is not that engaged in therapy, and the therapist may become quite discouraged. Yet, if the client is able to attend sessions fairly consistently, process some feelings, relate his or her experiences even minimally, and begin to make more positive behavioral choices for him or herself, the results, over time, may be substantial. In fact, in some cases, even a single session of trauma therapy may have positive impacts on the adolescent survivor, including possibly improving his or her perception of the benefits of future therapy. Whether the progress is major or not, these steps toward recovery are noteworthy and should be recognized and celebrated as such.

Managing Countertransference

Relational treatment can easily be compromised by therapist countertransference, perhaps especially in the face of an externalizing, angry, or self-destructive youth. Given the evocative quality of their suffering, adolescents may trigger strong emotions in clinicians, sometimes motivating a desire to parent, rescue, join, or even punish them. Some therapists may discover previously unrecognized biases against the client based on race, gender, or sexual orientation. The therapist even may become voyeuristic or aroused in the face of a sexualized young person who has learned that sexual appearance or behavior can provide a modicum of control over otherwise powerful people (Briere, 1996a; Dalenberg, 2000).

These various forms of countertransference can, at minimum, decrease the accuracy of the clinician's assessment and reduce the effectiveness of treatment. At worst, they can lead to clinician boundary violations and revictimization of the youth. Even when they do not have obvious negative impacts on the therapy, strongly activated memories or schema are hard on the clinician, making it difficult to avoid cynicism, vicarious traumatization, or burnout.

Managing countertransference with traumatized youth usually revolves around several related activities.

- *Vigilance*: It is important that the clinician regularly monitor himself or herself in work with traumatized youth: Is he or she experiencing

    o Strong, out-of-context or out-of-character emotional states?
    o Behavior patterns that frequently arise in interactions with certain clients?

- ○ A desire to argue with the client that seems to occur on a regular basis?
- ○ An overinvestment in the client or the issues with which the client is struggling?
- ○ Feelings that are clearly based on the therapist's history or unprocessed issues?

- *Behavior control*: Upon discovering significant countertransference, the obvious next step for the clinician is to inhibit any enactment of these feelings, reactions, or biases during the therapy session. Generally, this means that the clinician realizes that he or she inappropriately wants to argue with, dismiss, withhold from, overengage, or overprotect the client and, therefore, works hard to make sure that none of these outcomes ensue. Although it is difficult to provide good therapy while struggling with activated thoughts and feelings, this is, of course, the prime directive—to, above all, do no harm.

- *Access compassion*: When the clinician's responses seem to involve excessive judgment or rejection, it may be helpful to specifically work to increase his or her compassionate appreciation for the client's predicament—whether it be abuse-related anger at authority figures, neediness or demandingness based on early neglect or abandonment, or inappropriately applied survival behaviors that appear as manipulation. Various writers have described ways in which the clinician can engender compassion and nonjudgment in work with challenging clients (e.g., Briere, in press; Germer, Siegel, & Fulton, 2005; Gilbert, 2009).

- *Supervision/consultation*: When countertransference is identified, inhibited, and countered, the clinician may be able to greatly reduce its effects on the therapeutic relationship. However, each of these steps can be facilitated in regular supervision or consultation with someone who can point out issues of which the therapist is unaware and provide meaningful advice. In fact, we strongly suggest that all clinicians and trainees working with traumatized youth receive regular input from a trauma-trained mentor, supervisor, or consultant.

- *One's own psychotherapy*: If countertransference arises from the therapist's own trauma or maltreatment history, it is often helpful for the clinician to seek out his or her own psychotherapy. As the clinician's history is processed in treatment, his or her reactivity to trauma triggers associated with psychotherapy typically lessen significantly—providing benefits for the youth in terms of more accurate and attuned therapy and for the therapist, as he or she is able to engage his or her profession with greater equanimity and self-acceptance.

9

Safety Interventions

Some traumatized youth continue to be at serious risk of victimization, injury, or even death at the time of seeking therapeutic services. This danger may reflect the risks associated with community violence, gang activity, or prostitution, as well as specific life threats from previous perpetrators, boyfriends, stalkers, abusive parents, or drug dealers/abusers. Adolescent women are at significant risk of being raped or otherwise sexually abused by relations, partners, peers, or relative strangers. Openly gay or transgendered adolescents and racial/ethnic minorities may be assaulted in the context of hate crimes. In addition, the adolescent may be self-destructive; either passively through drug abuse, unsafe sexual practices, or involvement in other risky behaviors, as well as through more directly suicidal behavior. The client's behaviors may increase the chance of HIV or hepatitis C infections or, in some states, botched abortions. Homeless adolescents especially run a number of these risks, as do others who spend much of their time on the streets (see the National Child Traumatic Stress Network webpage on homeless youth, http://www.nctsnet.org/nccts/nav.do?pid=ctr_aware_homeless, and Schneir et al., 2007). These dangers are present for most adolescents; they escalate for those who have been previously abused or otherwise traumatized. As noted earlier, childhood maltreatment and other relational traumas are associated with a greater likelihood of subsequent substance abuse, unsafe sexual practices, prostitution, suicidality, and aggression toward others, as well as a greater risk of sexual revictimization.

Given this reality, the clinician must be vigilant to safety issues when working with traumatized youth and must be prepared to act on safety concerns before and during psychological treatment. In fact, ensuring safety is the first requirement of trauma therapy—certainly this includes adolescent and young adult victims. The primary interventions in this area are presented here.

Suicide Assessment and Prevention

Suicidal thoughts and behaviors are relatively common among abused or traumatized individuals (Tiet, Finney, & Moos, 2006; Zlotnick, Donaldson, Spirito, & Pearlstein, 1997), perhaps especially in the context of ongoing adverse conditions (Molnar et al.,1998). In some cases, suicidal behaviors are subtle, for example, when the client engages in high-risk activities and/or fails to protect himself or herself in dangerous situations. In other cases, there may be repeated suicide attempts. The therapist is advised to be alert to the possibility of suicidal behavior when working with any traumatized adolescent and to ask about suicidal lethality (e.g., suicidal plan, available means, and intent; Berman, Jobes, & Silverman, 2006) and previous suicide attempts whenever the client discloses suicidal ideation or is clinically depressed.

In any instance of suicidality, the clinician should develop (or reaffirm) a safety contract with the youth, involving the client's agreement to contact the therapist (or in his or her absence, a preidentified suicide hotline) in the event of any possibility of suicide. When suicidal lethality (i.e., actual likelihood of a fatal attempt) is assessed to be relatively low, further intervention may be limited to discussion of the underlying reasons for considering death and attempting to problem-solve other, less drastic options. When suicidal lethality is greater, psychiatric consultation, evaluation, medication, or hospitalization may be indicated.

On occasion, the client will deny suicidal thoughts or behaviors upon interview, yet endorse them on psychological testing. In the typical tests administered to traumatized youth, this will be evident on critical items of the Trauma Symptom Checklist for Children or the Trauma Symptom Inventory. In addition, the new Trauma Symptom Inventory-2 has a specific *Suicidality* scale.

Child Protection or Law Enforcement Services for Victims of Intrafamilial Abuse

Because most nonemancipated adolescents under age 18 are considered children by state law, those who are being maltreated by parents, caretakers, or other family members are subject to intervention by child protection agencies. As well, older youth victimized by partners, peers, or adults typically have the option of making a police report and seeking protection. Although the client may be opposed to the involvement of child protective services or the police—especially if they have had negative experiences with such officials in the past—the clinician has a legal and ethical duty to report child endangerment to such agencies (Meyers, 2002).

Although there may be no duty for the therapist to report peer victimization to the police, this is not always true. For example, in some jurisdictions, intimate partner violence must be reported to authorities. In any event, the clinician should always seek legal consultation when there is any possibility of harm to the client or others. In the best case, the client's safety is dramatically increased, and the perpetrators are addressed by the criminal justice system.

In some cases, an adolescent or young-adult client will disclose abuse that has not been previously reported to child protection services or law enforcement. When the therapist makes the appropriate report, the client may appreciate that their concerns and safety are being taken seriously by the clinician and become more trusting and engaged with the therapist. Such an occasion may be the first (or at least most significant) experience of being protected by an adult, thereby typically improving the therapeutic relationship. In the worst case, the client may feel betrayed and abruptly terminate his or her relationship with the therapist. More often, however, the clinician can negotiate this process with the adolescent, supporting him or her through the reporting experience and maintaining an enduring therapeutic relationship. In some cases, in fact, the youth and the clinician can even make the report together, thereby increasing the client's sense of collaboration and involvement in his or her own treatment and well-being.

Assistance in Separating From Gangs

Gang involvement is often a double-edged sword for adolescents living in inner-city environments. On one hand, it may offer protection from other gang members and may provide a context for affiliation with peers (Cummings & Monti, 1993). On the other, it is associated with both engaging in violence and being physically injured or killed by others. Although the clinician almost always wants the client to avoid gang affiliation, or to extract himself or herself from gang activity, the youth may be quite ambivalent about doing so, and/or may fear retribution from gang members if he or she leaves. The therapist can probably be most helpful by working with the client in a pragmatic, problem-solving sort of way, providing opportunities for the youth to determine what he or she wants, consider his or her best options, and, if the decision is to try to leave the gang, facilitate that process. In some cases, the client can be referred to groups or agencies that assist young people in finding alternatives to gang involvement and that provide a social support system that can substitute for gang affiliation. These agencies may also provide school-based services for youth at high risk of (or already having) gang involvement. This approach especially assists adolescents who would otherwise avoid mental health–based agencies or centers.

Working With Prostitution Issues

It is not uncommon for homeless (often runaway) adolescents, especially those with histories of childhood sexual, physical, or emotional abuse, to become involved in prostitution or other exploitation by the sex industry (Farley, 2003; Webber, 1991; Widom & Kuhns, 1996; Yates, MacKenzie, Pennbridge, & Cohen, 1988). In some cases, the youth may be recruited and controlled by a pimp. In others, the survivor may exchange sex for drugs, food, or shelter. Although prostitution is almost always a very negative experience—in many cases requiring the client to abuse drugs in order to continue it—and is associated with an elevated risk of assault, disease, depression, and posttraumatic stress (Farley, 2003), clinician entreaties that the adolescent just stop such behavior are often less than effective. Instead, the therapist may be most helpful by (a) providing therapeutic support and opportunities to process child abuse-related memories and assumptions that increase the likelihood of involvement in the sex industry, (b) facilitating exploration of other possible options for survival that are less injurious than prostitution, (c) forming a safe and caring relationship that can be antidotal to the survivor's other, more detrimental and exploitive relationships with customers, pimps, and other adolescents caught in prostitution, (d) increasing access to social and medical services, including referral to agencies or shelters specifically created for sexually exploited youth, (e) in some cases, helping to develop safety plans (see the following section) regarding escape from pimps, and (f) providing assistance with any related substance abuse problems (Schneir et al., 2007; Thompson, McManus, & Voss, 2006; Yates, MacKenzie, Pennbridge, & Swofford, 1991).

Safety Plans in Cases of Ongoing Child Abuse, Exploitation, or Domestic Violence

If the adolescent currently lives with an abusive parent figure or a physically or sexually abusive partner, or is under the control of some other potentially violent or sexually exploitive person, it is a good idea for the therapist and client to create a "safety plan" (Jordan, Nietzel, Walker, & Logan, 2004)—whether or not the client believes it is necessary. For younger adolescents, this may involve identifying a teacher, relative, or other trusted adult whom the child can contact in a specific manner if he or she feels endangered. For older adolescents, this may include developing a detailed strategy for exiting the home or environment when imminent danger is present (e.g., prepacked bags, planned escape routes, hidden cash) and finding a new, safer, environment, whether at a friend's home, a domestic violence shelter, or a drop-in center for the homeless. A preplanned escape option allows the youth to immediately enact a well-thought-out plan in an emergency, without having to devise one at the last minute. Client-therapist problem-solving activities that involve safety planning are often helpful not only because they increase the survivor's safety, but also because the process itself is often empowering (Jordan et al., 2004).

Intervening in Substance Abuse

As noted earlier, substance abuse is a common problem among traumatized adolescents. The comorbidity of trauma symptoms and use of drugs or alcohol can be an issue for treatment, because substance use can interfere with trauma processing, and high levels of trauma symptoms can reduce the capacity of survivors to tolerate internal states without the use of drugs or alcohol (Ouimette & Brown, 2003). Unfortunately, the usual clinical recommendation that substance-abusing clients be drug and alcohol abstinent before undergoing trauma therapy is problematic for many clients, including marginalized, multiproblem adolescents who may be quite reluctant to discontinue the use of agents that numb distress. Instead, although ITCT-A encourages clients' avoidance of chemical dependency, it does not require it—the youth is "taken as he or she is" and assisted within the constraints of what he or she will accept or tolerate—while at the same time offered the option of referral to a self-help program (e.g., Alcoholics Anonymous or Narcotics Anonymous) or a substance abuse treatment program. Of course, a client who is truly unable to engage in trauma-focused treatment, and is seeking treatment for substance abuse, should be referred for substance abuse treatment. In such cases, it should be clearly indicated to the client that he or she is welcome to return to trauma-focused treatment when he or she is more able to benefit from trauma processing.

For the majority of traumatized youth with substance abuse problems, who can engage in ITCT-A, intervention usually involves greater titration of cognitive and exposure-based processing of trauma, as outlined in later chapters, as well as greater attention to the development of affect regulation skills (see Chapter 11) and processing of trauma-related cognitions (see Chapter 12); interventions that may, eventually, remove the need for substance abuse. A highly recommended version of this approach is Najavits's (2002) "Seeking Safety" model for treating substance-abusing trauma survivors, even though that approach significantly deemphasizes the need for memory processing, per se.

Self-Mutilatory Behavior

Perhaps one of the most troubling behaviors seen in traumatized youth is self-mutilation. Usually involving nonsuicidal cutting or burning of the extremities, but also sometimes nonlethal self-injury to sexual areas and/or the trunk of the body, significant self-mutilatory behavior (SMB) often begins in adolescence (Briere & Gil, 1988) and becomes less prevalent as the trauma survivor ages. In many cases, SMB occurs after the adolescent has encountered perceived abandonment in a relationship and/or following a relational conflict (Briere, 1996a). Importantly, although sometimes accompanying suicidal ideation or behavior, self-cutting or burning is often nonsuicidal in nature and may even be used by the youth as a way to survive overwhelming emotion so that suicidality is not required. A series of three studies by Briere and Gil (1988) found that SMB is relatively common among clinically presenting child (especially sexual) abuse survivors and often is engaged in as a way to reduce emotional distress, posttraumatic symptoms, and unwanted dissociation. In fact, in the study of 93 chronic self-mutilators, 77 percent reported an improvement in negative emotional states following SMB, although most stated that they would like to stop using SMB if they could.

As for substance abuse, the primary intervention approach for SMB is to insure immediate safety—even including, if necessary, hospitalization when SMB is severe and disfiguring or life-threatening. Unfortunately, as many therapists will agree, SMB can be a chronic behavior for traumatized youth and young adults, who may engage in burning or cutting of the extremities on a regular basis as a way to reduce triggered emotional distress. In such instances, short of hospitalization, and/or immediate intervention around the triggering event, there is often little that the clinician can do to make the client "give up" such behaviors, at least in the immediate-term. Instead, as is true for other motivated avoidance strategies, the most effective ITCT-A interventions often are (a) de-escalation of the current crisis state, involving problem-solving, support, and use of distress-reducing activities like grounding or breath-based relaxation, (b) ongoing emotional processing of painful memories, so that, when triggered, they no longer have the power to engender SMB, and (c) the development of affect regulation capacities and behaviors, so that triggered distress is less overwhelming and thus more manageable without the need for SMB. The reader is referred to Chapters 11 and 13 for ITCT-A components often helpful in reducing SMB and other tension-reduction activities in youth.

Supporting Safer Sexual Behavior

Childhood abuse in general, and sexual abuse in particular, is associated with involvement in unsafe sexual behavior (i.e., involving risk of HIV/AIDS or other serious diseases, as well as sexual revictimization), along with substance abuse that may, in turn, lead to risky sexual activities (Koenig, O'Leary, Doll, & Pequenat, 2003). Prior victimization places the adolescent at increased risk in many ways. He or she may seek out unsafe intimate relationships that, as a result of early maltreatment, paradoxically feel safer than other, less exploitive relationships, due to their familiarity. The effects of abuse on self-esteem also may lead the youth to assume that current relational maltreatment is all that he or she can expect and that their sexuality, being of little worth, is easily traded for food, shelter, or protection. If he or she lives on the streets, sex may even appear to be the adolescent survivor's best (or only) commodity for exchange.

In general, ITCT-A interventions in this area involve providing psychoeducation on safer sex practices; increasing self-esteem, including building a sense of entitlement to positive treatment from others; desensitizing traumatic memories that, when activated, can lead to substance abuse or tension-reduction behaviors; cognitive processing of abuse-related cognitive distortions that lead to reduced self-assertion or self-protection; problem-solving around how to accomplish the greatest level of safety even while on the streets and/or involved in prostitution; and working with specific substance abuse issues (Briere, 2003; Koenig et al., 2003). Less effective are therapist attempts to push the client to immediately cease all dangerous sexual practices (i.e., repeated insistence that the youth "just say no"), moralistic or shaming statements, scare tactics, or repetitive arguments with the client regarding his or her dysfunctional thinking. Such behaviors are especially likely to be unsuccessful when they ask the client to do something that he or she is not able or ready to do, such as resisting sexual demands or aggressive sexual behavior in situations where he or she feels little power to do so.

As is potentially true for other self-endangering or risky behavior the youth may engage in, some jurisdictions may expect the therapist to inform parents of their children's unsafe sexual practices. On the other hand, there are obviously confidentiality issues at stake as well, and some older adolescents may have the right to keep discussions with their therapists private. We suggest that the reader seek legal consultation in this and any other context where there may be a duty to report.

Referral to Shelters and Programs

A final safety intervention is referral. Because older adolescents' environment may be dangerous in the ways outlined in this chapter, especially if he or she has no access to safe, reliable, and at least semipermanent housing, referral to a shelter may be indicated. Depending on the region, large cities in the United States frequently have outreach programs for runaway, homeless, substance-addicted, prostitution-involved, or physically endangered youth who lack parental supervision. Not only do such agencies offer a degree of safety, they typically provide specialized interventions for adolescents with these problems. In this regard, it is important that referral options for traumatized youth be "kid friendly" and able to deal with the typical problems and issues presented by this population (Schneir et al., 2007). Unfortunately, funding and governmental support for quality programs is often limited, despite their importance. When available, they can make a serious difference for multiply traumatized youth.

10

Psychoeducation

Although therapy for trauma-related problems often involves the processing of traumatic memories, psychoeducation can also be an important aspect of trauma treatment. Many adolescent survivors of interpersonal violence were victimized in the context of overwhelming emotion, narrowed or dissociated attention, and, in many cases, at a relatively early stage of cognitive development; all of which potentially reduced the accuracy and coherence of their understanding of these traumatic events. In addition, interpersonal violence frequently involves a more powerful figure who justifies his or her aggression by distorting objective reality, for example, by blaming victimization on the victim. These fragmented, incomplete, or inaccurate explanations of traumatic events are often carried by the survivor into adolescence and beyond.

Therapists can assist in this area by providing accurate information on the nature of trauma and its effects and by working with the youth to integrate this new information and its implications into his or her overall perspective. Although often presented relatively early in treatment, psychoeducational activities are helpful throughout the therapy process. Supportive partners and/or caretakers may also be engaged in psychoeducation when it is appropriate and helpful for the client. The use of psychoeducation is also addressed in Chapters 17 and 18, regarding interventions with family members and caretakers, as well as Chapter 19, in terms of group therapy.

Handouts

Whether it occurs in individual therapy or in a guided support group, psychoeducation sometimes includes the use of printed handouts. These materials typically present easily understood information on topics such as the prevalence and impacts of interpersonal violence, common myths about victimization, and social resources available to the survivor.

The therapist should keep several issues in mind when deciding what written material to make available and how it should be used (Briere & Scott, 2006):

- The quality of the materials
- The reading level required
- The language of the materials
- The cultural appropriateness of the information or depictions
- The risk of insufficient cognitive-emotional integration—especially if the materials are merely handed out without sufficient discussion or application to the client's own history or current situation

Most importantly, handouts should be considered tools in the psychoeducation process, not stand-alone sources of information. Didactic material, alone, may not be especially effective in changing the beliefs or behaviors of a victimized individual. Instead, the therapist should ensure that the information is as personally relevant to the youth as possible, so that whatever is contained in the handout or media is directly applicable to his or her life and thus has greater implicit meaning. Further, we recommend that such material be actively discussed between client and therapist, so that misunderstandings can be corrected, and the applicability of the material to the youth's actual experience can be emphasized.

Books and Other Materials

Clinicians may also refer clients to readily available books that are "survivor friendly." Although obviously limited to those with adequate reading skills (a significant problem for some traumatized adolescents), such books allow clients to "read up" on traumas similar to their own. Some books may be too emotionally activating for youths with unresolved posttraumatic difficulties, however, at least early in the recovery process. Others may contain erroneous information or suggest self-help strategies that are not, in fact, helpful. For these reasons, the clinician should personally read any book before recommending it to the adolescent; not only to make sure that it is appropriate to his or her needs, and is factually accurate, but also in terms of its potential to activate significant posttraumatic distress in those unprepared for such emotional exposure. Therapists may also use DVDs, YouTube files, or other media designed to address victimization issues (e.g., recognizing abusive behavior in dating relationships, portrayals of abuse and neglect). As an example, a MCAVIC therapist working with high-risk, traumatized youths in school settings used film footage from a sporting event, depicting the negative effects of violence on the athletes involved, to educate clients— who were more responsive to films than books—on the dangers of violent behavior toward others. Importantly, whenever using such materials in sessions, it is essential that there be sufficient time after viewing the material for the client to process his or her feelings and reactions as well as how the information may be helpful to him or her.

Verbal Information During Therapy

Although written psychoeducational materials can be helpful, it is often more useful for the therapist to provide such information verbally during the therapy process. This is especially true for "street kids" and youth who, for whatever reason, have not progressed far, or well, in the educational system. Because the information is directly imbedded in the therapeutic context, it is often more relevant to the client's experience and thus more easily integrated into his or her understanding. Additionally, psychoeducation provided in this manner allows the therapist to more easily monitor the client's responses to the material and to clear up any misunderstandings that might be present.

General Focus of Psychoeducation

Whether through written or verbal means, clinicians often focus on several major topics when working with adolescent (and other) trauma survivors. These include the following:

- The prevalence of the trauma (e.g., in contrast to the youth's impression that only he/she has been victimized)
- Common myths associated with the trauma (e.g., that victims ask for or deserve victimization)
- The usual reasons why perpetrators engage in interpersonal violence (e.g., to address their own needs or as a reflection of their own inadequacies)

- Typical immediate and longer-term responses to trauma (e.g., posttraumatic stress, depression, intimacy issues, or substance abuse)
- Reframing substance abuse and "acting out" or tension-reduction behaviors as adaptive strategies that, nevertheless, may have serious negative repercussions
- Warning signs of unsafe situations, such as peer physical or sexual assault, and strategies for keeping oneself safe and nonviolent toward others
- Normal sexual development and safer sexual practices
- Resources available to the trauma survivor (e.g., printed information, self-help groups, shelters, advocacy groups, or supportive legal or law enforcement personnel)

As is noted in the chapter on cognitive processing, psychoeducation is probably best understood as a component of a larger strategy: an attempt to assist the youth in updating (and/or actively countering) the understandings, beliefs, and expectations that he or she developed during earlier adverse experiences. In some cases, the adolescent is provided with information that is more accurate than what he or she believes (psychoeducation). In other instances, therapy may involve opportunities for the client to directly work with these thoughts and beliefs until a more benign and reality-based understanding arises (i.e., through the cognitive interventions described in Chapter 12). In many cases, these two approaches are combined. Regardless of what and how psychoeducation is delivered, it should be integrated into the ITCT-A treatment process according to the client's individual ability and readiness to receive such information, much in the way that therapeutic exposure should be titrated to the survivor's existing affect regulation capacities.

11

Distress Reduction and
Affect Regulation Training

Adolescents and young adults with complex trauma exposure often
experience chronic and intense emotional distress as well as more
classic posttraumatic symptomatology. Many also describe extremely negative emotional responses to trauma-related stimuli and memories—feeling
states that are easily triggered by later relationships and dangerous environments. When faced with overwhelming negative emotions and trauma
memories, the youth is often forced to rely on avoidance strategies such as
substance abuse, tension-reduction activities, or dissociation (Briere, Hodges,
& Godbout, 2010).

Unfortunately, high levels of avoidance appear to interfere with psychological recovery from the effects of trauma (Briere, Scott, & Weathers, 2005;
Polusny, Rosenthal, Aban, & Follette, 2004). In the worst case, the need to
avoid additional posttraumatic distress may cause the emotionally overwhelmed client to avoid threatening or destabilizing material during therapy,
or to drop out of treatment altogether. This scenario is exemplified by the
psychosocially overwhelmed youth who either is so involved in avoidance
behaviors that his or her participation in treatment is minimal, or who
attends therapy for one or two sessions, then disappears.

The interventions in this chapter have two foci: the reduction of acute,
destabilizing emotions and symptoms (distress reduction) and increasing
the client's more general capacity to regulate negative emotional states (the
development of affect regulation skills). This material is presented before the

71

chapters on cognitive and exposure-based processing because, in some cases, low affect regulation capacity must be addressed before more classic trauma therapy (e.g., therapeutic exposure) can occur (Cloitre et al., 2010; Pearlman & Courtois, 2005). In this regard, the overwhelmed, often highly avoidant adolescent may require a "track record" of safe and positive interactions with the therapist, some level of environmental safety, and considerable exposure to grounding, stress reduction, and affect regulation interventions before any substantial processing of memory material can be done.

Acute Distress Reduction

Acute stress reduction involves techniques that reduce triggered, overwhelming states that can emerge during therapy, such as panic, flashbacks, intrusive emotional states (e.g., terror or rage), dissociative states, or even transient psychotic symptoms. These internal processes can be frightening—if not destabilizing—to the young survivor and can diminish his or her moment-to-moment psychological contact with the therapist. At such times, it may be necessary to refocus the client's attention on to the immediate therapeutic environment—with its implicit safety and predictability—and the therapist-client connection.

These interventions may also be of use to the trauma survivor outside of the therapy session. For example, learning to "ground" oneself or induce a more relaxed state may be helpful when the youth encounters potentially threatening or destabilizing experiences in his or her life, such as in conflicts with others, exposure to trauma triggers, at school, or even when applying for a job or going on a first date.

Grounding

Grounding involves focusing the client's attention away from potentially overwhelming negative thoughts, feelings, and memories. The ability to disengage from intrusive, escalating internal states can be learned and then applied when necessary. As noted earlier, the therapist can teach the adolescent or young-adult client how to ground himself or herself during treatment sessions, when triggered memories produce potentially overwhelming emotional states. This skill can then be used by the client to address destabilizing states outside of treatment.

Grounding typically involves the following steps:

1. Ask the adolescent to *briefly* describe his or her internal experience. For example, "Susan, is something going on/upsetting you/happening right now?" If the adolescent is clearly frightened or responding to distressing internal stimuli, but can't or won't describe them, go to Step 2 below. If the client is able to talk about the internal experience, however, it is often helpful for him or her to generally label or broadly describe the experience. This does not mean the survivor should go into great detail—detailed description of the flashback or dissociative state may increase its intensity, thereby reinforcing the response rather than lessening it.

2. Orient the youth to the immediate, external environment. This often involves two, related messages: (a) that the client is safe and not, in fact, in danger, and (b) that he or she is here (i.e., in the room, in the session, with the therapist) and now (i.e., not in the past, actually experiencing the trauma). In some cases, the client can be assisted by reassuring statements, typically using the client's name as an additional orienting device (e.g., "Susan, you're okay. You're here in the room with me. You're safe.") In others, grounding may involve asking the client to describe the room or other aspects of the immediate environment (e.g., "Susan, let's try to bring you back to the room, OK?" followed by "Where are we?" "What time is it?" or "Can you describe this room?"). The client might be asked to focus his or her attention on the feeling of the chair or couch underneath him or her, or of his or her feet on the floor. Some clinicians place a hand on the client's shoulder or arm, so that the sensation of physical touch can both reassure and "bring him or her out" of an escalating internal state. This is generally not recommended, however, unless the clinician knows how touch will be interpreted by the client. For some victims of sexual or physical assault, for example, touch may trigger memories of the assault and increase, rather than decrease, negative internal states.

However accomplished, the client's reorientation to the here and now may occur relatively quickly (e.g., in a few seconds) or may take substantially longer (e.g., a number of minutes).

3. If indicated, focus on breathing or other methods of relaxation (described later in this chapter). Take the adolescent through a relaxation or breathing exercise for as long as is necessary (typically for several minutes or longer), reminding the client of his or her safety and presence in the here and now.

4. Repeat Step 1, and assess the client's ability and willingness to return to the therapeutic process. Repeat Steps 2 and 3 as needed.

If it is possible for therapy to return to its earlier focus, the clinician should normalize the traumatic intrusion (e.g., as a not-unexpected part of trauma processing), use the grounding activity (e.g., as a simple procedure for focusing attention away from intrusive events), and continue trauma treatment, albeit at a temporarily reduced level of intensity. It is important that the youth's temporary reexperiencing or symptom exacerbation be neither stigmatized nor given greater meaning than appropriate. The overall message should be that trauma processing sometimes involves the intrusion of potentially upsetting memories, thoughts, and/or feelings, but that such events are part of the healing process, too.

Relaxation

One of the most basic forms of arousal reduction during therapy is learned relaxation. Strategically induced relaxation can facilitate the processing of traumatic material during the therapy session by reducing the adolescent's or young adult's overall level of anxiety. Reduced anxiety during trauma processing lessens the likelihood that the client will feel overwhelmed by trauma-related distress and probably serves to countercondition traumatic material, as described in Chapter 14. In addition, relaxation can be used by the survivor outside of treatment as a way to reduce the effects of triggered traumatic memories. It is likely, however, that relaxation training alone is insufficient for trauma treatment (Taylor, 2003). Its primary function in ITCT-A is to augment the other components outlined in this book.

Progressive relaxation. This technique involves clenching and then releasing muscles, sequentially, from head to toe, until the entire body reaches a relaxed state (Rimm & Masters, 1979). As clients practice progressive relaxation on a regular basis, most are eventually able to enter a relaxed state relatively quickly. Some practitioners begin each session with relaxation exercises; others teach it initially in treatment and then utilize it only when specifically indicated, for example, when discussion of traumatic material results in a high state of anxiety. It should be noted that, in a small number of cases, the client may experience increased anxiety during relaxation training (Young, Ruzek, & Ford, 1999). In most instances, however, this anxiety passes relatively quickly, especially with reassurance. When it does not, the clinician may choose to discontinue this approach or use the following breath training method.

Breath training. When stressed, many individuals breathe in a more shallow manner, hyperventilate, or, in some cases, temporarily stop breathing altogether. Teaching the youth "how to breathe" during stress can help restore more normal respiration and, thus, adequate oxygenation of the brain. Equally important, as the client learns to breathe in ways that are more efficient and more aligned with normal, nonstressed inhalation and exhalation, there is usually a calming effect on the body and the autonomic nervous system.

Breath training generally involves a guided exercise that teaches the client to be more aware of his or her breathing—especially the ways in which it is inadvertently constrained by tension and adaptation to trauma—and to slow and deepen his or her breath so that more effective and calming respiration can occur. The following is one approach to breath training, adapted from Briere and Scott (2006).

First,

1. Explain to the client that learning to pay attention to breathing, and learning to breathe more slowly and deeply, can both help with relaxation and be useful for managing anxiety. Note that when we get anxious or have a panic attack, one of the first things that happens is that our breathing becomes shallow and rapid. When we slow down fearful breathing, fear, itself, may slowly decrease.

2. Explain that, initially, some people become dizzy when they start to breathe more slowly and deeply—this is a normal reaction. For this reason, they should not try breathing exercises standing up until they have become experienced and comfortable with them.

Then,

1. Have the client sit in a comfortable position.

2. Go through the following sequence with the client—the whole process should take about 5 to 10 minutes. After each step, "check in" as appropriate to see how the client is feeling and if there are any problems or questions.

    a. If the client is comfortable with closing his or her eyes, ask him or her to do so. Some trauma survivors will feel more anxious with their eyes closed and will want to keep them open. This is entirely acceptable and should be normalized as such.

    b. Ask the client to try to stay in the present while doing breathing exercises. If his or her mind wanders (e.g., thinking about school or about an argument with someone), he or she should gently try to bring his or her attention back to the immediate experience of breathing.

c. Ask the client to begin breathing through the nose, paying attention to the breath coming in and going out. Ask him or her to pay attention to how long each inhale and exhale lasts. Do this for five or six breaths.

d. It is usually helpful for the clinician to breathe along with the adolescent at the beginning of the exercise. You can guide him or her for each inhalation and exhalation, saying "in" and "out" to help him or her along.

e. Instruct the client to start breathing more into his or her abdomen. This means that the belly should visibly rise and fall with each breath. This sort of breathing should feel different from normal breathing, and the client should notice that each breath is deeper than normal. Do this for another five or six breaths.

f. Ask the youth to imagine that each time he or she breathes in, air is flowing in to fill up the abdomen and lungs. It goes into the belly first and then rises up to fill in the top of the chest cavity. In the same way, when breathing out, the breath first leaves the abdomen and then the chest. Some people find it helpful to imagine the breath coming in and out like a wave. Do this for another five or six breaths.

g. Explain that once the client is breathing more deeply and fully into the belly and chest, the next step is to slow the breath down. Ask the client to slowly count to three with each inhalation and to three for each exhalation—in for three counts, hold for a second, and then out for three counts. Inhaling 1 . . . 2 . . . 3 . . . and hold and then exhaling 3 . . . 2 . . . 1 . . . and hold. With practice, the client may begin to slow his or her breath even further. Tell him or her that there is no specific amount of time necessary for each inhalation and exhalation, only that he or she try to slow his or her breathing. Do this for five or six breaths.

3. Ask the client to practice this sequence at home for 5 to 10 minutes a day. He or she should choose a specific time of day (e.g., in the morning, before work or school) and make this exercise a regular part of his or her daily routine. The client should sit or lie down at home in a comfortable position, with no distractions, for this practice.

Eventually, the youth can choose to extend this exercise to other times in the day as well, especially when relaxation would be a good idea, e.g., in stressful social situations or whenever he or she feels especially anxious. Remind the client to internally count during each inhalation and exhalation, since counting, itself, often serves to trigger the relaxation response.

Visualization. A third approach to relaxation does not involve learning to breathe or relax, per se, but rather how to imagine a peaceful or pleasant scene in sufficient detail that relaxation naturally follows. The adolescent or young adult may be encouraged to sit with eyes closed (if possible) and visualize a day at the beach, a mountain lake, or walking in a forest. Often, the therapist verbalizes this scene while the youth attends to it, and then the client continues to imagine it for several minutes while the therapist is silent. Later, at moments of stress, the client can "go back" to the scene, if only for a few seconds or minutes. Some clinicians refer to this as the client going to their "special place," although not all older adolescents or young adults may value this terminology. Importantly, this skill is not useful in a crisis or emergency where the client must react quickly but, rather, when the stress is expected, and the youth has a chance to do this exercise beforehand. It may also be useful for a tape or CD to be made, recording the therapist guiding the client though the imagery. Some clients also find this approach helpful as a sleep technique at night.

Paradoxical anxiety. Because relaxation and breath training, visualization, and meditation (described later) involves decreasing muscle tension, reduced hypervigilance, and potentially increased awareness of internal states, a minority of traumatized youth experience a temporary upsurge in anxiety when beginning these exercises. Typically, individuals experiencing such paradoxical anxiety appear to interpret relaxation or related activities as vulnerability or underpreparedness for danger. If the youth appears especially anxious at such times, redirect his or her attention to outside stimuli or events, much as is described for grounding, and gently terminate the exercise. If it is possible for the youth to try the exercise again without too much distress, the clinician should normalize the anxiety as not unusual, typically transient, and not detrimental, and encourage him or her to try again.

Increasing General Affect Regulation Capacity

Above and beyond immediate methods of distress reduction, such as grounding and relaxation, there are a number of suggestions in the literature for increasing the general affect regulation abilities of trauma clients. All are focused on increasing the survivor's overall capacity to tolerate and down-regulate negative feeling states, thereby reducing the likelihood that he or she will be overwhelmed by activated emotions. In some cases, such affect regulation work may be necessary before any significant memory processing can be accomplished (Briere & Scott, 2005).

Identifying and Discriminating Emotions

An important aspect of successful affect regulation is the ability to correctly perceive and label emotions as they are experienced (Blaustein & Kinniburgh, 2010; Cloitre, Cohen, & Koenen, 2006; Linehan, 1993). Many adolescent survivors of complex trauma have trouble knowing exactly what they feel when triggered into an emotional state, beyond, perhaps, a sense of feeling "bad" or "upset." In a similar vein, some may not be able to accurately discriminate feelings of anger, for example, from anxiety or sadness. Although this sometimes reflects dissociative disconnection from emotion, in other cases it represents a basic inability to "know about" one's emotions. As a result, the youth may perceive his or her internal state as consisting of chaotic, intense, but undifferentiated emotionality that is not logical or predictable. For example, the youth triggered into a seemingly undifferentiated negative emotional state will not be able to say "I am anxious," let alone infer that "I am anxious because I feel threatened." Instead, the experience may be of overwhelming and unexplainable negative emotion that comes out of nowhere. Not only may the unknown quality of these states foster a sense of helplessness, but it often prevents the adolescent from making connections between current emotional distress and the environmental or historical conditions that produced it. Without such insight, the youth is unlikely to be able to intervene in the causes of his or her distress or improve his or her situation.

The clinician can be helpful in this area by regularly facilitating exploration and discussion of the client's emotional experience. In fact, "checking in" with the client multiple times per session is a regular part of ITCT-A. Often, the young survivor will become more able to identify feelings just by being asked about them on a regular basis. On other occasions, the therapist can encourage the client to do "emotional detective work," involving attempts to hypothesize an emotional state based on the events surrounding it or the bodily states associated with it. For example, the client may guess that a feeling is anxiety because it follows a frightening stimulus or is accompanied by hyperventilation, or anger because it is associated with resentful cognitions or aggressive behaviors. Affect identification and discrimination also may occasionally be fostered by the therapist's direct feedback, such as "It looks like you're feeling angry. Are you?" or "You look scared." This last option should be approached with caution, however. There is a real risk of labeling a client's affect as feeling A when, in fact, the client is experiencing feeling B—thereby increasing confusion rather than effective emotional identification. For this reason, it is recommended that, in most instances, the therapist facilitate the client's exploration and hypothesis testing of his or her feeling state, rather than telling the client what he or she is feeling. The critical issue here is not usually whether the client (or therapist) correctly identifies a particular emotional state but, rather, that the client explores and attempts to label his or her feelings on a regular basis. Typically, the more this is done as a general part of therapy, the more skillful the adolescent survivor becomes at accurate feeling identification and discrimination. As the client feels supported in his or her own exploration of feelings, rather than the therapist telling him or her what he or she feels, the therapeutic relationship also may be strengthened.

Identifying and Countering Thoughts That Underlie Negative Emotional States

Not only should the client's feelings be monitored and identified, the same is true for his or her thoughts. This is most relevant in situations when a cognition triggers a strong emotional reaction, but the thought is somehow unknown to the survivor. Affect regulation capacities often can be improved by encouraging the client to identify and counter the cognitions that exacerbate or trigger trauma-related emotions (Linehan, 1993). Beyond the more general cognitive interventions described in Chapter 12, this involves the survivor learning how to identify whatever thoughts mediate between a trigger and a subsequent negative emotional reaction. For example, an adolescent survivor of sexual abuse might think "she wants to have sex with me" when interacting with an older woman and then experience revulsion, rage, or terror. In such cases, although the memory itself is likely to produce negative emotionality, the associated cognitions often exacerbate these responses to produce more extreme emotional states. In other instances, thoughts may be less directly trauma-related, yet still increase the intensity of the client's emotional response. For example, in a stressful situation, the client may have thoughts such as "I'm out of control," or "I'm making a fool of myself" that produce panic or fears of being overwhelmed or judged.

Because triggered thoughts may be out of superficial awareness, their role in subsequent emotionality is not always clear to the survivor. As the client is made more aware of the cognitive antecedents to overwhelming emotionality, he or she can learn to lessen the impact of such thoughts. Often, the mindfulness interventions outlined later in this chapter can facilitate identification of specific cognitions, and recognition that they are just thoughts, not necessarily important information about self or the world. In addition to dismissing such intrusions as "just thoughts," however, the client can learn to explicitly disagree with them (e.g., "nobody's out to get me" or "I can handle this") or explicitly label them as "old movies" rather than accurate perceptions. In this regard, one of the benefits of what is referred to as insight in psychodynamic therapy is often the self-developed realization that one is acting in a certain way by virtue of erroneous, "old" (e.g., trauma- or abuse-related) beliefs or perceptions—an understanding that may lessen the power of those cognitions to produce distress or motivate problematic behavior in the present.

When the thoughts that underlie extremely powerful and overwhelming emotional states are triggered by trauma-related memories during the session, the therapist can focus on these intermediate responses by asking questions such as "What happened just before you got [scared/angry/upset]" or "Did you have a thought or memory?" If the client reports that, for example, a given strong emotion was triggered by a trauma memory, the therapist may ask him or her to describe the memory (if that is tolerable) and to discuss what thoughts the memory triggered, much in the way that is described for trigger identification and intervention in Chapter 13.

In other cases, the triggered emotional state may have occurred in the past, and the therapy discussion centers around a detailed exploration of why the response was as intense as it was. Ultimately, this may involve exploration and discussion of five separate phenomena:

1. *the environmental stimulus* that triggered the memory (e.g., a teacher's angry expression);

2. *the memory itself* (e.g., maltreatment by an angry parent);

3. *the thought associated with the memory* (e.g., "She hates me," "I must have done something wrong," or "She is blaming me for something I didn't do") and the associated feeling (e.g., anger or fear);

4. *analysis of the etiology of these thoughts* (e.g., developed in response to perpetrator statements at a time when the child had few other sources of information and relatively limited cognitive capacities); and

5. *the relative accuracy of the thoughts in the here and now*: a process that will be facilitated by the client describing his or her childhood-based beliefs out loud, where he or she can hear them in the context of therapeutic support and information.

This process is often best facilitated when the exploration is done primarily by the client, with nonjudgmental, guiding support of the therapist as needed. As the client learns to identify these cognitions, place them in some realistic context, and view them as remnants of the past as opposed to data about the present or future, he or she is indirectly developing the capacity to forestall extreme emotional reactivity and thereby better regulating his or her emotional experience.

Meditation

This component, often used in ITCT-A, is in some ways more ambitious than those previously described in this chapter, because it takes more effort and practice. On the other hand, the actual technique is relatively simple and quite effective (e.g., Greenland, 2010; Huppert & Johnson, 2010). Meditation accomplishes more than relaxation; also learned is *mindfulness*— the ability to observe one's internal experience with less judgment; to "let go" of upsetting thoughts, feelings and memories; and, with practice, become less reactive (Germer, Siegel, & Fulton, 2005; Semple & Lee, in press)—all skills that can be helpful for traumatized youth and adults (Briere & Scott, in press; Goodman, 2005). Nevertheless, not all adolescents will want to meditate, and not all therapists will feel comfortable or qualified in teaching it. Importantly, meditation training in ITCT-A should be provided by clinicians who, themselves, have personal, ongoing experience with this practice (Greenland, 2010; Semple & Lee, in press).

The most basic steps of meditation, which can be presented to the youth, are outlined below. The clinician can offer these instructions at the beginning of each session, so that the youth can practice with the therapist on a weekly basis, without distraction from what may be a chaotic, external environment. After the first two or three weeks, the clinician typically invites the youth to practice meditation at home, ideally three or four times a week. This will not be possible, however, if the youth's environment is dangerous; for example, on the streets or in the context of family violence. In such cases, meditation is probably best practiced in the context of therapy sessions only.

If meditation is possible at home, advise the adolescent to find a quiet place where he or she feels safe and can be alone, without interruption, for five minutes or longer.[1] Suggest he or she use this same place every time he or she meditates.

Instructions (Paraphrase as Needed)

Sit in a chair, or on the floor, with your back straight and your hands in your lap. You can lie down, if you wish, but this may make you sleepier.

1. See if you can close your eyes or at least lower your eyelids. If this makes you anxious, it is fine to leave them open.

2. Focus your mind on your breathing and just your breathing: feel the air going into your lungs and then going out.

3. Count each breath, from 1 to 10. As you breathe in, feel the air going in; as you breathe out, feel the air going out and think "1." As you breathe

in again, feel the air going in; as you breathe out again, feel it going out and think "2." Each time you breathe out, think the next number. Do this until you have gotten to "10," and then start over again with "1."

4. When your mind wants to think about other things, just remind yourself to go back to your breathing, watching and feeling the breath go in and out, counting each time you breathe out. Usually people have a hard time just paying attention to their breath and counting. Their mind wanders. That's what minds do. Don't criticize yourself when this happens, just notice what you are doing and go back to watching and feeling yourself breathe in and out, counting from 1 to 10, and over again. Let thoughts and feelings come and go, without thinking they are important, or even true. They are neither good nor bad, right or wrong; they are just thoughts or feelings. Notice them and then return to your breathing.

5. Try to do this for at least five minutes a day, every other day. You can keep a clock or watch next to you to keep track of the time, but try not to look at the time too much. If it has been less than five minutes, just go back to paying attention to your breath and counting. Eventually, you may want to spend more than five minutes mediating or to meditate more times per week. It is up to you.

Mindfulness. The process of meditation often leads to increased *mindfulness*: the moment-by-moment awareness of ongoing experience, without judgment and with acceptance. As the youth learns to focus his or her attention on the breath, he or she becomes more able to sustain attention or concentration for longer periods of time. Also gradually learned is the ability to identify thoughts and feeling that arise during meditation, acknowledge them as such, and then return attention to the breath. This process teaches *metacognitive awareness* (Teasdale, Segal, & Williams, 1995): the capacity to view thoughts, feelings, and memories as temporary, naturally arising phenomena of mind— not necessarily as information about what is actually true of the world or oneself. During meditation, the adolescent or young adult may discover that negative thoughts about self, anxious feelings, or memories of the past emerge into awareness in a seemingly random fashion and don't always "mean" anything: they are just thoughts, feelings, or memories.

Metacognitive awareness can be reinforced before (or after) meditation periods by having weekly, brief discussions with the client about the idea that cognitions are, in the words of one adolescent, "just thoughts, not facts." We suggest paraphrasing the following, varying the material each time you use it, and asking the youth to discuss this information in the context of his or her own specific experience of meditation. As the client becomes more conversant with this material, it may need to be reinforced less often. Instead, for example, the clinician might increasingly refer to this material while addressing self-esteem issues with cognitive interventions presented in Chapter 12. Adjust the syntax and word usage to match the developmental age of the youth: mindfulness is a little hard to convey to anyone, at first, let alone to a young person. But it can be done and can be very helpful.

> When you are doing meditation, it is sometimes good to notice that you are thinking. As you meditate, your thoughts kind of come and go, in your mind, right? That's normal, that's what your brain does—it makes thoughts. Lots of them. But these thoughts are just thoughts, they come out of nowhere, we think them, and then they go away. Then new thoughts come!
> [Engage client in discussion of his or her own experience]
> When you meditate, see if you can just let those thoughts come and go, and realize that they are just thoughts, not always facts about anything that is real. Sometimes we get into trouble by thinking that our thoughts are true. Sometimes they are true, but sometimes they aren't. If you think you are bad, or that everyone hates you, you believe it because you're thinking it, right? But, sometimes, it's just thoughts, things you learned a long time ago that aren't true. It's like you are hearing a CD or watching a movie in your mind, but you believe it!
> [Engage client in further discussion of his or her own experience]
> When you meditate, see if you can see those thoughts floating around, and remind yourself that they don't necessarily mean anything. . . . They are just thoughts, memories, things you say to yourself that, lots of times, don't have anything to do with your life right now. Just notice them, and then go back to paying attention to your breath.

In this way, mindfulness becomes, among other things, an affect regulation device: if the youth's emergent or triggered internal experiences are not necessarily accurate perceptions, but rather "just" productions of the mind, then they can be less frightening, anger-inducing, or depressing (Briere, in press). Similar to "trigger work" (described in Chapter 13), mindfulness allows the youth to be less reactive in response to internally experienced, trauma-related material or processes, as he or she comes to see that they are only what they are.

Although mindfulness is generally developed in the context of meditation, it can also be learned through other exercises or skill development activities. The reader is referred to Goodman (2005), Linehan (1993), and Saltzman and Goldin (2008), for more explicitly focused interventions to increase mindfulness and metacognitive awareness in children and youth, and to Greenland (2010) and Semple and Lee (in press) for fully structured, meditation- and exercise-based approaches to increasing mindfulness in children. Also recommended is Biegel's (2009) stress and mindfulness workbook, written expressly for teenagers, and Blaustein and Kinniburgh's (2010) exercises to increase clients' self-monitoring and self-awareness.

Resistance to Tension-Reduction Behaviors

Another way in which affect regulation skills can be learned is by the youth intentionally forestalling tension-reduction behaviors (TRBs) or other avoidance strategies when the impulse to engage in them emerges (Briere, 1996a). In general, this involves encouraging the client to "hold off," as long as possible, on engaging in behaviors such as self-mutilation, impulsive sexual behavior, substance abuse, or binging/purging that he or she might normally use to down-regulate or avoid triggered distress—and then, if the activity must be engaged in, doing so to the minimal extent possible. Although preventing TRBs entirely would obviously be the best course, in reality the clinician's ability to stop such behavior may be limited, short of hospitalizing the client (although that is sometimes indicated, in extreme cases). Despite the fact that adolescents and young adults have access to more destructive means than do children, and typically have less supervision, it is also true that they have more cognitive capacity and are more able to learn how to problem-solve their impulses. At the same time, it is an unavoidable fact of clinical life that tension-reduction and other avoidance behaviors are—sometimes paradoxically—survival-based and, therefore, not easily given up entirely by the overwhelmed, multiply victimized youth.

In general, it is recommended that the therapist take a clear stand on the harmfulness (but not immorality) of certain behaviors and work with the client to terminate, or at least decrease, their frequency, intensity, and injuriousness. Because TRBs serve to reduce distress, client attempts to delay their use provide an opportunity to develop a small amount of affect tolerance, as well as a growing awareness that the distress triggering TRBs is actually bearable when experienced without behavioral avoidance. For example, if a survivor is able to forestall binge eating or acting on a sexual compulsion—if only for a few minutes beyond when he or she would otherwise engage in such activity—four things may happen:

1. The client is exposed to a brief period of sustained distress, during which time he or she can learn a small amount of distress tolerance.

2. During this time period, the distress—although experienced as overwhelming—does not, in fact, do anything more than feel bad; no catastrophic outcome ensues.

3. The impulse to engage in the TRB may fade, since the emotionality associated with the urge to engage in the TRB often lessens if not immediately acted upon.

4. As the survivor is more able to forestall TRBs and other avoidance activities, he or she may develop greater feelings of self-efficacy and an increasingly positive sense of self.

With continued practice, the period between the initial urge to tension reduce and the actual TRB may be lengthened, the TRB itself may be decreased in severity, and affect tolerance may be increased. Importantly, the goal of decreasing (and then ending TRBs) is seen as not stopping "bad" behavior, per se, but rather as a way for the client to learn affect regulation and to get his or her behavior under greater personal control.

Affect Regulation Learning During Trauma Processing

Finally, affect regulation and tolerance can be learned implicitly during longer-term exposure-based trauma therapy. Because, as discussed in later chapters, trauma-focused interventions involve the repeated activation, processing, and resolution of distressing but nonoverwhelming emotions, such treatment gradually teaches the adolescent survivor to become more "at home" with some level of painful emotional experience and to develop whatever skills are necessary to de-escalate moderate levels of emotional arousal. As the client repetitively experiences titrated (i.e., not overwhelming) levels of distress during exposure to trauma memories, he or she may slowly develop the ability to self-soothe and reframe upsetting thoughts, learn that negative states are survivable, and call upon relational support. In addition, by working with the client to de-escalate distress associated with activated memories, the therapist often models affect regulation strategies, especially those involving normalization, soothing, and validation. However developed, this growing ability to move in and out of strong affective states, in turn, fosters an increased sense of emotional control and reduced fear of negative affect.

Note

1. The relatively short meditation advocated here, relative to the often suggested 20 minutes for adults, reflects the fact that younger people (especially early adolescents) often cannot tolerate longer meditation periods, at least initially. If the youth becomes more adept at meditation, however, longer periods may be recommended by the therapist.

12

Cognitive Processing

As noted earlier, victims of interpersonal violence can be prone to a variety of negative cognitive phenomena, including self-blame, guilt, shame, low self-esteem, overestimation of danger, and other negative beliefs and perceptions. The adolescent survivor of childhood physical and emotional abuse may view his or her maltreatment as just punishment for being "bad." A teenage woman battered by her live-in partner may assume that she deserves to be beaten. Individuals who have been repeatedly exposed to situations in which they were helpless to escape or otherwise reduce their trauma exposure often develop a sense of having little power to affect future potentially negative events. Some adolescent and young-adult survivors view their posttraumatic symptoms as evidence of being mentally ill. Victims of sexual trauma often feel ashamed and isolated by their experiences, partially as a function of socially transmitted myths about rape.

In general, cognitive therapy of posttraumatic disturbance involves the guided reconsideration of negative perceptions and beliefs about self, others, and the environment that arose from the trauma. As these negative assumptions are reevaluated, a more affirming and empowering model of self and others can take their place. At the same time, the client may develop a more detailed and coherent understanding of the traumatic event, a process that is generally associated with clinical improvement. In some cases, considerable cognitive work may need to be done—especially to reduce self-hatred and helplessness—before the youth can engage in the emotional processing described in Chapter 14.

Cognitive Reconsideration

In ITCT-A, trauma-related cognitive disturbance is generally addressed through a detailed verbal exploration of the traumatic event and its surrounding circumstances. As the survivor repeatedly describes the trauma in the context of treatment, he or she, in a sense, relives the past while viewing it from the perspective of the present. By verbally recounting the traumatic event, the adolescent (with the assistance of the therapist) has the opportunity to "hear" the assumptions, beliefs, and perceptions that were encoded at the time of the trauma and to compare them with what he or she now knows. Together, the client and therapist can then work to create a more accurate cognitive model of what occurred. Borrowing from the Self-Trauma model (Briere, 2002; Briere & Scott, 2006) this process is referred to here as *cognitive reconsideration*.

Cognitive reconsideration may foster more positive self-perceptions, as the client comes to reinterpret former "bad" behaviors, deservingness of maltreatment, and presumed inadequacies in a more accurate light. For example, the client who has always interpreted her behavior just prior to a rape as "sluttish" or "asking for it" may gain from the opportunity to revisit and review what actually happened and to see if her judgments about herself seem valid. Exploration of the events prior to the rape may reveal that she was not behaving in a "seductive" manner, nor is she likely to recall actually wanting to be abused or otherwise hurt.

In addition, increased awareness of what one could reasonably have done at the time of the trauma—i.e., what one's options actually were—can be antidotal to inappropriate feelings of responsibility, self-blame, or self-criticism. For example, describing memories of childhood abuse in detail—while at the same time listening to them from the perspective of an older adolescent—may lead the adolescent to the realization that he or she had few options other than accommodation at the time of the abuse. The notion that "I should have done something to stop it," for example, can be countered by a greater understanding of the size and power differentials inherent in an adult forcing himself on a seven-year-old child.

Finally, blaming or shaming statements made by an assailant may eventually lose their power when examined in the context of a safe environment and a caring listener. Many victims of interpersonal violence tend to, on some level, accept rationalizations used by the perpetrator at the time of the assault. These include rapist statements that the victim was asking to be sexually assaulted, child abuser statements that physical abuse was merely appropriate punishment for bad behavior, or emotionally abusive parental or peer statements that the youth was bad, fat, ugly, or worthless. As the client and therapist discuss the circumstances of the event, and consider perpetrator statements in the absence of danger or coercion, the objective lack of support for these statements may become more apparent to the client.

Because the therapist is often more able to see these cognitive distortions than is the client, he or she may feel pressed to voice an opinion regarding the lack of culpability of the victim or the obvious cruelty of the perpetrator. This is understandable and, in small doses, appropriate. But, rarely will such statements, in and of themselves, substantially change the client's opinion. In fact, clinical experience suggests that cognitive therapy is rarely helpful when the clinician merely disagrees (or argues) with the client about his or her cognitions or memories or makes definitive statements about what reality actually is. Rather, cognitive interventions are most effective when they provide opportunities for the client to experience the original trauma-related thoughts and self-perceptions (e.g., feelings of responsibility and guilt when recalling being beaten by a parent), while, at the same time, considering a more contemporary and logical perspective (for example, that the beatings were, ultimately, about the parent's chronic anger, alcoholism, and feelings of inadequacy and not due to the client's failure to be a good child or show proper respect).

As suggested by various writers, the reconsideration of trauma-related assumptions, expectations, or beliefs is probably most effective when it occurs while the adolescent or young adult is actively remembering the trauma and reexperiencing the thoughts and feelings that he or she had at the time (Briere & Scott, 2006; Resick & Schnicke, 1993). Merely discussing a traumatic event without some level of emotional memory activation is less likely to change the cognitions related to the memory. In contrast, active recall and description of a traumatic event probably trigger two parallel processes: (1) observation of one's own trauma-related attributions regarding the specifics of the event and (2) activation of the emotions associated with the event. The second component of this response is covered in detail in the next chapter, under the heading of *titrated exposure*. However, it is important to acknowledge it here because emotional activation allows the client to more directly relive the traumatic event, such that any cognitive interventions are more directly linked to specific memories of the trauma.

There are two major ways that the youth can remember and, to some extent, reexperience traumatic events during the process of treatment: by describing them in detail and by writing about them. In the first instance, the therapist asks the client to describe the traumatic event or events in as much verbal detail as is tolerable, including thoughts and feelings he or she experienced during and after the victimization experience. As noted in Chapter 14, this is an important component of titrated exposure. It also facilitates cognitive processing, however, if it includes discussion of conclusions or beliefs the survivor formed from the experience. In response to the client's description, the therapist generally asks open-ended questions that are intended to make apparent any cognitive distortions that might be present regarding blame, deservingness, or responsibility. As the youth responds to these questions, the therapist provides support and encouragement and, when appropriate, carefully offers information that might counter the negative implications or self-perceptions that emerge in the client's responses (see, e.g., Chapter 10). The client might then have responses that lead to further questions from the therapist. Or, the topic might shift to the client's emotional processing of the implications of any new information, insights, or feelings that arose from the discussion process.

The second major form of cognitive processing involves the use of homework. The adolescent is asked to write about a specific topic related to the trauma, bring it to the next session, and read it aloud in the presence of the clinician. In this way, the client has the opportunity to continue therapeutic activities outside of the session, including desensitization of traumatic memories and continued cognitive reconsideration of trauma-related assumptions and perceptions. In addition, research suggests that the mere act of writing about an upsetting event, especially if done on multiple occasions, can reduce psychological distress over time (Pennebaker, 1993). See Chapter 14 for an example of trauma processing homework, adapted from Resick and Schnicke (1993).

It should be noted, however, that although therapeutic homework is a mainstay of various cognitive-behavioral therapies, self-exposure to trauma-related thoughts or feelings (i.e., without a therapist present) may be challenging, if not overwhelming, for some adolescent or young-adult survivors. If writing about a trauma activates extreme anxiety, self-hatred, or other sufficiently strong negative states, certain youths (e.g., those with low affect regulation capacity) may become "retraumatized"—sometimes then engaging in deleterious avoidance or tension-reduction behaviors, such as substance abuse, self-injury, or binge eating. This is not a common scenario; most traumatized adolescents appear capable of processing trauma-related memories and cognitions on their own, between sessions. Nevertheless, it is recommended that such homework be offered only to those clients who appear able to tolerate it and that their emotional response during and after homework be specifically investigated.

Another potential problem with homework is whether the client has a safe home in which to do it. Some adolescents live in abusive or dangerous environments (e.g., on the streets) where there may be no safe place to write or where the processing of trauma-related material would occur in the context of anxiety or hypervigilance (e.g., in households where there is ongoing violence) and thus potentially result in *re*sensitization of a memory by pairing it with fear. As well, some youth's homework may involve writing about abuse in a home where the perpetrator of that abuse could discover it, thereby placing the adolescent in greater danger. When homework cannot be done in safety, it should not be offered to the client. Or, alternatively, as was sometimes done at MCAVIC-USC, writing exercises can occur in an extended session, perhaps in the first or last 15 minutes of therapy.

However implemented, the goal of writing and/or verbally presenting trauma narratives is to activate the client's memories of the traumatic event and to facilitate their cognitive processing. Such discussions often center around a series of gentle, usually open-ended inquiries that allow the client to progressively examine the assumptions and interpretations he or she has made about the victimization experience.

Typical questions, in this regard, stimulate detailed discussion of the following:

• The youth's thoughts during and after the trauma, including why he or she came to think those things at that time

• Ways in which those thoughts may have become current assumptions, despite their relatively unexamined nature

• The extent to which the trauma may have prevented clear thinking at the time (e.g., the youth's relative lack of power when the event occurred and/or the ability of the perpetrator to control the client's thinking)

• Whether negative cognitions about himself or herself "make sense," given what the adolescent now knows and given the perspective associated with the client's now greater age and current greater safety

• Whether, in light of the specific aspects of the trauma (e.g., the client's youth, lesser power/strength/social entitlements, relative unavailability of help, etc.), there was little the client could have done other than what he or she did do

• Whether he or she actually deserved what happened (e.g., was what happened appropriate punishment, abusive behavior, or a good way to treat a child?)

• Whether, in fact, he or she "asked for it," including whether the client can recall wanting to be raped, beaten, or maltreated or, if the trauma was sexual victimization, whether he or she can remember actually desiring sexual contact with the abuser

- Whether the adolescent's judgments of himself or herself can be generalized to others (e.g., if the trauma happened to another child, would the survivor come to the same conclusions about the other child's badness/stupidity/unacceptability?)

- If the adolescent has internalized the statements of the perpetrator or the responses of other unsupportive people, whether these individuals would generally be people whom the client would take seriously or trust regarding their opinions on other topics

The intent of such cognitive exploration is for the youth to update his or her trauma-based understanding—not to incorporate the therapist's statements or beliefs regarding the true state of reality or the client's thinking errors. Although therapist feedback about the presumed reality of things may sometimes be helpful, much of the knowledge the client acquires in therapy is best learned from himself or herself. By virtue of the opportunity to repeatedly compare "old" trauma-based versions of reality with newer understandings, especially in the context of a safe and supportive environment, the client can often revise his or her personal history—not in the sense of making things up, but by updating beliefs that were made under duress and never revisited in detail. Importantly, good cognitive therapy is not an argument between client and therapist; instead, it represents an opportunity for the adolescent to reconsider previous assumptions and beliefs in the context of current safety, support, gentle inquiry, and new information. As is true for other treatment components as well, this process is likely to be more effective if a positive therapeutic relationship has been established.

The therapist may stimulate these discussions as the description of the trauma unfolds or after the client's verbal rendition is completed. Often the latter approach is especially helpful: encouraging the client to describe the trauma in detail and then following up with questions and detailed exploration. In doing so, the client is more able to fully expose himself or herself to the story, with its associated emotional triggers, and the therapist has a better chance of determining what the client thinks about the trauma without the rendition being affected by therapist responses.

Cultural and developmental issues. Throughout treatment, it is important that the therapist consider cultural factors that might inhibit or encourage the cognitive aspects of therapy. For example,

- Is the client able to describe the trauma in his or her primary language? This may not be possible and still produce a positive outcome, but it is possible that first-language processing is more effective.

- Does the client's culture contribute to the harmful trauma-related beliefs he or she holds? If the youth's sociocultural environment supports ideas about appropriate sexual conduct that reinforce shame or guilt, for example, it may be harder (but not impossible) to help the client reassess the validity of these ideas or attributions.

- Do racial or cultural differences between client and therapist make it hard for the client to process beliefs or assumptions arising from exposure to racism or other forms of oppression? When the therapist is of the majority race or ethnicity and the client is not, client distrust and/or expectations of judgment may make it more difficult to address and process these issues in treatment.

Similarly, developmental differences between younger and older adolescents (e.g., neurobiology [especially level of prefrontal functioning], expressive skills, capacity to cognitively process memories, the extent to which the therapist's verbalizations are understood) can have significant impacts on how cognitive reconsideration is applied and received. The clinician must always monitor the developmental appropriateness of his or her verbal interacts and expectations so that they match the level of cognitive development of the client. For example,

- Is the clinician using language that is too complex or too simple?

- Is the understanding that he or she wants for the client possible for someone of the client's psychological or chronological age?

- Is the therapist asking the client to do something that is either too childlike or too adult for him or her to accept?

Nonjudgment. However accomplished, the intent of cognitive therapy in this domain is to assist the client to more fully and accurately explore his or her beliefs or assumptions, without lecturing, arguing, or labeling such beliefs as "wrong." Instead, such cognitions should be viewed (and reflected back to the client) as entirely understandable reactions to overwhelming events that involved extreme anxiety and distress, incomplete information, coercion, confusion, and, in many cases, the need for survival defenses. Trauma-related cognitions should be treated not as the product of client error but, rather, as logical initial perceptions and assumptions that require updating in the context of safety, support, and better/new information. Not only does such a therapeutic stance tend to be more effective than merely informing the client of his or her misperceptions of reality, it is less likely to alienate chronically traumatized youth who may have been on the wrong end of authoritarian power dynamics for many years.

Normalizing or reframing symptomatology. While addressing cognitive distortions about the event and what it means to the client, the clinician also may encounter attributions the client has formed regarding the meaning of symptoms he or she is experiencing. In general, these involve beliefs that the intrusive-reliving, numbing/avoidance, and hyperarousal symptoms of traumatic stress represent loss of control or major psychopathology. In the style outlined earlier for trauma-related cognitions, the therapist can facilitate cognitive reconsideration of these perceptions or beliefs by asking the adolescent or young adult—especially after some level of psychoeducation has transpired—about

- what might be a nonpathologizing explanation for the symptom (e.g., the survival value of hypervigilance or the self-medicating aspects of substance abuse),

- whether the symptom(s) actually indicate psychosis or mental illness (e.g., whether flashbacks are the same thing as hallucinations or whether it is really "paranoid" to be fearful about trauma-reminiscent situations, especially if trauma is still possible), and

- whether it is better to actively experience posttraumatic stress (especially reexperiencing) than to "shut down" or otherwise avoid trauma memories (Briere & Scott, 2006).

These and other questions may stimulate lively and clinically useful conversations, the goal of which is not for the clinician's view to prevail, but for the client to explore the basis for (and meaning of) his or her internal experience.

Development of a Coherent Narrative

In addition to the cognitive processing of traumatic memories, therapy can provide broader meaning and context. Client descriptions of past traumatic events often become more detailed, organized, and causally structured as they are repeatedly discussed and explored in therapy—including during cognitive reconsideration. Increased narrative coherence is often associated with reduced posttraumatic symptoms (Foa, Molnar, & Cashman, 1995; Siegel, 1999). As the client is increasingly able to describe chronologically and analytically what happened, and to place it in a larger context, he or she may experience an increased sense of perspective, reduced feelings of chaos, and a greater sense that the universe is predictable and orderly, if not entirely benign. Creating meaning out of one's experiences may provide some degree of closure, in that they "make sense" and thus may not require further rumination or preoccupation. Finally, a more coherent trauma narrative, by virtue of its organization and complexity, may support more efficient and complete emotional and cognitive processing. In contrast, fragmented recollections of traumatic events that do not have an explicit chronological order and do not have obvious cause-effect linkages can easily lead to additional anxiety, insecurity, and confusion—phenomena that potentially interfere with effective trauma processing.

The development of a coherent narrative usually occurs naturally during the cognitive aspects of trauma-focused therapy. As the traumatic event is discussed repetitively and in detail, a process sometimes referred to as *context reinstatement* may occur (Briere & Scott, 2006)—a detailed trauma description often triggers recall of additional details that, over time, provide a story that is more internally consistent and "hangs together."

Although a more coherent narrative often arises naturally from repeatedly revisiting the trauma in therapy, the clinician can work to further increase the likelihood of this happening. This generally involves gentle, nonintrusive questions regarding the details of the trauma and support for the client's general exploration of his or her thoughts and feelings regarding the event—in the same manner described earlier for cognitive processing. In partial contrast to cognitive processing interventions, however, narrative interventions explicitly support the development of broader explanations and a "story" of the traumatic event, its antecedents, and its effects.

A tool often used in ITCT-A to assist in the development of a coherent trauma narrative is the *trauma timeline*. This intervention involves the client mapping out on a horizontal line (typically using a large piece of paper) his or her ages (and the associated dates) when traumatic, neutral, and positive events happened in his or her life. For example, at age seven years, the adolescent's grandmother passed away and the family moved out of her house, which then led to the mother moving in with a physically abusive boyfriend. The boyfriend then sexually abused the client for the next three years. When the client was age 11, the boyfriend was arrested for driving under the influence of alcohol and accidentally killing another driver, at which point the family had no financial support and had to move into a shelter. Although this produced many additional challenges (the most significant are also mapped), this was the beginning of a time when the family grew closer, in the absence of violence (also mapped).

It should be reiterated that timelines or other narrative supports should not specify bad things alone. Throughout the narrative, it is important that the client include key people who were mentors, role models, or especially supportive in some way, and include positive events as well as traumatic ones. It is important that the client not feel that the therapist is only interested in traumatic events, nor that the client's life has only involved trauma. The inclusion of positive people and events lightens the narrative process (which also may titrate the associated distress associated with speaking of hurtful things) and decreases the likelihood that the client will infer pessimism and helplessness from recountings of the past.

Cognitive Changes Arising From Nonoverwhelming Emotional Activation During Treatment

Not all cognitive effects of trauma therapy involve verbal reconsideration of traumatically altered thinking patterns—it is also possible for the survivor's beliefs to change during the process of remembering and processing upsetting memories (Foa & Rothbaum, 1998). In the context of processing traumatic memories in therapy, the client repetitively experiences three things: (1) anxiety that is conditioned to the trauma memory, (2) the expectation that such anxiety signals danger and/or is, itself, a dangerous state and must be avoided, and yet (3) an absence of actual negative outcome (i.e., he or she does not actually experience physical or psychological harm from anxiety or what it might presage). This repetitive *disparity* (a technical term that will be discussed in greater detail in the next chapter) between the expectation of anxiety as signaling danger and the subsequent experience of nondanger probably changes the expectation over time. Beyond its cognitive effects on beliefs and assumptions associated with the specific trauma memory, the repetitive experience of feeling anxious during trauma therapy—in the context of therapeutic safety—can change the experience of what anxiety actually means. In many cases, the client becomes less anxious about anxiety; coming to see it as merely an emotion and not necessarily as a harbinger of danger, loss of control, or psychological disability. To paraphrase one young survivor, "I thought feeling all this stuff would kill me. It doesn't."

13

Trigger Identification
and Intervention

Many of the difficulties that trauma-exposed adolescents and young adults experience in the world arise when stimuli or situations in their immediate environment trigger upsetting memories, with their associated thoughts and emotions. Once these memories are triggered, the youth may experience a cascade of thoughts involving, for example, helplessness, imminent danger, betrayal, abandonment, or need for retribution. Along with these may be emotions the client experienced at the time of the trauma, such as fear, anger, shame, or sadness. The end effect of these processes may be an episode of "acting out" or tension-reduction behavior as a way for the youth to reduce distress associated with these memories. For example, a young man is insulted by a peer, which triggers memories of parental maltreatment and extreme, unfair criticism, which, in turn, activates feelings of low self-esteem and thoughts about "getting even." These thoughts and memories may then activate anger and motivate an action (e.g., aggression) that is out of proportion to the actual insult by the peer: he has been triggered and now is involved in an act that is more relevant to his childhood than his current situation. Examples of other triggers and responses are (1) the breakup of a dating relationship triggering early memories of abandonment with associated desperation and emptiness, leading to a suicide attempt; (2) a consensual sexual activity triggering flashbacks of childhood sexual abuse, resulting in intense fear or disgust; or (3) criticism at work by an employer triggering physical and psychological abuse memories, resulting in the youth throwing something and quitting his or her job.

This tendency for current events to trigger extreme emotions and behaviors related to childhood maltreatment is a serious problem for some adolescents and young adults. The suggested clinical approach to this issue might have appeared in previous chapters on affect regulation training, cognitive interventions, or mindfulness but is outlined separately here because of its importance. Additional information and perspectives on triggers, and trigger identification, can be found in other sources as well, including DeRosa and Pelcovitz (2008) and Blaustein and Kinniburgh (2010).

Trigger awareness and intervention can help the survivor maintain internal equilibrium in his or her daily life by teaching him or her how to identify and address triggers in the environment that activate posttraumatic reliving. Successful trigger identification during ITCT-A can facilitate a greater sense of control and better interpersonal functioning by helping the adolescent to avoid or alter situations in which triggering might be likely or, in the event triggering has occurred, to change his or her experience of—and response to—the associated internal cascade of negative thoughts and/or feelings. The adolescent is supported in learning to (a) identify instances when he or she is being triggered, (b) reframe triggered reactions as archaic, as opposed to contemporary (i.e., "real" versus "not real"), and then (c) respond to these archaic/"unreal" experiences as, in fact, internal events rather than accurate perceptions of the external world.

Trigger identification and intervention training usually occurs during the therapy session and is then called upon later when the survivor encounters triggers in his or her environment. In other words, it is often difficult to figure out exactly what to do when one has been triggered; it is better to have previously identified the trigger, its meaning, and its solutions in the context of therapeutic guidance and support and then call upon that information as needed.

The Trigger Grid

In session, the client and therapist work through the *trigger grid*, presented in Appendix VI as *What Triggers Me?* This is done in a sequential way, as the client and therapist go over each question in the grid, with the client (not the therapist) providing answers. Although not answering trigger grid questions, the therapist uses the questions to facilitate the youth's exploration of triggering phenomena. In many cases, this will provide opportunities for discussions about triggers and responses that are at least as helpful as the specific act of completing the grid. The trigger grid may be amended or added to over time, as the client discovers and/or reports additional triggers and responses.

The goal of the trigger grid exercise is for the client to accomplish the following:

(1) learn about triggers, including their "unreal" (i.e., non-here-and-now), yet understandable, historic nature,

(2) identify specific instances during which he or she has been triggered,

(3) determine, based on this exploration

    (a) what seem to be the major triggers in his or her life and

    (b) how to identify when he or she is being triggered, and

(4) problem-solve strategies that might be effective once triggering has occurred.

Identifying Triggers

In response to the trigger grid, clients typically identify a number of trauma-related triggers, including, for example,

- interpersonal conflict,
- sexual situations or stimuli,
- angry people,
- intoxicated people,
- perceived narcissism,
- seemingly arbitrary criticism or accusations,
- rejection,
- perceived abandonment,
- interactions with an authority figure,
- people with physical or psychological characteristics that are in some way similar to the client's past perpetrator(s),
- boundary violations,
- sirens,
- gunshots, and
- the sound of crying.

Identifying Triggered States

One of the more challenging parts of the trigger grid for the adolescent trauma survivor is the question, "How do I know I've been triggered?" Some answers are relatively easy; for example, it may not be difficult to recognize an intrusive sensory flashback of a gunshot as posttraumatic. In others, however, the reexperiencing may be more subtle, such as feelings of anger or fear, or intrusive states, for example feelings of helplessness that emerge "out of nowhere" during an interpersonal interaction. Among the qualities of triggered as opposed to contemporary ("real") responses are the following:

- A thought/feeling/sensation that doesn't fully "make sense" in terms of what is happening around the survivor

- Thoughts or feelings that are too intense, based on the current context

- Thoughts or feelings that carry with them memories of a past trauma

- An unexpected alteration in awareness (e.g., depersonalization or derealization) as these thoughts/feelings/sensations occur

- A physical reaction such as heart "pounding" in the chest, shortness of breath, suddenly feeling hot or blushing, a prickly sensation on the back of the neck, sweaty palms, dry mouth, a sudden headache or upset stomach, etc.

- A situation in which the adolescent often gets triggered

The section on *What happens after I get triggered?* provides an opportunity for the client to explore the thoughts, feelings, and behaviors associated with each major trigger, so that triggering becomes more obvious to him or her, and his or her responses to the trigger are better understood as reactions to the past, not the present. This exercise may help the client to discriminate triggered states from "real" (i.e., here and now) ones and, thus, have less reactivity to them.

Problem-Solving Triggered States

The final question on the grid is "What could I do or say to myself so that I wouldn't get triggered, or for the trigger to be less bad?" This question is answered for each of the major triggers that the client has identified earlier. Among possible answers to this section are the following:

- Changing the scenario or using "timeouts" during especially stressful moments (e.g., leaving a party when others become intoxicated; intentionally minimizing arguments with authority figures—even removing oneself if that is possible and appropriate; learning how to discourage unwanted flirtatious behavior from others).

- Analyzing the triggering stimulus or situation until a greater understanding changes one's perception and thus terminates the trigger (e.g., carefully examining the behavior of an individual who is triggering posttraumatic fear, and eventually becoming more aware of the fact that he or she is not acting in a threatening manner; or coming to understand that a given individual's seemingly dismissive style does not indicate a desire to reject or ignore as much as it does interpersonal awkwardness).

• Increasing support systems (e.g., bringing a friend to a party where one might feel threatened or calling a friend or AA sponsor to debrief an upsetting situation).

• Positive self-talk (e.g., working out beforehand what to say to oneself when triggered, such as, "I am safe," "I don't have to do anything I don't want to do," "This is just my past talking, this isn't really what I think it is," or "I don't have to stay here/put up with this. I can just walk away").

• Relaxation-induction or breath control, as described in Chapter 11.

• Remembering the lessons of meditation and mindfulness (also presented in Chapter 11), such that the triggers and subsequent thoughts are seen as "just" replayed memory and "only" reactions to that memory—not things that necessarily have relevance to the youth's current experience.

• Strategic distraction, such as starting a conversation with a safe person, reading a book, or going for a walk, as a way to pull attention away from escalating internal responses such as panic, flashbacks, or catastrophizing cognitions.

• Using physical and creative activities, such as sports, yoga, dance, music, or art to reduce anxiety and increase self-efficacy, thereby decreasing reactivity to triggers.

As the adolescent or young adult becomes more conversant with triggers and their associated feelings and behaviors, and progressively completes more of the trigger grid over time, triggered states can be more recognizable as such—as replayed "movies" or ancient computer programs rather than perceptions of the contemporary/"real" world. This increased distance from the triggered experience often serves to reduce the power of the feeling and lessen the likelihood that problematic behaviors will emerge. Further, by working out strategies beforehand, the triggered survivor less often has to figure out what to do—instead he or she can call on the fruits of previous problem-solving and, to the extent it is possible in any given triggering circumstance, respond in a more effective and self-protective manner.

Although the trigger grid remains in the client's chart, many adolescents find it helpful to create and write down their own list of triggers—and what they can do when triggered—on a separate piece of paper or in a journal. This list of triggers and responses can then be kept by the client and referred to when appropriate.

14

Titrated Exposure

I n addition to the interventions described in the previous chapters, most child and adolescent trauma treatments include some form of therapeutic exposure, given its established helpfulness in treating posttraumatic stress (Berliner, 2005; Cohen, Berliner, & March, 2000). In general, therapeutic exposure refers to a procedure wherein the client is exposed to memories of a traumatic event, and the emotional responses that emerge are desensitized or habituated over time until they no longer can be activated by the memory. A specific type of therapeutic exposure, *titrated exposure*, can be defined as therapeutic exposure that is controlled so that the activated emotions do not exceed the client's affect regulation capacity and, thus, do not overwhelm the trauma survivor. In this context, the Self-Trauma model (Briere, 2002) and ITCT-A additionally refer to the *therapeutic window* and *intensity control*, both of which are described in this chapter.

Despite the frequent usefulness of exposure in trauma treatment, however, a previous point bears repeating. Although emotional processing is a very important aspect of trauma therapy, it should only be applied to the extent that the youth can tolerate it. The emotionally overwhelmed and avoidant adolescent or young adult may not be ready to immediately process all memories of a hurtful past. As will be noted, there are clear counterindications to full or prolonged exposure therapy for some individuals, sometimes even procedures involving titrated exposure and intensity control. In such cases, the relational, cognitive, and affect regulation components of ITCT-A may be more relevant than what is usually thought of as trauma work. On the other hand, temporary avoidance of formal exposure activities with the overwhelmed adolescent does not mean that the youth should not talk about or process the past *at all*, only that this process may be limited until he or she can tolerate greater levels of access to trauma material.

The Therapeutic Window

The therapeutic window represents the psychological midpoint between inadequate and overwhelming activation of trauma-related emotion during treatment: it is a hypothetical "place" where therapeutic interventions are thought to be most helpful (Briere & Scott, 2006). Interventions within the therapeutic window are neither so trivial or nonevocative that they provide inadequate memory exposure and processing, nor so intense that they become overwhelming. In other words, interventions that take the therapeutic window into account are those that trigger trauma memories (i.e., through therapeutic exposure) and promote processing, but do not overwhelm the client's internal protective systems and motivate unwanted avoidance responses. Because many traumatized adolescents and young adults with complex posttraumatic outcomes have affect regulation problems, the therapeutic window is an important aspect of ITCT-A.

Interventions that *undershoot* the therapeutic window are those that unnecessarily avoid discussion of traumatic material or are focused primarily on support and validation with a youth who could actually tolerate greater exposure and processing. Undershooting is rarely dangerous (unless the client is avoiding describing current victimization); it can, however, waste time and resources at a time when more effective therapeutic interventions would be possible. It also may communicate to the client that the clinician does not want him or her to discuss trauma, or that the therapist is not empathic about—or interested in—the youth's previous upsetting experiences.

Overshooting the window, on the other hand, occurs when the clinician either (1) inadvertently provides too much therapeutic exposure and, therefore, too much emotional activation relative to the client's existing affect regulation resources or (2) is unable to prevent the young person from flooding himself or herself with overwhelming traumatic distress. Interventions that are too fast-paced may overshoot the window because they do not allow the adolescent to adequately accommodate and desensitize previously activated material before exposing him or her to new memories. When therapy consistently overshoots the window, the survivor often has to engage in avoidance maneuvers in order to keep from being overwhelmed by the therapy process. For example, a therapist may be overshooting the window by pushing for processing of material that the client is not ready to explore, which then causes the client to retreat from therapy. Most often, the youth will increase his or her level of dissociation (e.g., through disengagement or "spacing out") or cognitive avoidance during the session, or will interrupt the focus or pace of therapy with arguments, by "not getting" obvious therapeutic points, by distracting the therapist with various dramatic, sexualized, or aggressive behaviors, or by changing the subject to something less threatening. In the worst case, he or she may drop out of treatment. Although the clinician may interpret these behaviors as "resistance" or "borderline behavior," such avoidance often represents appropriate protective responses to therapist process errors.

The client's need for avoidance can easily impede treatment by decreasing his or her exposure to memory material and the ameliorative aspects of therapy, especially if the client is unable to sustain regular attendance at therapy sessions. In contrast, effective therapy for traumatized adolescents and young adults provides carefully titrated exposure to traumatic material while maintaining the safety and support necessary to eventually extinguish trauma-related emotional responses. By carefully adjusting the amount of therapeutic exposure so that the associated emotional activation does not exceed the survivor's emotional capacities, treatment within the therapeutic window allows the youth to slowly process trauma memories without being retraumatized and needing to shut down the process.

Intensity Control

Intensity control refers to the therapist's awareness and relative control of the level of emotional activation that occurs within the session. As noted in Chapter 7, it is recommended that—especially for youth with significant affect regulation difficulties—emotional intensity be highest at around mid-session, whereas the beginning and end of the session should be at the lowest intensity (Briere & Scott, 2006). Ideally, at the beginning of the session, the client gradually enters the process of psychotherapy; by the middle of the session, the focus has shifted to relatively more intense processing and activation; at the end of the session the client is sufficiently dearoused that he or she can reenter the outside world without needing later avoidance activities. The relative safety of psychotherapy sessions may allow some clients to become more affectively aroused than they would outside of the therapeutic environment. As a result, it should be the therapist's goal to leave the client in as calm an affective state as is possible—ideally no more emotionally activated than he or she was at the beginning of the session. This may involve, in some cases, using one of the grounding or breathing exercises described in Chapter 11, particularly if the client is agitated at the session's end.

The need for the client to experience upsetting feelings and thoughts during trauma-focused treatment requires that the therapist carefully adjust the level of emotional activation he or she experiences, at least to the extent that this is under the therapist's control. From the therapeutic-window perspective, intense affect during treatment pushes the client toward the outer edge of the window (i.e., toward an increased possibility of being overwhelmed), whereas less intensity (or a more cognitive focus) moves the client toward the inner edge (i.e., toward reduced exposure and emotional processing). The goal is to keep the survivor near the "middle" of the window—to feel neither too little (i.e., to dissociate or otherwise avoid to the point that abuse-related emotional responses and cognitions cannot be processed) nor too much (i.e., to become flooded with previously avoided emotionality that overwhelms available affect regulation resources and is retraumatizing).

Constraints on Therapeutic Exposure

As noted in this and other chapters, exposure to trauma memories and the associated distress can be quite challenging. In most instances, titrated exposure is tolerable to the extent that it occurs within the therapeutic window. In some cases, however, almost any level of memory processing overshoots the window, irrespective of the clinician's efforts. When this occurs, it is usually because (a) the trauma is so recent or severe, or there are so many trauma memories, that emotional activation is innately overwhelming, (b) the client has insufficient affect regulation capacities, and/or (c) the client generally suffers from such high levels of comorbid emotional distress, symptomatology, or negative cognitive preoccupation that additional trauma-related distress is incapacitating.

For these reasons, detailed exploration of traumatic material is not always immediately appropriate. Therapeutic exposure to trauma memories may be contraindicated for those experiencing very high levels of anxiety, severe depression, acute psychosis, major suicidality, overwhelming shame associated with the traumatic event, especially impaired affect regulation capacity, very recent and substantial trauma exposure, or substance intoxication (e.g., Briere & Scott, 2006; Bryant & Harvey, 2000; Cloitre et al., 2002; Najavits, 2002;

Pitman et al., 1991). When these conditions preclude exposure therapy, the clinician is advised to focus on the therapeutic relationship, as well as the various other interventions outlined in this book—especially distress reduction and affect regulation (Chapter 11) and cognitive interventions (Chapter 12)—until exposure is more indicated. In some cases, psychiatric medication also may be appropriate (Briere & Scott, 2006; Stamatakos & Campo, 2010).

The Components of Titrated Exposure

Assuming that none of the constraining conditions just presented are in force, or that they have been sufficiently diminished, titrated exposure can occur. For the purposes of this book, the processing of traumatic memory within the therapeutic window will be divided into five components: *exposure, activation, disparity, counterconditioning,* and *desensitization/resolution.* These components do not always follow a linear progression. In fact, in some cases interventions at a "later" step may lead to further work at an "earlier" step. In other instances, certain steps (e.g., counterconditioning) may be less important than others (e.g., disparity). And, finally, as described in Chapter 11, the therapy process may require the youth to learn (or invoke previously learned) affect regulation techniques in order to down-regulate distress when emotional responses inadvertently become potentially overwhelming.

Exposure

Exposure refers to any activity engaged in by the therapist or the client that provokes or triggers client memories of traumatic events. Several types of exposure-based therapies are used by clinicians to treat traumatic stress. In the ITCT-A version, the therapist typically asks the client to recall non-overwhelming but moderately distressing traumatic experiences in the context of a safe therapeutic environment, generally encouraging greater detail and emotional exploration over time. This approach usually does not adhere to a strict, preplanned series of extended exposure activities, nor does it necessarily focus on only one trauma or trauma memory in a given session. Intensity of exposure is adjusted on an ongoing basis, because the youth's ability to tolerate exposure may vary considerably as a function of outside life stressors, level of support from friends, relatives, and others, and, most importantly, the extent of affect regulation capacities available to him or her at any given point in time. In Self-Trauma (Briere, 1996, 2002) language, the "size" of the therapeutic window may change within and across sessions.

In general, therapeutic exposure involves the adolescent or young adult recalling and discussing traumatic events with the therapist and, in some cases, writing about them at home and then reading them out loud in the next session. Although some other forms of trauma therapy focus on memories of a single trauma (e.g., of a motor vehicle accident or physical assault), and discourage much discussion of other traumas, the approach advocated in ITCT-A is considerably more permissive. It is quite common and acceptable for trauma survivors to "jump around" from one memory to another, often making associations that are not immediately apparent to the therapist—or even, in some cases, the client. Especially for youth with histories of multiple, complex, and extended traumas, the focus of a given session may move from a rape experience to earlier childhood maltreatment to an experience of violence during an arrest. A young man may begin the session with a memory of being beaten in the context of prostitution and find himself, 20 minutes later, describing being physically abused by his father when he was a child.

In some cases, perhaps especially for younger adolescents, exposure can occur through the use of art or collage activities in therapy sessions, such as the client drawing the traumatic event(s) or creating a collage (of photos and words provided by the therapist, cut from magazines) that depicts what occurred. Older clients who have difficulty providing trauma narratives also may be more able to generate emotionally arousing material in this more projective manner, as opposed to verbalizing or writing about the experience. These activities can be quite emotionally evocative in some cases and may require several sessions for the client to complete. While engaging in these activities, and after completing them, the client is encouraged to describe any emotions and cognitions that arise and to examine the connection between these experiences and the emotions and thoughts that he or she had at the time of the trauma.

Whether through verbal or nonverbal means, the broader exposure activities of ITCT-A reflect the complexity of many trauma presentations. Although an adolescent may come to treatment in order to address a recent assault experience, it may soon become apparent that either (a) an earlier trauma is actually more relevant to his or her ongoing psychological distress, or (b) his or her presenting distress is due to the interacting effects of multiple traumas. A young heroin user, for example, might seek treatment for the effects of a violent rape by an acquaintance and soon discover that this rape activates memories of a number of other distressing experiences, as well as the childhood incest experiences that may have partially determined her current addiction. In such instances, insisting that the client focus exclusively on a single trauma during therapy, or even on just one trauma at a time, may be contraindicated, let alone appreciated by the client. As well, recollections of early trauma are often fragmented and incomplete, if not entirely nonverbal in nature, precluding exposure to a discrete, coherent memory, per se. Instead of being limited to discussions of a single trauma, we suggest that the client be allowed to explore—and thereby expose himself or herself to—whatever traumatic material seems important at a given time or whatever memory—or part of a memory—is triggered by any other memory. In so doing, the client also may make connections between feelings experienced at the time of the trauma and feelings associated with later traumatic exposures, which tends to allow broader processing of cumulative trauma.

Explaining the value of titrated exposure. Although exposure is widely understood to be a powerful treatment methodology by clinicians, the adolescent or young adult may respond negatively to the idea of revisiting traumatic memories. Prior to therapy, the survivor is likely to have spent considerable time and energy controlling his or her distress by avoiding people, places, and situations that trigger posttraumatic intrusions and by trying to suppress or numb trauma-related distress. As a result, exposure techniques, wherein the client is asked to intentionally reexperience events and emotions that he or she has been avoiding, may seem counterintuitive, if not antisurvival. In this context, the clinician may easily overestimate the young person's actual willingness to undergo therapeutic exposure, at least prior to receiving further information and support.

For this reason, an important aspect of trauma therapy is *prebriefing*: explaining the rationale for therapeutic exposure, and its general methodology, prior to the onset of treatment. Without sufficient explanation, the process and immediate effects of exposure may seem so illogical and stressful that the client may automatically resist and avoid. On the other hand, if exposure can be explained so that he or she understands the reasons for this procedure, it usually is not hard to form a positive client-therapist alliance around this approach and a shared appreciation for the process.

Although the way in which exposure is introduced may vary from instance to instance, the clinician should paraphrase the following main points when preparing clients for exposure work:

- Unresolved memories of the trauma often have to be talked about and reexperienced or else they may not be fully processed and will be more likely to keep coming back as symptoms or unwanted feelings.

- Although the youth, understandably, would like to not think about what happened, and may have been avoiding upsetting feelings about the trauma, such avoidance (a) is usually impossible to maintain (hence the presence of symptoms) and (b) often blocks processing and thus, ironically, serves to keep the symptoms alive.

- If the client can talk about what happened enough, in the safety of treatment, the pain and fear associated with the trauma is likely to decrease. The clinician cannot, however, promise that this will occur.

- By its nature, exposure is associated with some level of distress, and some people who undergo exposure experience a slight increase in flashbacks, nightmares, and/or distressing feelings between sessions. This is normal and usually not a bad sign—it can even be reframed to the client as evidence that therapy is working. At the same time, it should be clearly stated that the youth should inform the therapist when new posttraumatic stress occurs, or previous distress intensifies, so that the clinician can monitor whether exposure has been too intense.

- The clinician will work to keep the discussion of these memories from overwhelming the client and remind him or her that he or she can stop talking about any given memory if it becomes too upsetting (an option sometimes not offered in more classic, prolonged exposure approaches). The youth need only talk about as much traumatic material as he or she is able to tolerate. However, the more he or she can remember, think, feel, and talk about nonoverwhelming memories during therapy, the more likely it is that significant improvement will occur.

Homework. As noted in the last chapter, trauma therapy sometimes includes homework assignments for older clients who are able to tolerate between-session exposure exercises. This adjunct to session-based treatment typically involves the youth writing about a specific traumatic event when at home (or wherever might be safe) and then reading it aloud in the next session. Along with providing additional opportunities to examine and process cognitions initially associated with the event (per Chapter 12), this activity requires that the client access the original trauma memory in order to write about it and, thus, provides significant therapeutic exposure. This exposure is then repeated when the client reads the narrative aloud to the therapist. Importantly, as noted in Chapter 12, some clients may not feel safe enough at home to do this homework there, in which case he or she may do it with the therapist during their session.

Adapting from Resick and Schnicke's (1993) book on cognitive processing for rape victims, the therapist is invited to copy Appendix V (*Written*

Homework About My Trauma) and provide it to the client, saying something like this:

> "Here is the homework sheet we discussed. Try to write answers to all the questions on it about the [rape/shooting/abuse incident/etc.] and what happened afterward. Write as much about what happened as you can remember, and be as specific as possible. After you're done writing, read it to yourself at least once before our next session. If it is too upsetting to read all at once, try reading as much as you can, and then read the rest later, when you are ready."

The client may be asked to repeat this writing exercise on several different occasions over the course of treatment, either completing the exercise for a different trauma on each occasion or repeating the exercise on multiple occasions for the same trauma. The specific timing and frequency of these writing and reading exercises may vary according to (a) the youth's capacity for written expression, (b) his or her readiness to directly confront the trauma, and (c) his or her immediate emotional stability and affect regulation capacity. The therapist's response to hearing the client's story should be characterized by support, validation, and appreciation for the client's willingness to engage in a potentially difficult task.

In some cases, the youth may even write a book about his or her life up to the present. The second author (CBL), for example, has worked with adolescents who read aloud, in the session, books on abuse written from the youth's perspective and then wrote their own version, sometimes with illustrations, in the same tone and format. This process not only allowed the client to desensitize and place in perspective his or her abuse history, but also to gain a little distance on it through the creative process.

Obviously, the writing approach is not possible for those who are not literate, non-English speakers, or too cognitively debilitated (e.g., by psychosis, severe depression, or hyperarousal) or impaired. As noted previously, the total number of times this exercise is done may increase if there are several different traumas in need of emotional processing. In general, these written renditions tend to become more detailed and emotionally descriptive upon repetition, and the client's emotional responses when reading the assignment aloud become less extreme over time. It should be reiterated, however, that homework involving exposure to trauma memories (and thus the associated feelings and thoughts) is only indicated for those who are unlikely to be overwhelmed by such activities, and who can do so safely. In general, it is best to discuss this activity with the client, and get his or her opinion about whether it would be possible and useful, rather than just prescribing it. As with any other exposure intervention, the client has the absolute right to refuse to engage in exposure homework.

Activation

If treatment is to be effective, some degree of activation must take place during exposure. Activation refers to emotional responses that are triggered by trauma memories, such as fear, sadness, or horror, and trauma-specific cognitive reactions, such as intrusive negative self-perceptions or sudden feelings of helplessness. Other related memories and their associated affects and cognitions may be triggered as well. A 14-year-old girl who is asked to describe a childhood sexual abuse experience, for example, undergoes therapeutic exposure to the extent that she recalls and describes aspects of that event during the therapy session. If these memories trigger emotional responses conditioned to the original abuse stimuli (e.g., fear or disgust), or associated cognitive intrusions (e.g., "I am so gross"), or stimulate further memories (e.g., of other traumas or another aspect of the abuse triggered by remembering certain aspects of it), therapeutic activation can be said to have taken place.

In order to extinguish emotional-cognitive associations to a given traumatic memory, such associations must be (a) activated, (b) not reinforced, and, ideally, (c) counterconditioned. As a result, therapeutic interventions that consist solely of the client narrating trauma-related memories, without emotional activation, will often fail to produce significant symptom resolution. In order for optimal activation to occur, there should be as little avoidance as is reasonably possible during the exposure process. On the other hand, as noted throughout this book, too much activation is also problematic because it generates high levels of distress (thereby linking memory to current emotional pain, rather than to safety or positive feelings) and motivates avoidance (thereby reducing further exposure and processing).

Because activated cognitive-emotional responses are, to some extent, the crux of trauma work, the following sections describe several interventions aimed at controlling the level of activation during treatment. These are described here in the context of verbal/narrative processing, but they may also be appropriate when the client reads homework material to the clinician—especially in terms of decreasing activation. The goal, in each case, is to work within the therapeutic window—to support emotional and cognitive activation that is neither too little nor too much for optimal processing.

Increasing activation. The therapist typically seeks to increase activation in instances when, despite available affect regulation capacity, the adolescent appears to be unnecessarily blocking some portion of his or her emotional responses to the traumatic material. It is not uncommon for avoidance responses to become so overlearned that they automatically, but unnecessarily, emerge during exposure to stressful material. In other instances, gender roles or socialization may discourage emotional expression in a young person who could otherwise tolerate it. When avoidance is not required for continued emotional homeostasis, yet appears to be blocking trauma processing, several interventions may be appropriate. In each case, the goal is increased awareness and, thus, increased activation.

First, the therapist may ask questions that can only be answered in a relatively less avoidant state. These include, for example, the following:

- "What were you feeling/how did it feel when that happened?"
- "What are you feeling now?"
- "Do you have any thoughts or feelings when you describe [the trauma]?"

In such cases, the youth's avoidance in the session may decrease, yet never be acknowledged by either therapist or client—an outcome that is entirely appropriate, since the primary intent is to keep activation at a reasonable level, not to label the client's reaction as problematic.

Second, the clinician can indirectly draw attention to the avoidance, without stigmatizing it, and ask the adolescent or young adult to increase his or her level of contact during the process of activation. This is often most effective when the client's avoidance, or the power of the triggered emotions, has previously been identified as an issue in therapy. This may involve encouraging suggestions such as the following:

- "You're doing well. Try to stay with the feelings."
- "Don't go away now. You're doing great. Stay with it."
- "I can see it's upsetting. Can you stay with the memory for just a few more minutes? We can always stop if you need to."

In other cases, for example, when it is not clear whether the client is dissociating, or when the client is more prone to a defensive response, the therapist may intervene with a question-statement combination, such as these two:

- "How are you doing? It looks like maybe you're spacing out a little bit."
- "It looks like you're going away a little bit right now. Are you?"

Although calling direct attention to avoidance is sometimes appropriate, it tends to break the process of exposure-activation, and it should be used only when less direct methods of encouraging activation (and thus reducing avoidance) have not been effective.

A third way that the clinician can increase activation is by increasing the intensity of the emotional experience. Often, this involves requesting more details about the traumatic event. As the youth provides more specific information, the opportunity for greater activation increases—both because greater details usually involve more emotionally arousing material and because greater detail reinstates more of the original context in his or her mind, thereby increasing the experience of emotions that occurred at the time of the trauma. For example, as the teenager describes her victimization by her brother in greater detail, the emotions (terror, anger, humiliation) she felt at the time may be increasingly triggered and, when expressed in the safety of therapy, more completely desensitized.

The clinician may also directly activate trauma-related emotions by asking the youth to describe the feelings (and, to a lesser extent, thoughts) that he or she had at the time of the trauma, as well as any feelings that arise during the session. This process should be followed carefully by the therapist, however, since the associated emotional activation may, on occasion, exceed the therapeutic window. The exact balance of emotional activation and safety is part of the art of trauma therapy, ITCT-A or otherwise.

Decreasing activation. If the therapist inadvertently triggers too much activation, or is unsuccessful in keeping the client's emotional activation to a tolerable level, the therapeutic window will be exceeded. This can be problematic because, as noted earlier in this chapter, and in Chapter 11, clients with reduced affect regulation capacities typically become overwhelmed in the face of especially upsetting memories. In general, when material exceeds the therapeutic window, the appropriate response is to either redirect the client to a less upsetting topic or, more subtly, directing the conversation to less emotionally charged aspects of the trauma. Once the client's emotionality has returned to baseline, careful exposure activities may be resumed, if appropriate.

Occasionally, overactivation (exceeding the window) may produce responses that are not sufficiently addressed by changing the focus or intensity of the therapeutic conversation. For example, the client may experience a transient dissociative response, engage in an angry emotional outburst, or begin to cry in a withdrawn manner. When such responses are extreme, the therapist should generally stop exposure-activation and focus on stabilizing interventions (e.g., breathing exercises, grounding, placing the process in perspective—described in Chapter 11) in order to reduce the impacts of whatever is triggering the response. In fact, if overshooting appears to be relatively common with a given client—despite the clinician's ongoing attempt to titrate emotional exposure—it may be appropriate to focus more on affect skill development and/or cognitive processing, or safety interventions, relationship building, and emotional support for a number of sessions, only returning to emotional processing when the client's capacity to tolerate distress has increased. In other cases, the problem may not be as chronic or severe: the client may have just completed a session the prior week that was particularly evocative, or encountered a new life stressor, and may need to take "a break" for a session or two before returning to higher levels of trauma processing.

Therapist activities that decrease activation might appear to deprive the youth of the opportunity to address the emotional sequels of major trauma. Such restraint, however, is one of the responsibilities of the therapist. If the clinician suspects—based on observation of the client—that activation is likely to exceed the therapeutic window in any given circumstance, it is important that he or she ensure safety by reducing the intensity and pace of the therapeutic process. This does not mean that the clinician necessarily avoids trauma processing altogether; only that the work should proceed slowly and carefully or be temporarily delayed. Fortunately, the need for such a conservative approach is usually transient. As the traumatic material is slowly and carefully processed, progressively fewer trauma memories will have the potential to activate overwhelming affect, and, as described in Chapter 11, the client's overall capacity to tolerate distress will grow.

Disparity

Exposure and activation are typically not, in and of themselves, sufficient in trauma treatment. There also must be some disparity between what the client is feeling (e.g., activated fear associated with a trauma memory) and what the current state of reality actually is (e.g., the visible absence of immediate danger) (Briere, 2002). For conditioned emotional responses to traumatic memories to be diminished or extinguished over time, they must consistently not be reinforced by similar danger (physical or emotional) in the current environment.

As described earlier, safety should be manifest in at least two ways. First, the adolescent should have the opportunity to realize that he or she is safe in the presence of the therapist. This means safety not only from physical injury and sexual exploitation, but also from harsh criticism, punitiveness, boundary violation, underappreciation of the client's suffering, or, conversely, appearing overwhelmed by the client's pain or difficulties. Because the client may tend to overidentify danger in interpersonal situations, the absence of danger in the session must be experienced directly, not just promised. In other words, for the client's anxious associations to trauma memories to lose their power, they must not be reinforced by current danger or maltreatment in the session, however subtle.

Second, safety in treatment includes protection from overwhelming internal experience. The client whose trauma memories produce destabilizing emotions during treatment may not find therapy to be substantially different from the original experience. As noted earlier, overwhelming emotion may occur because one or both of two things are present: (1) the memory is so traumatic and has so much painful affect (e.g., anxiety, rage) or cognitions (e.g., guilt or shame) associated with it that unmodulated exposure produces considerable psychic pain, or (2) the survivor's affect regulation capacities are sufficiently compromised that any major reexperiencing is overwhelming. In each instance, safety—and therefore disparity—can only be provided within the context of the therapeutic window. Because processing within the window means, by definition, that exposure to memories does not exceed the client's ability to tolerate those memories, reexperiencing trauma in this context is not associated with overwhelming negative affect, identity fragmentation, or feelings of loss of control.

It should be noted that it is not enough that disparity be present in the session; it also must be perceived as such. Thus, for example, although the 15-year-old incest survivor may be safe from abuse or exploitation during the psychotherapy session, he may not easily perceive that to be true. Instead, the hypervigilance associated with posttraumatic stress, characteristics of the clinician that are similar to those of the abuser (e.g., gender, age, appearance), or just being alone with a seemingly powerful adult, may cause the client to believe that he is in danger. In many cases, it is only after repeated experiences of safety in such contexts that the client will come to reevaluate his or her impressions and truly note disparity. Because very traumatized youth may reflexively view interpersonal situations as dangerous, and may have a myriad of potential triggers that can produce fear, it may take considerable time in therapy before the curative aspects of disparity are able to manifest themselves. As a result, the multitraumatized "street kid," survivor of severe and chronic child abuse, adolescent refugee previously sold into the sex trade, or young adult living in an unsafe, emotionally unsupportive home environment may require consistent, reliable treatment that far exceeds the safety and relational parameters of classic short-term trauma therapy.

Counterconditioning

Not only is it important that there be a visible absence of danger during trauma processing, in the best circumstances, there also should be positive phenomena present during therapy that are relatively antithetic to the experience of physical or psychological danger. Thus, for example, a teenager in therapy for problems related to ongoing violence from her boyfriend may expect her therapist to be critical or rejecting. When her fears are met not only with the absence of those things in treatment (i.e., the disparity associated with therapeutic safety), but occur, in fact, in the presence of acceptance, validation, and nurturing, as well as the therapist's consistently well-paced, and emotionally attuned responses, the activated distress may diminish in intensity because it is incompatible with the positive feelings that arise in therapy. As a result, the emotional associations to memories of being victimized are not only not reinforced, they are weakened by contradictory, positive feeling states that are present as the memories are evoked.

It is in this area that a caring therapeutic relationship is most important. The more positive and supportive the relationship, and compassionate the therapist, the greater the amount of positive emotionality available to countercondition previous negative emotional responses. For example, as the chronically unloved adolescent survivor interacts with a reliably caring therapist, the negative associations to relatedness, intimacy, interpersonal vulnerability, and attachment figures are repeatedly elicited and then, in a sense, contradicted by the ongoing experience of support and protection within the therapeutic process. It is often not enough that the therapist does not hurt or exploit; it is also important that attunement and caring be present. Such clinician responses must, of course, be carefully monitored and constrained so that they do not involve or suggest any level of intrusion, boundary violation, voyeurism, punitive disengagement, or self-gratification—any of which may convert counterconditioning into danger and an absence of disparity (see Chapter 15). For this reason, consultation or supervision and collegial interaction are often crucial to addressing and managing the therapist's countertransference issues.

A second form of counterconditioning may be the experience of safe emotional release. Crying or other forms of emotional expression in response to upsetting events typically produces relatively positive emotional states (e.g., relief) that can countercondition the fear and related affects initially associated with the traumatic memory. In other words, the common suggestion that someone "have a good cry" or "get it off of your chest" may reflect cultural support for emotional activities that naturally countercondition trauma-related emotional responses (Briere, 2002). From this perspective, just as traditional systematic desensitization often pairs a formerly distressing stimulus to a relaxed, anxiety-incompatible state in an attempt to neutralize the anxious response over time, repeated safe and validated emotional release during exposure to painful memories may pair trauma memories to the relatively positive internal states associated with emotional expression in a protected environment. For this reason, optimal trauma therapy typically provides gentle support for—and reinforcement of—expressed emotionality during exposure activities.

Importantly, however, the therapist should not "push" for emotional expression when the client is unable or unwilling to engage in such activity. The amount of emotional expression available to the client will vary from person to person, partially as a function of the client's affect regulation capacity, personal history, and socialization. Particularly in adolescence, clients may become disengaged, dissociated, or withdrawn and unable to express feelings through words, as opposed to behavior. In such cases, the client may require greater affect regulation skill development before any significant emotional expression can occur or may need to use a less verbal method to express feelings, such as through an art activity or playing board games. Multiply traumatized clients who have not been supported or encouraged to express emotions (or even have been punished for doing so) may be in special need of gentle support and creative ways to facilitate emotionality and emotional release. This may also require greater support from significant others in the youth's interpersonal world. For example, as caretakers or partners are engaged in therapy, and learn to be more supportive of the client, the survivor may feel more safe and accepted, allowing him or her to access feelings and gain from the counterconditioning aspects of emotional expression. More detailed discussion of this aspect of ITCT-A is included in Chapters 17 and 18.

Desensitization/Resolution

Together, the process of remembering painful (but not overwhelming) events in the context of safety, positive relatedness, emotional expression, opportunities for introspection, and minimal avoidance can serve to break the connection between traumatic memories and associated negative emotional and cognitive responses. As this occurs, environmental and internal events that trigger memories of traumatic experiences will no longer produce the same level of negative response. Once processed, traumatic memories become, simply, memories; their ability to trigger emotional distress is significantly diminished. In the case of the multiply trauma-exposed person, however, the process usually does not end with the resolution of a given memory or set of memories. Instead, especially in longer-term therapy, other memories—often those that are associated with even greater distress—tend to become more available for discussion, at which point the process may begin anew.

15

Relational Processing

We've suggested in this book that many of the relationship problems experienced by traumatized adolescents arise from early learning about—and adapting to—childhood maltreatment. Interpersonal issues are often especially challenging for young people, because, even for those who have not been abused or neglected, adolescence is a developmental period when relationships with peers become more important, and sexual, romantic, or pair-bonding dynamics typically emerge for the first time. Because child abuse and neglect usually involves maltreatment in the context of what should have been intimate relationships, these relational issues, associations, and yearnings can become powerful triggers for subsequent interpersonal difficulties in youth.

One of the earliest impacts of abuse and neglect is thought to be on the child's internal representations of self and others (Allen, 2001), inferred from how he or she is treated by his or her caretakers. In the case of abuse or neglect, these inferences are likely to be especially negative. For example, the child who is being maltreated may conclude that he or she must be inherently unacceptable or malignant to deserve such punishment or disregard, or may come to see himself or herself as helpless, inadequate, or weak. As well, this negative context may mean that he or she comes to view others as inherently dangerous, rejecting, or unavailable.

These early inferences about self and others often form a generalized set of expectations, beliefs, and assumptions, sometimes described as *internal working models* (Bowlby, 1988) or *relational schemas* (Baldwin, Fehr, Keedian, Seidel, & Thompson, 1993). Such core understandings are often relatively nonresponsive to verbal information or the expressed views of others later in life, since they are encoded in the first years and thus are generally preverbal in nature. For example, the young man who believes, based on early learning, that he is unlikable or unattractive to others, or that others are not to be trusted, will not easily change such views based on others' statements that he is valued by them or that they can be relied upon.

Because they become the default assumptions the adolescent carries in his or her interactions with others, these negative schema are easily activated and acted upon in current relationships, ultimately making it hard for the youth to maintain meaningful connections and attachments with other people. As a result, formerly abused or neglected youth may find themselves in conflictual and chaotic relationships, may have problems with forming intimate peer attachments, and may engage in behaviors that are likely to threaten or disrupt close relationships.

Because relational schemas are often encoded at the implicit, nonverbal level, and are primarily based in safety and attachment needs, they may not be evident except in situations where the survivor perceives abuse-similar interpersonal threats, such as rejection, abandonment, criticism, or physical danger (Briere & Scott, 2006). When this occurs, these underlying cognitions and emotions may be triggered, with resultant interpersonal difficulties. For example, a teenage girl who experienced separation or abandonment in early childhood may relate relatively well in a given occupational or intimate context until she encounters relational stimuli that suggest (or are in some way reminiscent of) rejection, empathic disattunement, or abandonment. These perceived experiences, because of their similarity to early neglect, may then trigger memories, emotions, and cognitions that—although excessive or out of proportion in the immediate context—are appropriate to the feelings and thoughts of an abused or neglected child (Briere, 1996a). This activation may then motivate behavior that, although perhaps intended to ensure proximity and to maintain the relationship, is so characterized by "primitive" (i.e., child-level) responses and demands and so laden with upsetting emotions that it challenges or even destroys that relationship.

The most dramatic example of chronic relational trauma activations may be what, in adults, is referred to as *borderline personality disorder*. Those identified as having borderline personality features are often prone to sudden emotional outbursts in response to small or imagined interpersonal provocation, self-defeating cognitions, feelings of emptiness and intense dysphoria, and impulsive, tension-reducing behaviors that are triggered by perceptions of having been abandoned, rejected, or maltreated by another person. Although many maltreated adolescents are too young to be diagnosed with this disorder (American Psychiatric Association, 2000), in some cases their symptomatic presentation may be very similar, and some may receive this diagnosis as they grow into adulthood.

A fair portion of "borderline" behavior and symptomatology can be seen as arising from triggered relational memories and emotions associated with early abuse, abandonment, invalidation, or lack of parental responsiveness, generally in the context of reduced affect regulation capacities (Allen, 2001; Herman et al., 1989; Linehan, 1993). Upon having abuse or neglect memories triggered by stimuli in his or her current context, the adolescent or young adult may attempt to avoid the associated distress by engaging in activities such as substance abuse, inappropriate proximity-seeking (e.g., neediness or attempts to forestall abandonment), or involvement in distracting, tension-reducing behaviors, as described in Chapters 11 and 13.

The ITCT-A approach to relational disturbance parallels, to some extent, those outlined in Chapters 12 and 14 for cognitive and exposure-based interventions. In the relational context, however, the components of trauma processing occur more directly within the therapeutic relationship. Because, in fact, most disturbed relatedness appears to arise from maltreatment early in life, and is often triggered by later interpersonal stimuli, it is not surprising that the most effective interventions for relational problems seem to be, in fact, relational (Pearlman & Courtois, 2005).

Among other things, the therapeutic relationship is a powerful source of interpersonal triggers. As the connection between the youth and the clinician grows, the client's increasing attachment to the therapist can increasingly trigger implicit (nonverbal, sensory, experiential) memories of attachment experiences in childhood. For many clients, these early attachment memories include considerable abuse or neglect, which may be reexperienced in the form of maltreatment-related thoughts and feelings during therapy. These "relational flashbacks" are largely implicit and are often misperceived by the adolescent not as memories but, rather, as feelings and information about the current therapist-client relationship (see Briere, 2002, and Briere & Scott, 2006, for more on these "source attribution errors"). Once activated and expressed, such cognitions and emotions can be discussed and processed in the context of the safety, soothing, and support associated with a positive therapeutic relationship.

As in work with more simple traumatic memories, the therapeutic processing of relational memories and their associations (e.g., attachment-level cognitions and conditioned emotional responses) can be seen as involving the exposure, activation, disparity, and counterconditioning described in Chapter 14:

> *Exposure*: during psychotherapy, the adolescent encounters stimuli that trigger implicit memories of early interpersonal abuse or neglect.

Therapy stimuli can trigger exposure to relational memories by virtue of their similarity to the original trauma, including the clinician's physical appearance, his or her age, sex, or race, and the power differential between client and therapist. Even positive feelings associated with the therapeutic relationship can trigger distress—the adolescent's caring feelings toward the therapist (or perception of similar feelings from the clinician) can activate intimate feelings or fears that invoke victimization-related memories, or perceptions of therapist support and acceptance can trigger fears of losing such experiences (i.e., of abandonment by an attachment figure). As well, therapists, like other people, may engage in momentary lapses in empathic attunement, distraction by personal problems, fatigue, or the triggering of their own issues by some aspect of the client's presentation—any of which may inadvertently expose the client to intrusive memories of earlier maltreatment or neglect.

Beyond these discrete triggers, the therapeutic relationship itself—by virtue of its ongoing nature and importance to the youth—may produce stimulus conditions similar to those of early important relationships, including the client's childhood need for attachment. To the extent that the earlier relationship was characterized by trauma, the current therapeutic relationship is therefore likely to trigger negative relational memories, with associated assumptions of neglect, rejection, or disattunement.

Importantly, just as noted in previous chapters for simpler trauma processing, exposure must occur within the context of the therapeutic window in order to address possible overshooting of the client's affect regulation capacities. The clinician may have to work actively, and pay very careful attention, to insure that his or her stimulus value or the characteristics of the therapeutic relationship do not produce so much exposure to negative relational memories that the adolescent becomes overwhelmed. Just as the therapist treating PTSD may titrate the amount of exposure the client undergoes regarding a traumatic memory of war or an assault, the clinician treating relational traumas tries to ensure that cued associations to the abusive environment, although virtually inevitable, are not overwhelming.

For example, adolescents with schemas arising from punitive parenting may require treatment that especially avoids any sense of therapist judgment. Similarly, the youth who has been physically or sexually assaulted may require (a) special, visible attention to safety issues, (b) therapist responses that especially stress boundary awareness and respect, or even (c) a greater-than-normal physical distance between the client's chair and the therapist's. A client with abandonment issues arising from early psychological neglect, on the other hand, may be less triggered when the clinician is especially "close" and psychologically available. On a more general level, therapists of chronically traumatized youth may need to devote greater attention than usual to avoiding behaviors that in some way appear to involve intrusion, control, or narcissism.

Unfortunately, some characteristics of the therapist may be such powerful triggers that the therapeutic process is especially challenged. For example, the female adolescent who was sexually abused by a man, or more recently raped by a male peer, may have considerable difficulty working in therapy with a male clinician. Regardless of the therapist's personal qualities and best intentions, his masculine stimulus value may trigger trauma memories of assaults by a male. Similar scenarios may occur when the therapist's ethnic or racial identity is the same as those who have maltreated or discriminated against the client. More subtly, the (usually middle-class) social status of the therapist may trigger negative feelings in the socially marginalized adolescent, based on a long history of not being understood, or of being judged as somehow less important, by people of the therapist's social position.

In many cases, exposure to memories involving victimization, social deprivation, or discrimination can be titrated. The male clinician treating an abused young woman will need to be careful to avoid interactions that are in any way sexually or physically reminiscent, let alone threatening;[1] the Caucasian therapist working with a young African American man may need to work hard to communicate a nonracist (and nondefensive) perspective; and the economically advantaged counselor should strive to consciously avoid making assumptions or judgments based on his or her background when interacting with economically impoverished clients. When social or gender differences almost inevitably emerge during treatment, the clinician can foster discussion of these issues in the context of acceptance, support, and a willingness to challenge his or her own biases if and when they appear—including the possibility that the therapist is unconsciously behaving in a way reminiscent of people who have hurt the client. It is important that the client feel encouraged and supported to share his or her feelings and reactions regarding the therapist's gender and cultural background and for the therapist to avoid making assumptions about the client's perceptions and experiences.

Whether involving exposure to memories of childhood maltreatment by a parent, or social injury by a devaluing culture, relational exposure thus refers to any aspect of the therapeutic relationship that causes the client to reexperience relational trauma memories. It is *titrated* exposure to the extent that the clinician modifies the degree to which the memory is triggered, generally by avoiding activities that increase the extent to which the current therapy stimuli are reminiscent of the original trauma. In most cases, this means that although the therapeutic relationship is intrinsically similar to the youth's early relationships by virtue of its dyadic nature, encouragement of intimacy, and association with early attachment dynamics, it is not similar in that the therapist is careful to avoid any behaviors, assumptions, or verbalizations that might imply rejection, abandonment, revictimization, or exploitation.

> *Activation*: as a result of therapeutic exposure, the client experiences emotions and thoughts that occurred at the time of the relational trauma.

Activated emotional responses to early relational memories during treatment are often notable for the suddenness of their emergence, their intensity, and their seeming contextual inappropriateness. Intrusive negative cognitions about self or the therapist may be activated, or attachment-related schema involving submission or dependency may suddenly appear. In some cases, such activation may also trigger sensory flashbacks and dissociative responses.

Cognitive-emotional activation can be easily understood by both client and therapist when it occurs in the context of a flashback involving an assault or disaster. When activation occurs in the context of triggered relational stimuli, however, the actual "reason" behind the client's intrusive thoughts, feelings, and or sensations may be far less clear. Because the original trauma memory (a) may have been formed in the first years of life, and therefore is not available to conscious (explicit) awareness, or (b) may be so associated with emotional pain that it is immediately avoided, neither client nor therapist may know why the adolescent or young adult is feeling especially anxious or angry or why he or she is suddenly so distrustful of the clinician. In fact, in instances where such activations are dramatic, they may appear so irrational and contextually inappropriate that they may be seen as evidence of significant psychopathology. Ultimately, however, these activations are logical, in the sense that they represent conditioned cognitive-emotional responses to triggered relational memories, albeit ones that may not be traceable to specific childhood events. And, more generally, they are necessary to effective treatment: trauma memories, relational or otherwise, can be processed only when exposure activates cognitions and emotions that are then addressed through disparity, as described here.

> *Disparity*: although the adolescent trauma survivor thinks and feels as if maltreatment, neglect, or abandonment is either happening or is about to happen, in reality the session is safe, and the therapist is not abusive, rejecting, or otherwise dangerous.

Although this component is often critical to trauma processing, youth who have been victimized interpersonally—especially if that victimization was chronic—may find disparity difficult to fully apprehend at first, let alone trust. There are a number of reasons for this. First, those exposed to chronic danger often come to assume that such danger is inevitable. The "street kid" or victim of ongoing abuse or neglect may find it very difficult to accept that the rules have suddenly changed and that he or she is safe—especially in situations that bear some similarity to the original dangerous context, such as in a relationship with a powerful other. Second, in many cases, the original perpetrator(s) of violence promised safety, caring, or support as a way to gain access to the victim. For example, the client who was sexually abused by her father may have been told by him that you can only "trust your family to take care of you" or that sexual abuse is what a father does to show his love. As a result, reassurance, declarations of safety, or expressions of caring may seem like just more of the same, if not a warning of impending danger. Finally, therapy implicitly requires some level of intimacy, or at least vulnerability, from the client; a requirement that—from the survivor's perspective—can be a recapitulation of past experience of intimate demands and subsequent injuries.

For these and related reasons, not only must disparity/safety be present, the adolescent must be able to perceive it. Although occasionally frustrating for the clinician, this sometimes means that considerable time in therapy will be necessary before enough trust is present to allow true relational processing. For example, the survivor of extended maltreatment may require many weeks or months of therapy before letting down her guard enough to significantly participate in trauma therapy. Similarly, the "street kid" may not immediately trust the therapist just because the clinician wants him to. In some cases, the youth may test the clinician for months before chancing the vulnerability associated with significant disclosure or relational connection.

Given these concerns, the therapist should be prepared for client disbelief, immediate rejection, or even further withdrawal in the face of statements like "You are safe here" or "I won't go away." This does not mean that the clinician shouldn't make such statements (when they are accurate and expressed in a nonintrusive, nondemanding way), yet the therapist should understand that such declarations rarely alter cognitions that have been repeatedly reinforced by prior adversity. In fact, for those hypervigilant to danger in interpersonal situations, disparity cannot be communicated; it must be demonstrated. Therapist statements that he or she should be trusted can even have the opposite effect on traumatized clients—because they have heard similar promises or protestations from ill-meaning people in the past, such statements may make them feel less safe, not more. Instead, when working with young survivors of chronic relational trauma, the therapist must behave in a consistent, reliably safe, and nonexploitive way, so that, over time, the youth can truly extrapolate safety into the future and imagine disparity. Behaving in a way that actually communicates disparity means that the therapeutic environment must be the antithesis of how injurious others have been in the adolescent's past—involving reliability and connection rather than abandonment; relational safety rather than maltreatment or exploitation; boundary respect versus psychological intrusion; and a diversity-supportive, culturally competent perspective rather than one that supports stereotypes or social discrimination.

The exposure-activation-disparity process may proceed in a stepwise fashion for the relational trauma survivor: Early in therapy, he or she may occasionally (and often inadvertently) reveal some small degree of vulnerability or suffering to the therapist and then reflexively expect a negative consequence. When this vulnerability is not, in fact, punished by the therapist, but is met with support and some carefully titrated level of visible caring, the adolescent may slowly lower his or her psychological barriers and express more thoughts or feelings. As these responses are likewise supported, and not exploited or punished, the client's willingness to process pain in "real time" (i.e., directly, in the presence of the therapist) generally increases. It should be stressed that this may take time, and therapist expressions of impatience may, ironically, subvert the process by communicating criticism or implied rejection.

In other cases—for example, when the client has experienced less extreme or less chronic relational trauma, when the conditions surrounding the victimization are clearly quite different (and perceivable as such by the youth) from therapy, or when there were supportive people in the client's environment in addition to the perpetrator(s)—disparity may be considerably easier to establish, and trauma processing may be more immediately possible. In any case, however, this is an assessment issue, as opposed to something that can be automatically assumed.

> *Counterconditioning*: relational triggering of negative emotional states occurs at the same time as the adolescent experiences positive emotional states associated with growing attachment to the therapist.

When counterconditioning was described in Chapter 14, the healing aspect of this phenomenon was described as the simultaneous presence of both (1) the activated distress associated with traumatic memory exposure and (2) the positive feelings engendered by a compassionate therapist in a positive therapy environment. When relational trauma is being processed, counterconditioning is potentially even more important. Activated negative relational cognitions (i.e., "he/she doesn't like me," "he/she will hurt/abandon me," or "I'll be taken advantage of if I become vulnerable") and feelings (e.g., associated fear of authority figures or intimacy) are directly—and, therefore, potentially more efficiently—contradicted by positive relational experiences. In other words, there may be something especially helpful about having fears and expectations of maltreatment in the specific context of nurturance, compassion, and acceptance. In the language of earlier psychodynamic theory, such real-time contradiction of activated schema and positive feelings may provide a "corrective emotional experience."

For traumatized youth in therapy, compassionate treatment appears to weaken negative emotional associations to previous trauma (Briere, in press). This may involve several different, but related phenomena:

- The therapist's visible, noncontingent caring may engage the client's inborn attachment system, which is sensitive to, and triggered by, loving attention from important relational figures (Bowlby, 1988).

- This process, in turn, activates biological self-soothing circuitry that down-regulates the activity of threat recognition/hypervigilance systems (Gilbert, 2009).

- The shift from fear to soothing eventually counterconditions anxiety associated with trauma-reminiscent stimuli in the session (Briere & Scott, in press).

There is, however, also a potential downside to the juxtaposition of negative expectations and positive experiences in therapy. Just as positive experiences in therapy may contradict earlier held beliefs about close relationships, it is also true that activated, negative relational cognitions can at least temporarily prevent the youth from identifying and accessing the positive relational phenomena that occur in therapy. Fortunately, this is rarely an all-or-none experience; in most cases, even the distrustful or hypervigilant youth will slowly come to reevaluate negative relational cognitions when therapist support and validation are visibly and reliably present. As is the case for client difficulties in perceiving therapeutic safety, the incremental process of "letting in" therapeutic caring and positive regard (and, thereby, positive attachment experiences) may require considerable time in treatment.

In some cases, activation of early thoughts and feelings may cause the client to "regress" to a more basic level of relational functioning with the therapist. However, it is important that the therapist understand this as attachment-level reliving, in the same way as a flashback to an assault is reliving. As described earlier, the goal is to work within the therapeutic window—providing sufficient relational contact, support, and positive regard such that the client has the opportunity to reexperience implicit childhood memories in the context of a distress-diminishing state. At the same time, however, the clinician must not provide so much quasi-parental support that early trauma-related distress is too strongly activated, or the youth's dependency needs are reinforced in a way that is detrimental to growth. The latter is probably best prevented by the therapist's continuous examination of his or her own needs to protect and/or rescue the client. In addition, obviously, the possible emergence of attachment-level feelings in the therapist requires special vigilance to the possibility of inappropriate sexualization or romanticization of the older youth or inadvertent exploitation of the younger client to meet the therapist's unmet attachment (including parenting) needs. Any such countertransference, if acted upon, both destroys disparity (i.e., eliminates safety) and reinforces trauma-related emotions and cognitions.

> *Desensitization*: the youth's repeated exposure to relational trauma memories, triggered by his or her connection with the therapist, in combination with the reliable nonreinforcement and counterconditioning of his or her negative expectations and feelings by the therapeutic relationship, leads to a disruption of the learned connection between relatedness and danger.

As described in Chapter 14, the process of exposure, activation, disparity, and counterconditioning, when repeated sufficiently in the context of the therapeutic window, can lead to the desensitization of relational trauma memories. However this occurs, the effect of the progressive activation and processing of implicit relational memories and their cognitive and emotional associations is to change the youth's reaction to his or her interpersonal world. Successful therapy, in this regard, means that the client is more able to enter into and sustain positive interpersonal relationships, because connection with others no longer triggers the same levels of fear, anger, distrust, and negative or avoidant behaviors. As a result, the client's interpersonal life can become more fulfilling and less chaotic—a source of support rather than of continuing stress or pain.

Note

1. In some cases, it may not be possible for the sexually abused client to view the male therapist as sexually nonthreatening, in light of prior experience. Especially for female clients, this may mean that—as we generally suggest—the preferable therapist will be a woman if the original perpetrator was a man (Briere, 1996a). This will vary from case to case, however, and client preference should be given great weight in this regard.

16

Interventions for Identity Issues

A s noted at various places in this book, survivors of early and severe childhood trauma or neglect often experience problems associated with an inability to access, and gain from, an internal sense of self. This may present in the adolescent or young adult, for example, as problems in (1) determining his or her own needs or entitlements, (2) maintaining a consistent sense of self or identity in the context of strong emotions or compelling others, and (3) having direct access to a stable model of self when external conditions or people are challenging or negative. Equally important, the valence of whatever self the youth can access is often negative, involving low self-esteem, self-blame, feelings of inadequacy, and little sense of entitlement to positive treatment from others (Briere, 1992).

Many of these difficulties develop in the early years of life, when the parent-child attachment relationship is disrupted by caretaker aggression or neglect (Bowlby, 1988). In addition to potentially negative impacts on the developing child's psychobiology (Pynoos, Steinberg, & Piacentini, 1999; Schore, 2003), childhood abuse and neglect can motivate adaptations and defenses that, in turn, reduce the child's development of a coherent sense of self (Briere & Rickards, 2007; Elliott, 1994).[1]

Probable reasons for identity disturbance include (1) the effects of early dissociation, (2) demands for other-directedness, and (3) the absence of benign interactions with others (Briere, 2002). Dissociating or otherwise avoiding trauma-related distress early in life may block the youth's awareness of his or her internal state at the very time that a sense of self is thought to develop in children. Further, the hypervigilance or other-directedness needed by the endangered child in order to ensure survival means that much of his or her attention is directed outward, a process that detracts from internal awareness. When introspection occurs, it is likely to be punished, since (a) such inward focus takes attention away from the environment and, therefore, increases danger, and (b) greater internal awareness means—in the context of ongoing trauma—greater emotional pain (Briere & Scott, 2006). Finally, most theories of self-capacities stress the role of benign others in the child's development—one may have to interact with caring others in order to form a coherent and positive sense of oneself (e.g., Stern, 2000). This is thought to occur when the loving and attuned caretaker reflects back to the child what the child appears to be feeling or experiencing, responds to the child's needs in a way that reinforces their legitimacy, and treats the child in such a manner that he or she can infer positive self-characteristics.

As the child develops into an adolescent, the growing complexity of his or her interactions with the social environment ideally bestows a growing sense of self and security in the context of others. Unfortunately, this progression into increasingly coherent identity may be less possible for those who were deprived of positive parenting. Self issues are often exacerbated in adolescence and early adulthood, when many young people—abused or otherwise—experience significant tumult as their sense of identity undergoes significant change.

Because much of self-development appears to involve interactions with caring others, the therapeutic relationship can be a powerful source of stimuli and support for the client's growing sense of self. In this context, the clinician may work to accomplish several tasks:

Provide relational safety. Introspection is, ultimately, a luxury that can only occur when the external environment does not especially require hypervigilance. For this reason, the clinical setting should provide those aspects of safety outlined in Chapter 9. Not only should the youth feel physically safe, he or she should experience psychological safety—the clinician should be psychologically noninvasive, careful to honor the client's boundaries, and reliable enough to communicate stability and security. When these conditions are met, the youth is more likely to trust the interpersonal environment enough to explore his or her internal thoughts, feelings, and experiences. The process of actually discovering that one is safe in treatment, however, may be protracted; many young trauma survivors—perhaps especially youth living on the streets, adolescents caught in the sex trade, gang members, and those exposed to years of victimization—may have to be in treatment for some time before they are able to accurately perceive the safety inherent in the session (see the discussion of disparity in Chapter 14). Even then, this sense of relative safety may wax and wane.

Support self-validity. Also helpful is the therapist's visible acceptance of the adolescent's needs and perceptions as intrinsically valid and his or her communication to the client regarding the client's basic relational entitlements, as noted in Chapter 8. To some extent, this may appear to contradict the need to challenge the client's negative self-perceptions and other cognitive distortions. However, the approach we advocate is to not argue with the youth regarding his or her "thinking errors" about self but, rather, to work with the client in such a way that he or she is able to perceive incorrect assumptions and reconsider them in light of current (therapy-based) relational experience. For example, even though the adolescent may view himself or herself as not having rights to self-determination, these self-perceptions will be contrary to the experience of acceptance and positive regard experienced in the therapeutic session. Such cognitions, when not reinforced by the clinician, are likely to decrease over time. Equally important, as the message of self-as-valid is repeatedly communicated to the client by the therapist's compassionate behavior, client notions of unacceptability are relationally contradicted (Briere, in press).

This general focus on the client's entitlements can help to reverse the other-directness the survivor learned in the context of abuse or neglect. During most childhood abuse, attention is typically focused on the abuser's needs, the likelihood that he or she will be violent, and, ultimately, on the abuser's view of reality. In such a context, the child's needs or reality may have appeared irrelevant, if not dangerous, when asserted. In a safe, client-focused environment, however, reality slowly becomes more about what the youth needs or perceives than what the therapist demands or expects. When the focus is on the client's needs, as opposed to the therapist's, he or she is often more able to identify internal states, perceptions, and needs, and discover how to "hang on to" these aspects of self even when in the presence of meaningful others (i.e., the therapist). By making it clear to the adolescent or young adult that his or her experience is the ultimate focus, and by helping the client to identify, label, and accept his or her internal feelings and needs, the therapist helps him or her to build a coherent and less negative model of self—to some extent in the way caretakers would have, had the client's childhood been more safe, attuned, and supportive.

Reinforce more secure attachment possibilities. Various writers (e.g., Siegel, 1999) suggest that sustained positive relationships—including longer-term psychotherapy—can allow individuals with adverse childhoods to develop greater attachment security, self-esteem, and capacity to form intimate relationships with others. ITCT-A supports a positive and increasingly secure sense of self by regularly exposing the youth to the unconditional positive regard and ongoing emotional support associated with a good therapeutic relationship. As noted in Chapter 15, when this occurs, the client has the opportunity to reexperience early attachment memories in the context of an antithetic, positive current relationship. In some ways similar to the formulations of Fonagy and others (e.g., Bateman & Fonagy, 2004), and not that different from cognitive-behavioral therapy for posttraumatic stress, therapy triggers the client's distorted internal working models of self and others—first developed during childhood maltreatment and/or neglect—and allows them to be contradicted and updated by the actual thoughts, feelings, and experiences that arise in the context of current therapeutic security and acceptance.

In practice, when the abused and/or neglected youth experiences the relational components of ITCT-A, he or she has the simultaneous experience of triggered negative perceptions of self (e.g., of inadequacy, unworthiness of love, and even self-hatred), while also experiencing the therapist's view of him or her as valuable, worthy of caring, and intrinsically good. Over time, this ongoing exposure to the inconsistencies between "old" models of self and "new," more positive inferences based on caring treatment, appears to cause a shift in the client's internal working model of who he or she actually is and what he or she is entitled to in the world. As this change solidifies, the youth is more likely to value himself or herself and feel secure, both in relationships and when alone.

Support self-exploration. As therapy facilitates self-exploration and self-reference (as opposed to defining self primarily in terms of others' expectations or reactions), the abused youth may be able to gain a greater sense of his or her internal topography. Increased self-awareness may be fostered particularly when the client is repeatedly asked about his or her ongoing internal experience throughout the course of treatment. This may include (as described in earlier chapters) multiple, gentle inquiries about the client's early perceptions and experiences, his or her feelings and reactions during and after victimization experiences, and what his or her thoughts and conclusions are regarding the ongoing process of treatment. Equally important is the need for the youth to discover, quite literally, what he or she thinks and feels about current things, both trauma-related and otherwise. Because the external-directedness necessary to survive victimization generally works against self-understanding and identity, the young survivor should be encouraged to explore his or her own general likes and dislikes, views regarding self and others, entitlements and obligations, and related phenomena in the context of therapeutic support and acceptance. As noted earlier, this exploration may be facilitated when the clinician conveys genuine interest, curiosity, and caring about the client's internal states and processes. It may be inhibited by overly analytic or detached therapist behaviors, especially to the extent that they appear to express judgment or criticism. The reader is referred to Blaustein and Kinniburgh (2010) for additional suggestions on increasing adolescents' sense of self through self-exploration.

Support self-actualization versus socially based devaluation. It may also be important to encourage discussion of the young person's beliefs, experiences, and perceptions regarding gender, cultural background, sexual orientation, and other sociocultural issues. Such interchanges ideally support the client's self-determination and self-acceptance and potentially negate cultural stereotyping or discrimination. This process of discerning who one is in the social matrix, and how one should relate to others' culturally based expectations, may not always be straightforward. For example, although the client may have the physical appearance of a certain culture/ethnic background, he or she may, in fact, identify with another culture or may have a sense of belonging in more than one culture if he or she has a mixed racial/cultural background. Gay, lesbian, or transgendered youth may have conflicting experiences of self, reflecting, in part, socially transmitted messages about the unacceptability of any sexual orientation not classically heterosexual. They may have undergone years of socialization to view "normal" sexuality as involving attraction to opposite-sexed partners based on biological gender, and to assume that the epitome of relational success is heterosexual marriage and the bearing of children. Similarly, youth whose ethnicity has been regularly devalued by Anglo American culture, whether based on skin color (e.g., those of African American or Hispanic descent) or cultural background (e.g., most recently in America, Middle Eastern), may have internalized what are essentially self-hating perspectives. In all these cases, the culturally aware clinician can work with the youth to develop self-perceptions that are positive, efficacious, and empowering— even if, in many cases, the client has to struggle against negative social messages and proscriptions.

In summary, the therapist's consistent and ongoing support for introspection, self-exploration, and self-identification allows the abused or marginalized adolescent to develop a more articulated and accessible internal sense of self. Ultimately, the therapist takes on the role of the supportive, engaged, helpful figure whose primary interest—beyond symptom resolution—is the development of the adolescent's internal life and self-determinism. As the client develops a stronger, more positive sense of self, his or her relational functioning also typically improves, generally allowing more social support and reinforcement. Part of the complexity of this process is that, although it encourages a sense of self that is less dependent on the views of others, it is necessarily anchored in the positive, supportive, and affirming responses of significant figures, including the therapist. This unfolding of self-awareness and internal referencing, although less based on specific therapeutic techniques or protocols, can be one of the more important aspects of treatment.

Note

1. Although this book implicates a strong sense of self in optimal psychological development, not all cultures endorse "self"-hood in equivalent ways (see Walsh, 1988). Yet, largely irrespective of culture, certain traits and capacities (e.g., self-esteem, self-confidence, self-efficacy, and interpersonal boundary awareness) are widely viewed as valuable, and their underdevelopment seen as problematic.

17

Family Therapy

The family therapy component of ITCT-A is indicated when problematic family dynamics or intrafamilial conflicts have a negative effect on the adolescent's psychological functioning. These interventions are often most helpful for adolescents who have not yet left the familial home. Further, appropriate candidates for family therapy should not be overwhelmed by posttraumatic symptoms and should have caretakers or family members who are willing to participate in treatment and are at least somewhat supportive of the client.

Unfortunately, a significant proportion of severely maltreated adolescents are separated or alienated from their families. This may be because intrafamilial abuse has made it difficult for the survivor to interact with caretakers (either because the youth is unwilling to do so or because the caretaker's maltreatment is ongoing and/or includes current neglect); the client has run away from home; the youth is functionally emancipated, and neither party views the caretakers as having a current role; the caretakers are separated from one another or otherwise have moved away; the caretaker no longer has custody of the adolescent, for example when an adolescent is placed elsewhere by child protective services; the adolescent's behavior has alienated the caretakers; or the caretaker is overwhelmed with his or her own trauma or suffers from a major psychological disorder, such that he or she cannot contribute positively to the adolescent's therapy.

Although these issues may make family therapy at least temporarily impossible or ill-advised, it is still important to involve the caretakers in the youth's treatment as much as possible. Even if caretakers are nonprotective or emotionally abusive, or are seemingly undermining the adolescent's therapy, attempts should still be made to involve them in collateral sessions (see Chapter 18)—while assuring the adolescent client that, with the exceptions associated with mandated reporting and extreme suicidality, what he or she shares with the therapist is kept confidential. In the absence of family therapy, a therapist who can engage with caretakers and form a therapeutic alliance, while maintaining a strong connection with the client, is more likely to facilitate positive change in the family system and to improve the outcome of the adolescent's therapy (Gil, 1996; Karver et al., 2008).

Engaging traumatized adolescents and their families in family therapy may be difficult, for the reasons just outlined. However, especially after the youth has had some individual therapy and the caretakers have attended collateral and/or parenting (and perhaps group) sessions, family therapy is often appropriate, and the involved family members may be amenable to treatment. Family sessions may occur concurrently with individual, collateral, and group therapy. Generally, the focus is on improving family communication patterns, exposing and attempting to resolve family conflicts that impact the adolescent, clarifying appropriate boundaries, attempting to increase the general level of attunement and emotional support within the family, and preventing further traumatization of the adolescent.

Family therapy can facilitate system change as well as increase the youth's sense of well-being and functioning. However, it is essential that all participating members feel safe and supported. Hughes (2007) suggests that the therapist have an attitude of relaxed engagement that includes qualities of playfulness, acceptance, curiosity, and empathy (PACE). Emotionally attuned interactions between therapist and participating family members enhance the therapeutic relationship and model secure attachment relationships (Byng-Hall, 1999; Hughes, 2007). As ITCT-A activates these "old" attachment patterns within the context of "new" caring and attunement, trauma-related behaviors and feelings can be processed in somewhat the same manner described in Chapter 15, leading to more secure and healthy attachment relationships between caretakers and their children.

A particular challenge in doing family therapy arises when multiple children or adolescents have been victimized, are all considered primary clients, and have been assigned to individual therapists. We advise that, following a significant course of individual therapy, all therapists and clients participate in family therapy. The individual therapists may feel particularly attuned and allied with each of their clients, to the extent that they have difficulty relating or connecting with other family members. For example, the second author (CBL) has encountered instances when, during family therapy, each therapist appears to be mirroring the behavior and stance of his or her specific client.

In one instance, the therapist of the acting-out youngest child was more impulsive or distracting in family therapy sessions, in a manner similar to that of his or her client, whereas the therapist of the oldest adolescent—who was overly responsible in the family—became more structured, initiated more directives, and otherwise "took charge" in a manner similar to that of his or her client. In such cases, or whenever working with complicated family dynamics, presession planning and postsession debriefing by all therapists involved becomes paramount. This includes clinicians reflecting on the therapeutic process, specific events, and countertransferential feelings, and being open to feedback from the other therapists and consultants/supervisors regarding ways in which the family's dynamics may influence the therapist's perceptions and actions.

Cultural factors are often relevant in family and caretaker therapy. Caretakers and other family members may have been raised in social-cultural contexts in which issues like acceptance of corporal punishment, rigid sex roles, and parental authoritarianism—or seeming insufficient supervision—result in considerable strain with family members (often including the youth) who do not endorse these perspectives. As noted by Gil and Drewes (2005), it is important for the therapist to transform cultural knowledge into appropriate therapeutic behaviors. The cultural background of the client and their family may vary within a given family, resulting in different family members identifying with different cultures. For example, a client who is biracial (African American/Latino) may identify more with Latino culture because of important family relationships, whereas a sibling who is African American/White may identify more with African American culture. In addition, even for caretakers within a given supposed cultural group, for example, "Latino" or "Hispanic," each may be from a different subgroup (e.g., with ancestors in Mexico, Central America, South America, Puerto Rico, or Cuba) and thus endorse widely different perspectives, histories, and languages or dialects. Religious/spiritual beliefs may also vary within the family and can influence the extent to which family members value therapy. For this reason, it is often important to ask the client and family members how they perceive themselves regarding cultural/ethnic issues, as opposed to making potentially erroneous assumptions. We refer the reader to Gil and Drewes (2005) for specific advice on how to adjust interventions according to the specific cultural background of the client and his or her family. Other resources for the therapist wanting to understand effects of cultural background and associated family values include Fontes (2005) and McGoldrick, Giordano, and Pierce (1996). All of these resources directly describe specific aspects of a wide range of cultures and provide guidelines for appropriate assessment and treatment.

The family may be impacted by other systems issues, such as police or child welfare involvement regarding possible child abuse or domestic violence, and ongoing legal processes, such as family members being involved in the criminal justice system. There may be custody, dependency, foster parent, and reunification issues that present further complications. Many of these issues and concerns can be worked out, to some extent, if there is motivation, good family communication, and sufficient support. As communication increases, all family members have a chance to understand why things are happening as they are and how some problematic family patterns can be changed. Dynamics such as scapegoating, splitting, inappropriate or excessive expectations of the adolescent or caretaker, and indirect aggression, can be brought to light and hopefully reduced or eliminated over time.

The adolescent client's role in all this is complex. On one hand, he or she is the "identified patient," officially responsible—by virtue of his or her problems, symptoms, and behaviors—for the family being in treatment. This is especially true when the youth has been abused or neglected within the family. Intrafamilial sexual abuse, in particular, seems to involve more complicated family system issues (Gil, 2006), including isolation and lack of outside support systems, extensive denial in the family, a "nonoffending" caretaker who is dissociated and disengaged, blurred boundaries and inappropriate roles (including parentification of children), alliances by family members with the perpetrator, secrecy, poor communication, and lack of empathy for each other. In this and other instances, the adolescent client may be blamed for family dynamics that may not be his or her "fault" and, in fact, may be the source of some of his or her behavior.

On the other hand, it is often the adolescent who shakes up what is already a dysfunctional family system and who brings in assistance from others. He or she may inadvertently begin a process that reveals hidden family violence, abuse of other children, emotional neglect, covert substance abuse, and significant parental psychological disturbance. As these issues are identified and processed in therapy, the youth's role as the problematic member may shift, to his or her (and the family's) benefit. Effective family therapy may result in increased support for, and understanding of, the adolescent trauma survivor, as well as more general positive outcomes for the rest of the family.

ITCT-A Family Therapy Interventions

There are many good books on family therapy, although only a few are focused on treating the traumatized youth from this perspective. Books that specifically address family therapy with child and adolescent abuse or trauma survivors include Friedrich (1990), Gil (1996, 2006), and Pearce and Pezzot-Pearce (2007). Presented here are family interventions that have proven to be especially useful in ITCT-A.

The time line. Just as it is helpful for the client to create a time line of traumatic and nontraumatic events over his or her lifetime thus far (see Chapter 12), this intervention also can be helpful in family therapy sessions. A version of the time line technique can be found in Families Overcoming and Coping Under Stress (FOCUS; Saltzman, Babayon, Lester, Beardslee, & Pynoos, 2008)—a family therapy model used at MCAVIC for medically traumatized clients and their families, involving the FOCUS first author.

In this approach, each family member creates their own time line, demarking all specific traumatic events or losses that he or she has experienced. In this way, family members can explore their different perceptions and feelings associated with traumatic experiences and update each others' recollections of shared—but differently experienced—events. For families with multiple traumatic exposures, it may also be helpful to identify on the time line which events have had the greatest impact on each family member. In some cases, the clinician can suggest that a "total time line" be created, which is a compendium and integration of all the time lines created by individual family members. In blended or fragmented families, this overall time line may document events that some family members may not have experienced or even been aware of, and it may provide insight to family members in terms of things that affect the family but are not known to all.

The genogram. One way that family members can become more aware of the intergenerational transmission of trauma and loss, as well as relationships between family members, is to create a genogram (McGoldrick, Gerson, & Shellenberger, 1999). The genogram is a graphic representation of a family tree that maps out current and former members and their relationship to one another. Depending on their complexity, genograms may denote a wide range of people, events, and even the transmission of behavior (e.g., child abuse) from parent to offspring, across multiple generations. For example, family members can contribute information and impressions regarding positive and negative relationships between family members, psychological traits, conflicts, abuse and violence, neglect, substance abuse, losses, deaths, medical and psychiatric illnesses, and family themes and secrets across several generations. This activity, sometimes completed over more than one session, supports family members' exploration of their perceptions, experiences, and feelings relative to one another, while also becoming more aware of how family dynamics and history have contributed to their trauma and distress.

Family drawings. Family members can be instructed to each create a drawing of their family doing something (Kinetic Family Drawing) or depicting how they might appear in a photograph ("family snapshot"). Sometimes family members will express more information regarding family relationships and issues through drawings than they might through strictly verbal communication. Information on who is included in the drawing, their size relative to one another, and their proximity and demeanor can (a) increase the therapist's understanding of family relationships and dynamics and (b) facilitate discussion and increased awareness among family members.

For example, in one instance, previously undisclosed information was revealed in a family session through drawings by a mother and her adolescent daughter, the latter of whom had been sexually abused by mother's live-in partner. The mother drew a picture of herself, her partner (who had been removed from the home), her adolescent daughter, and infant daughter, living together in a house with a sun representing "God smiling down" upon the household. The daughter drew a picture of her head only, within a picture frame, her mother's head in a separate frame, and the younger sister's head in a third picture frame, all with spaces between them. The adolescent daughter also drew a calendar, noting dates of unmonitored visits involving her, her mother, and her mother's partner—none of which had been sanctioned by the child protection worker. This information was communicated to the adolescent's worker, who then ensured that no further visits involving the adolescent occurred. It also allowed the teenage daughter to have a more frank discussion with her mother about her feelings regarding the mother's continuing relationship with her partner.

Role playing. This exercise involves family members playing the roles of other family members, under the therapist's guidance, with a goal of increasing their understanding or appreciation of the other person's experience. For example, a mother might role-play the adolescent son who "sits around on the couch all day," while he role-plays her "telling me what to do all the time." While taking on each other's persona, and speaking from that person's position, the mother might come to understand better the depression and hopelessness her son has experienced since the loss of his father, and the son might gain an inkling of the pressure his mother feels at now being the sole provider in the family and her anxiety about his well-being. Not only may such interchanges increase each family member's insight, they may lead to more openness to communication and a greater willingness to problem-solve conflicts as they inevitably emerge during family life.

Family Therapy Module

The following is a six- to eight-session family therapy module that usually occurs after a course of individual therapy for the adolescent and weekly collateral therapy sessions for the caretakers. Each session is briefly summarized in terms of the primary topic, goals for the session, and sample interventions. The order of sessions may vary, but, unless specifically irrelevant, the following topics should be included. If trauma includes child abuse and/or family violence, additional attention should be directed at increasing caretaker protectiveness and reducing the risk of further victimization. Six sessions of family therapy are a minimum in most cases; for some families, additional sessions might occur immediately or at a later date.

Primary foci for family therapy, which are interwoven across sessions, are the following:

- Effective communication

- Appropriate caretaking, including safety and protection of the child and age-appropriate expectations

- Affect management

- Boundaries and roles

- Attachment/relationship issues

- Parental empathy, support, and emotional attunement

Session 1: Assessment of Family Functioning, Family Therapy Goals, and Planning

- Each family member has an opportunity to describe areas he or she would like to see addressed in the family sessions and goals he or she would like for treatment. It is important that the family begin sessions with a sense of hope and optimism that they can feel better, more supported, and cared for in their family. Each member (regardless of age) should have an opportunity to express feelings and concerns about the sessions and how their family is currently operating.

- The therapist(s) begins to engage all family members in the family therapy process, ensuring that all feel welcome.

- The therapist(s) reviews plans for future sessions with the family, taking into account their stated goals.

- The therapist begins to gain a sense of how the family is functioning (if this is not already known) by reviewing a typical day—routines, mealtimes, bedtimes, assigned chores, afterschool activities, how homework is completed, etc., as well as problems that have arisen and how traumatic events have affected family functioning. For example, if a family member is dealing with a chronic, debilitating illness or traumatic injury, it is important to know how this is affecting family relationships and functioning. Family members also have an opportunity to briefly describe how they have been traumatized or maltreated and why they are at the clinic or therapist's office receiving treatment—e.g., a son witnessed a shooting of a friend, a daughter was sexually abused by a stepfather, a mother was battered by a boyfriend. By briefly stating what they have experienced at the onset of therapy, the message is communicated that difficult things will be talked about in a safe place. This is especially important when there are family members (e.g., a caretaker or sibling) who have not attended any therapy sessions previously.

- Cultural beliefs and practices, as well as the role of religion or spirituality, should be assessed and integrated into the plan for family therapy. Respect for cultural differences is essential, although the mandating reporting responsibilities of the therapists, regardless of culture, should be noted.

Session 2: Effective Communication and Expression of Feelings

- Each family member is encouraged to express feelings that they are having regarding the traumatic event(s) that brought them to treatment.

- Communication among family members is facilitated by the therapist redirecting family members to express feelings directly to the person concerned. When family members make blaming statements, typically beginning with "You . . . ," they are, instead, encouraged to use "I . . ." statements, to convey how they feel in a way that others can hear. Often, role-plays are helpful at this stage to describe situations at home and for the therapist to coach better communication skills (e.g., expressing feelings and developing listening skills).

- Better communication can be an ongoing challenge throughout the duration of the family therapy sessions. But communication should be especially focused upon at the beginning of treatment, in order to create an environment of safety for later processing of trauma and other difficult material.

- Caretakers are encouraged to be more visibly empathic toward their children—initially, it may only be possible to begin this process, which will continue throughout family therapy. As caretakers become more caring and attuned, the caretaker-adolescent attachment relationship can become more secure. For those caretakers who have particular difficulty understanding their adolescent emotionally, regular individual therapy and/or caretaker collateral sessions may be required concurrently throughout the time that family therapy sessions are conducted.

Session 3: Roles and Boundaries (May Require More Than One Session)

• Following intrafamilial abuse, but also as a result of other types of trauma (e.g., community violence, medical trauma), there may be a reversal of roles and/or inappropriate expectations of children vis-à-vis their caring for parents. An example of this is *parentification*, whereby an adolescent is required to perform duties and tasks beyond his or her developmental level and is expected to care emotionally for adults and other children, rather than having his or her own emotional needs cared for in an age-appropriate manner. Emotional abuse and neglect by caretakers may also lead the adolescent to experience himself or herself as devalued except in terms of what he or she can do for others. A goal at this point in family therapy is to attempt to reorient the adult(s) toward taking better care of themselves and nurturing their children in a consistent, emotionally attuned manner. For more dysfunctional families, a number of sessions may be necessary for roles and boundaries to be significantly realigned. Most typically, more traumatized caretakers may especially struggle with being less demanding and more nurturing of their children.

• Family drawings and collages can further clarify roles and boundaries, for example, having each family member draw their family as they currently perceive it, and then as they would like to be in the future. Such drawings can convey roles of family members as well as relationships, connections, expectations, and emotional status. An adolescent may draw himself or herself as isolated from the rest of the family, much larger or smaller than adult members, or with very little attention to detail for family members while the background is elaborate and highly detailed. Family drawings can also reveal feelings that family members have toward each other and provide opportunities for more relational processing.

• Role-plays can also be employed whereby (a) all family members reverse roles, or (b) members enact a situation at home (e.g., discipline situation or adolescent wanting emotional support) and, with coaching by the therapist(s), learn alternative, more age-appropriate and role-appropriate ways of managing situations that arise.

Session 4: Exploration of Trauma Exposures (May Require More Than One Session)

- Once communication, roles, and boundaries—and increased support of children by caretakers—are evident, it is important that each member of the family have further opportunities to describe the relevant traumatic event(s) and how they, specifically, were impacted emotionally.

- As events are described, they can be mapped out on paper as a time line (described earlier), with each family member's feelings indicated for each point in time. This exercise often helps members to gain a better understanding of how all family members experienced shared and/or separate traumatic events.

- Family members can participate together in creating a genogram—especially once family dynamics have improved and safety is more salient—showing multiple generations, relationships, and trauma exposures throughout the family system. This may help the family to understand the broader history and context of traumatic experiences and may even help them to prevent further trauma in the future.

- For some families, especially those with younger children, it may be helpful for family members to engage in drawings, board games, and other play-oriented means of describing traumatic events.

Session 5: Enhancing Family Relationships, Increasing Support Network, and Further Trauma Processing (May Require More Than One Session)

- Most families will require further opportunities to process their traumatic experiences and express associated feelings, perhaps continuing relevant activities from Session 4.

- At this time, the therapist(s) may provide further opportunities for the adolescent to experience their primary caretakers as being more empathic, supportive, and emotionally attuned to them.

- When adequate communication skills have been acquired, and care-takers are expressing more empathy for their children, it may be helpful to have extended family members (e.g., aunts, uncles, grandparents) attend the session. For example, if family members are dealing with a recent loss or new traumatic event (e.g., incarceration of a family member) or require support beyond the immediate family, this larger family session can be very beneficial. An extended family meeting may also counteract, to some extent, emotionally abusive or neglectful behaviors by caretakers who continue to struggle with emotionally supporting their children.

- Because the formation and continuation of more secure attachments is important for the adolescent's healing (Byng-Hall, 1999), family therapy can be focused, at this stage, on further developing and reinforcing the primary attachments in the adolescent's (and other family members') life. This is typically accomplished as the caretaker demonstrates emotional attunement and emotional support of the youth, rather than focusing on their own needs. For some families, more sessions will be required to further explore and develop attachment relationships.

- Caretakers may also benefit from attending concurrent group sessions for themselves (see Chapter 18), wherein they can explore further their own traumatic experiences, receive support from other adults who have had similar experiences, and become more emotionally available to their families.

Session 6: Goals for the Future, Reinforcing Treatment Gains

- At this point, all family members review with the therapist(s) their progress thus far, goals for the future, and the possibility for further therapy. If indicated or desired, family therapy sessions may be extended at this point or resumed again at a later time after the adolescent client and collateral(s) have made more progress in individual therapy. Further sessions may be especially indicated if further safety or protection issues arise, new trauma disclosures occur, reunification or visitation with an alleged perpetrator becomes an issue, or clients are exhibiting or expressing heightened anxiety, requiring further relational processing within the family context. Similarly, if further traumatic events occur during family therapy (e.g., death in family, sudden hospitalization of chronically ill parent or child, contact by perpetrator), a decision may be made to extend current sessions in order for the family to process this new material.

- Finally, during the process of ongoing family therapy, it may become clear that additional issues must be addressed in treatment. These may include

  o cultural factors that provoke identity and communication issues for members of the family, such as acculturation stress and generational differences in beliefs regarding acceptable parent and adolescent behaviors;
  o the need to broaden the family's social network, including increasing interests and support for the family and its members, identifying respite resources for the caretaker(s), and increased contact with external systems, such as church or community groups; and
  o issues arising from the needs and issues of foster parents, as well as the impacts of the adolescent's history of multiple placements and multiple caretakers on his or her response to the current family milieu.

It is important that the therapist balance the needs of the family system, while not overlooking the needs of the primary adolescent client, who, in most cases, is also undergoing ongoing individual therapy. There may be things that he or she has to say to other family members, requests he or she wants to make, or explanations he or she wants to hear regarding ways in which the family may have mistreated him or her. On the other hand, the rest of the family may be outspoken or preoccupied with issues relatively unrelated to the adolescent's concerns. In such instances, the clinician should be careful to include the adolescent's desires or specific goals for treatment when working with the family as a whole. Information on the adolescent's specific family-related issues will not always arise in the context of the family session—it may come from his or her work in individual therapy, in which case the therapist should communicate this material to the adolescent's family therapist(s) with the adolescent's permission. In other cases, this information may become apparent during the assessment phases of treatment, and the Assessment-Treatment Flowchart–Adolescent (ATF-A) may be helpful in determining the priorities for family treatment.

18

Interventions With Caretakers

W hen possible, ITCT-A involves the trauma survivor's parents or
caretakers in treatment. Although interventions for caretakers and
families differ, each is ultimately focused on the same goal: assisting the
traumatized young person by increasing his or her access to relational support, healthy attachments, and a positive parenting environment.

In contrast to earlier chapters, which address adolescents and young
adults up to age 21, this chapter, like the last, is most concerned with youth
who still live in a dependent role within a family unit. Thus, it is less relevant
to youth who live on the streets or in shelters or who, for whatever reason,
are separated or emancipated from their caretakers. Even in these cases,
however, therapy involving caretakers may still be helpful, since many separated adolescents continue to have significant contact with their parents and
thus continue to be influenced by them.

Support, Education, and Parenting Skills

An important part of working with caretakers is increasing their understanding of the adolescent's difficulties and behaviors, so that they may be more
supportive. Many parents experience considerable distress, and sometimes
desperation, at their child's externalizing behavior and may have almost
given up hope at the severity or chronicity of his or her depression, self-
destructiveness, or aggression. Many lack information about what the effects
of abuse are and the logic behind what appears to be "bad" behavior. As

well, they may not understand developmental issues that complicate the adolescent's reactions to abuse.

Caretaker issues often impact the course of the young person's treatment as well. In general, low caretaker involvement and emotional support typically extends and complicates the treatment of traumatized youth (Friedrich, 1990; Gil, 1996, 2006). At the most basic level, many adolescents (especially younger ones) are unable to attend sessions without their caretaker's consent and/or are dependent on a caretaker to bring them to sessions. More subtly, it is important that caretakers not undermine their children's therapy by belittling the process, discounting or arguing against therapist statements or recommendations, or just by failing to support the youth as he or she undergoes treatment.

In many cases, the clinician will also find it necessary to improve the caretaker's ability to parent the youth, so that he or she can provide developmentally appropriate emotional support, attachment resources, discipline, and protection from further victimization. In most cases, it is not just child maltreatment or peer assaults that negatively impact the adolescent; it is also the degree to which he or she experiences support, caring, attunement, and protection from his or her parents or caretakers.

Given the stress and demands associated with raising a traumatized youth, it is especially important to provide caretakers with opportunities to discuss and ventilate feelings and reach out to helpers and peers for support. The unsupported caretaker is unlikely to be as good a parent as otherwise might be possible and may be more reactive to the challenges of raising an adolescent. Thus, it is not only the humanitarian impulse to assist beleaguered people that should motivate the therapist to work with caretakers, but also the indirect effects on the youth of having caretakers who feel supported and who have resources to call upon.

When caretakers were not directly involved in major maltreatment of the child,[1] and are willing to engage in the process, individual and group meetings can be quite helpful. As noted earlier, a significant number of caretakers of adolescent trauma survivors lack good parenting skills and may treat their own children in the way they, themselves, were treated in their own dysfunctional or abusive families of origin. When caretakers themselves have significant trauma histories, and/or suffer from significant psychological symptomatology, their care of their children may be further compromised by behavioral withdrawal, instability, substance abuse, chaotic parenting styles, or negative mood states.

Most problematic is the possibility that the disengaged or angry caretaker will choose to prematurely discontinue therapy for the traumatized youth. For this reason, among others, the therapist should make special efforts to engage the caretaker in the therapy process. This may involve soliciting his or her opinion about the basis for the youth's difficulties, as well as how the therapist can be most useful to both the adolescent and the caretaker. Also important will be explicit efforts on the therapist's part to recognize and support the caretaker's feelings about the youth's trauma. By facilitating the caretaker's expression of his or her own feelings about what transpired (e.g., guilt and/or anger), while not overly confronting any denial he or she may need to engage early in the process, the clinician can help the caretaker feel like an important collaborator in the child's treatment and will increase the extent to which the caretaker can support the youth. The reader is referred to specific guidelines by Pearce and Pezzot-Pearce (2007) for facilitating support from caretakers following disclosures of abuse, especially for younger adolescents.

Another reason to engage the caretaker early in the treatment process is to proactively intervene in his or her response to the youth's trauma-related "bad" or problematic behavior. Stressed caretakers, and those whose childhood experience or cultural background support physical discipline, may require specific counseling and education regarding what is acceptable punishment for the adolescent's transgressions. Personal or cultural values can contribute to disciplinary behavior that might escalate to physical child abuse, requiring the therapist to report the caretaker to a child protection agency. From the first appointment, adolescent clients and their caretakers should be informed of what legally constitutes child abuse and under what circumstances a suspected child abuse report must be made. Equally important, the therapist should explore with caretakers alternative, positive parenting practices that will not only not traumatize the youth, but also help him or her to learn more functional behaviors. Regardless of culturally or historically based parenting practices, however, it is important for caretakers to understand that positive reinforcement for appropriate behavior can contribute to a more positive relationship with their adolescent child.

ITCT-A provides two modalities of caretaker intervention: individual collateral meetings and caretaker groups. Individual parent/caretaker sessions usually occur on a weekly to biweekly basis, often for 30–45 minutes per meeting, and may either be for a limited number of sessions or may extend for the full duration of the adolescent's treatment. These sessions typically involve some combination—depending on caretaker needs—of support, parenting skills development, psychoeducation on abuse and the adolescent's response to it, and general developmental issues.

If the caretaker(s) appears to have mental health issues, and/or their own history of childhood trauma, it may be appropriate to refer them to another agency for separate therapy. However, for more disadvantaged and traumatized caretakers, it may be important for therapy to be provided at the same agency where the adolescent client attends individual therapy. When services are provided at one agency, opportunities for closer coordination and collaborative treatment planning are maximized. With appropriate consents between agencies (whether legally required or not), collaboration between the youth's and his or her caretaker's therapist may be both efficient and specifically helpful. Finally, when both caretakers and children receive treatment at the same general time at the same place, the likelihood of regular attendance typically increases. We discuss issues associated with caretaker individual therapy later in this chapter.

Caretaker Groups

At MCAVIC-USC, caretaker groups generally ran for 12 weeks, on a weekly basis. Caretakers sometimes repeated a group module a second time, leading to a total of 24 weeks, or advanced to a second series of group sessions focused more on their own issues as trauma survivors. Two types of groups are typically offered in ITCT-A: a didactic parenting group, adapted to address specific cultural issues, and a caretaker support group. In some cases, an older adolescent client is also a parent. When this is true, the youth may concurrently attend his or her own individual therapy sessions as well as participate in a caretaker group.

Didactic parenting groups can be especially helpful for caretakers who can benefit from material and discussion focused on increasing their ability to manage behavior, increase communication, and improve age-appropriate expectations of their children, yet do not want to address trauma-focused issues and feelings in depth. Other caretaker groups, especially those more focused on addressing trauma-related issues, can provide support that, ultimately, facilitates the caretaker's readiness to seek his or her own individual therapy.

In many cases, grandparents, aunts, uncles, or other relatives are the legal guardians and primary caretakers and thus should be included in caretaker collateral sessions and caretaker groups. These caretakers often are guardians because the biological parent or parents have abandoned the youth, become incarcerated or incapacitated due to illness or substance abuse, have died, or chose to remain allied with an abusive partner—necessitating the minor being placed with relatives. In such instances, there is usually much to talk about, gain support for, learn about, and process. Foster parents also should be encouraged to attend individual collateral sessions and caretaker groups. However, a minority may not be interested—at least initially—in participating in the adolescent's treatment. In those situations, the therapist should nevertheless make every attempt to encourage their participation in (or at least support for) the adolescent's treatment. Supportive phone calls can sometimes facilitate this process, as does collaboration with child protection workers to encourage the foster parent to attend appointments.

Caretaker support groups typically involve multiple topic areas, including interactions with systems (e.g., law enforcement), parenting, identity issues, their own history of trauma, reactions to their child(ren)'s trauma exposures, gender and cultural issues, sexuality and relationship issues, and prevention strategies. Materials such as *The Mother's Book* (Byerly, 1985), which continues to be quite relevant despite its age, can be useful with caretaker support groups—especially with mothers of sexually abused adolescents. The sense of isolation and shame that a nonoffending caretaker may feel can be reduced through participation in a group with other caretakers who have experienced similar issues.

The following model is used for caretakers of adolescents (or, in another context, younger children; Lanktree & Briere, 2008b) who have been sexually or physically abused or exposed to domestic violence. Although this is a suggested sequence for group sessions, more sessions may be devoted to a particular topic area, or the order of sessions may also be adjusted according to the needs of group members. We recommend 12 to 16 weeks of group sessions in this model.

Therapists may wish to administer the Trauma Symptom Inventory-2 or a similar measure to determine the extent of trauma-related distress and disturbance of individual group members, in part as a way to design the focus of specific group sessions. Although the 12-session group model presented below focuses more on the dynamics and impacts of sexual abuse, the majority of adolescents treated with the ITCT-A model have experienced more than one type of trauma, for example, exposure to domestic violence and/or caretaker substance abuse, physical abuse, emotional abuse, significant losses, and/or community violence.

This group is typically used with caretakers who have had a successful course of parenting classes, or a parenting-focused support group, and have attended regular collateral sessions so that they are more able to address their own trauma issues. Although sessions include some didactic material, and attention to parenting issues, the focus is more on the exploration of the caretaker's own trauma history, family-of-origin concerns, attachment issues, as well as more general discussion and support among group members. This model is designed to increase self-awareness and positive identity, facilitate more in-depth trauma processing, explore sex role/gender issues, develop relaxation and coping skills, explore relationships with partners, and increase safety for themselves and their families. Group members may, or may not, journal their experiences in the context of the group.

The recommended session-by-session structure of the caretakers group is as follows:

- **Session 1: Introductions and Planning**

Topics and activities: Introductions, overview of the group, confidentiality, and rapport/trust building. Group members describe how they were referred to the group and why they are attending. Each member completes a written "contract" stating his or her goals for attending the group and his or her commitment to attend all planned weekly sessions, arrive on time, and stay for the entire session each week. Group rules about respecting one another, not interrupting, limits of confidentiality, and limiting communication with each other to sessions are discussed. Group members complete self-portraits and share how they are feeling about participating in the group. An overview of the group sessions is provided and discussed. Group members are encouraged to provide input so that the topics for all sessions will meet their needs.

- **Session 2: Information Regarding Child Abuse and Domestic Violence/ Dealing With Systems**

Topics and activities: Psychoeducation regarding common reactions to child abuse and domestic violence; processing activated experiences; and strategies for dealing with systems. Didactic information is provided regarding short- and long-term impacts of child abuse and domestic violence on children and themselves, including symptoms, feelings, and behaviors. Because many caretakers are raising younger children as well as adolescents, developmental differences are also included in the discussion. This session also may include viewing a DVD on the impacts of abuse, in order to promote more in-depth discussion and understanding about ways in which their children may have been affected. If this resource is used, caretakers should have the opportunity to express any feelings that may have been activated. Group members also describe and debrief one another regarding their experiences and strategies for coping with various systems such as Criminal Court, Dependency Court, Family Court, law enforcement, and child protection agencies.

- **Session 3: Understanding the Dynamics of Abuse and Abusers**

Topics and activities: Activities and discussion to increase caretakers' understanding of the dynamics of abuse and those who abuse, as well as the impacts and feelings associated with child abuse and domestic violence. Group members discuss dynamics and impacts of sexual abuse, domestic violence, or physical abuse, on their children and their family. Members explore the impacts of trauma on their relationships (parent-child, other children in their family, and extended family). Feelings related to the offender(s), including betrayal, grief, loss, and anger, are explored. Members of the group discuss how and when the abuse happened and the reactions they had to the disclosures.

- **Session 4: Parenting Issues and Strategies**

Topics and activities: Psychoeducation, discussion, and role-plays to improve group members' parenting skills and to explore the influence of their own trauma history on parenting. Behavioral management strategies are discussed, along with other ways that members can increase their support and empathy for the youth. Group members consider how their own trauma history may have contributed to their parenting issues. Strategies for better boundaries and communication are discussed. Group members may role-play situations they have encountered with their children and explore better ways of resolving caretaker-child conflicts. Members discuss ways to increase their functioning as caretakers, including the development of more affect regulation skills and increased self-awareness. At the end of the group session, members participate in a meditation, breath training, or relaxation activity (see Chapter 11) that de-escalates activated emotions, facilitates greater acceptance of self, and builds optimism about themselves as caretakers.

- **Session 5: Coping Skills and Self-Care**

Topics and activities: Discussion and role-plays to increase healthy coping skills, self-awareness, and ability to care for themselves and others. Group members discuss the idea of using coping skills in order to be less reactive with children and youth and practice affect regulation skills and trigger identification (see Chapters 11 and 12). They also explore how they can further develop mindfulness in their parenting and in other aspects of their lives. Group members may engage in more role-plays to practice skills they have learned through the group, including ways that they can be more assertive and empowered. Caretakers explore and develop strategies and skills to increase safety for themselves and their families. This may also include developing a safety plan (see Chapter 9) to protect them from further abuse and/or violence. Finally, members may engage in a meditation, breath training, or relaxation activity to further develop affect regulation capacities.

- ## Session 6: Families of Origin

Topics and activities: Group members complete family genograms and discuss family issues and themes. Group members explore issues related to their own family-of-origin and attachment relationships. Each member presents his or her family genogram, with special attention to family-of-origin relationships, intergenerational issues related to trauma and loss, role models, strengths acquired, and ways in which his or her parenting has been influenced by his or her experiences while growing up.

  - ## Sessions 7 and 8: Trauma Narratives *(Note: This session and the following one may occur earlier in the sequence if group members are ready to process their traumatic experiences at an earlier point in the group.)*

Topics and activities: Members share their narratives through writing activities, and/or creating a collage or time line, and discussion. To the extent they are comfortable doing so, each group member briefly describes his or her personal trauma or neglect history, explores how the youth's trauma (presently or in the past) may have triggered memories of his or her own victimization, and provides support for other members during this disclosure process. Beyond direct disclosures, this also may be done by sharing journal entries, writing and reading letters to the offender, or engaging in (and sharing) other writing activities. Members also may create a time line (as described in Chapter 12) or a collage, focusing on their trauma experiences and ways they have used their strengths and resources to survive traumatic experiences.

- ## Session 9: Gender and Cultural Identity Issues

Topics and activities: Group members explore their sense of self related to gender and cultural background and practice increasing assertiveness. This session is focused on increasing self-awareness, self-esteem, assertiveness, and positive coping skills.

Gender issues, sex roles, cultural beliefs and background, and spirituality are discussed and explored. Members may complete a collage representing their culturally based self-perceptions as a child or youth, as well as their current views of themselves. If relevant, discussion also may include members' experiences of racial, gender, or economic discrimination.

- **Session 10: Attachment Relationships**

Topics and activities: Group members explore their attachment relationships from childhood and in their current lives and discuss ways to improve their attachment relationships with their children. In this session, members describe their relationships with their children, partners, and others (e.g., family members, friends, coworkers), and explore ways in which their childhoods may have made it difficult to form and maintain secure relationships—including with their children. Group members discuss ways in which members might improve their relationships with others and provide supportive feedback to one another.

- **Session 11: Intimacy/Sexuality**

Topics and activities: Group members discuss issues related to dating, sexuality, intimacy in relationships, and maintaining their personal safety and the safety of their children. Trust issues are explored, and group members discuss the challenges they face in dating or ongoing relationships with sexual/romantic partners. Members explore self-protection and prevention strategies in instances where a partner or date might become abusive or violent and discuss how they could increase the safety of their children and themselves. Members may also want to explore feelings associated with sexual and intimacy issues arising from their trauma histories.

- **Session 12: Celebration and Planning for the Future**

Topics and activities: Overview/recap of the group. Group members review the goals written in their contracts at the beginning of the group and their progress in meeting those goals. Members may choose to share their journal entries from the time that they were in group. Each group member briefly discusses his or her goals for the future. Members complete self-portraits and the TSI-2 (if also administered at the beginning of the group) and discuss positive changes they have noticed in themselves and others over the course of the group.

Caretaker Therapy

The psychological treatment of caretakers proceeds in essentially the same way as it would for any other adult client. However, this work may be most helpful to the adolescent if the caretaker is able to explore any of his or her own trauma experiences, feelings, and reactions in much the same way that his or her adolescent son or daughter is hopefully doing in his or her own therapy sessions. The caretaker with unresolved trauma and/or a dismissive/disorganized attachment to his or her child is likely to benefit from opportunities to increase affect regulation skills and self-capacities, as well as to explore and process his or her own traumatic experiences cognitively and emotionally. The reader is referred to recent sources on the treatment of adolescents and adults with complex trauma (e.g., Blaustein & Kinniburgh, 2010; Briere & Scott, 2006; Cloitre et al., 2006; Courtois & Ford, 2009; Habib, 2009) for further information on how these goals might be accomplished.

Because of the interpersonal complexities, boundary issues, and role conflicts inherent in a single clinician treating multiple family members, it is strongly recommended that someone other than the adolescent's therapist be assigned to treat his or her caretaker(s). This is particularly important for the older adolescent, whose relationship with his or her therapist could be compromised if the caretaker (who may have contributed to the youth's trauma) is also seeing his or her therapist in individual collateral sessions. Similarly, if siblings are also participating in individual sessions, they should be treated by different therapists. When this is not possible within an agency, individual family members should be referred to other clinics or practitioners.

Note

1. The notion of the "nonoffending parent's" role in treatment can be complex. Although we do not suggest that especially abusive caretakers (e.g., sex offenders) should be involved in the youth's treatment, it is not always clear where this dividing line actually resides. For example, a neglectful or psychologically abusive caretaker may still be included in conjoint or family therapy, depending on the severity of the actions against the child. Much of this determination involves clinical judgment, as well as, in some cases, the determinations of the legal system.

19

Group Sessions

G roup therapy is another modality of ITCT-A, although it is not applied with all traumatized adolescents. Typically, group treatment augments individual therapy; it is generally not used in isolation.[1] This is because many adolescent and young-adult survivors of complex trauma suffer from relatively intense symptomatology, including posttraumatic stress and painful relational memories—phenomena that, along with the specific activities of trauma group therapy, can be triggered by interactions with other group members. In the absence of concomitant individual therapy or a previous course of trauma-focused individual therapy, these triggered cognitive and emotional states may become very challenging for both the client and the group.

Especially activating may be descriptions by group members of abuse incidents that prematurely expose the client to his or her own unprocessed memories, often before he or she has sufficient affect regulation capacities to handle such material. The youth may become so flooded by negative internal states that he or she either redirects the group leaders' (and the group's) attention to his or her responses (thereby altering group dynamics) or leaves the group session in an emotionally compromised state. In the absence of an individual therapist to whom the client can go for support and further intervention, the net effect of group therapy for such individuals occasionally may be negative.

If a therapist is providing individual therapy in the same agency or elsewhere, it is important that collaboration occur between the group therapists and the therapist, outside agencies, or other professionals, e.g., phone consultations subsequent to signed consents for exchange of information at the beginning and midpoint of the group and as termination approaches. Some group members who have terminated individual therapy, or have reduced the frequency of individual sessions, may feel triggered in group sessions. If this occurs, group cotherapists may choose to offer debriefing with the triggered group member after a given session. Alternatively, the group member may be advised to resume regular individual therapy sessions while also continuing the group therapy sessions.

Despite the potentially activating aspects of being triggered by hearing about other members' traumas, group therapy has advantages over individual therapy alone. These include reduced isolation and stigmatization, normalization of material previously viewed as shameful, the development of interpersonal trust, and identification with a supportive network of other, similarly traumatized or maltreated individuals (Briere, 1996a). Some clients may only be able to discuss and process previously undisclosed details, feelings, and psychological concerns in the context of the support and structure of trauma-focused groups.

ITCT-A group models discussed here relate most to "Stage Two" (focus on trauma processing) and "Stage Three" (focus on interpersonal relationships) interventions described by Herman (1992) and Mendelsohn et al. (2011). These foci complement the work that is accomplished in ITCT-A individual and family therapy.

Group sessions also may be conducted in school settings with adolescent students who have been traumatized. In such instances, intervention may overlook the injunction that group treatment not occur in the absence of current (or previous) individual therapy. Although this is not preferable, in some cases this is the only way some traumatized youth will have access to any form of therapy. In this context, if concomitant individual therapy is not possible, the sessions should focus more on community violence, traumatic loss, parental substance abuse, or witnessing domestic violence, rather than child abuse, particularly sexual abuse. In this regard, MCAVIC provided school-based groups with high-risk youths who otherwise would not or could not participate in clinic-based treatment (Lanktree, 2008a). Fortunately, therapists were able to provide crisis interventions and debriefing with group members following group sessions at school sites, as well as facilitating referrals for individual therapy when indicated.

In some cases, even when adolescent clients are seen in school settings, individual sessions are possible. For example, group treatment combined with individual therapy sessions was provided by MCAVIC at "storefront" (alternative) school settings in a milieu-type setting. In this context, therapists provided daily visits to the school site, where they offered support, behavior management training, and consultations to school social workers, teachers, and counselors (Lanktree, 2008a; Neale & Aguila, 2004). This adaptation of ITCT also is possible in residential treatment settings, where contact with family members is not possible or may be contraindicated.

Assuming that, in most cases, individual therapy is also available, group therapy can be a powerful tool in the adolescent survivor's recovery. As noted, some group members may be able to process their trauma in ways not possible during individual therapy, and most can gain greater empathy for others, feel less isolated, and have greater compassion for themselves. We present below some central principles and parameters for ITCT-A groups. In addition, Appendix VII provides examples of clinic-based and school-based groups—both of which can be adapted for use in residential settings.

Before the specifics of ITCT-A group therapy are described, another helpful group model for youth with complex trauma exposure deserves mention here. This approach, Structured Psychotherapy for Adolescents Responding to Chronic Stress (SPARCS; DeRosa & Pelcovitz, 2008; Habib, DeRosa, & Labruna, 2009), is a 16-session group intervention for adolescents aged 12 to 19 years. It addresses issues associated with a history of chronic interpersonal trauma, and was designed for adolescents living in the context of significant, ongoing stressors. SPARCS is present-focused, does not involve a systematic exposure component (although trauma is discussed), is strength-based, and incorporates a focus on increasing mindfulness and self-regulation. It does not include ITCT-A's requirement of individual therapy prior to, or during, group participation. Preliminary data, and our own impressions, indicate that SPARCS is a helpful group methodology. For this reason, although we describe a specific group component of ITCT-A below, the SPARCS approach may be substituted for (or used to augment) this component when appropriate.

Screening and Assessment

Initial screening interview. For all types of ITCT-A groups, it is essential that prospective group members be interviewed by both cotherapists, so that clients know what to expect regarding group session topics, structure, and attendance requirements and have an opportunity to discuss their goals for group. Referrals are typically received in school settings from school counselors and social workers and in clinic settings from individual ITCT-A therapists. The individual interview is also an opportunity for cotherapists to evaluate the client's readiness for trauma-focused work in the group, as well as the extent of his or her coping strategies and affect regulation skills. Screening occurs at the time of the referral and during the initial interview. We recommend that treatment commence as soon after the interview process as possible.

Clients who are currently in crisis and experiencing significant difficulties regulating affect, have significant substance abuse issues (i.e., at the level of drug or alcohol addiction), or are acutely suicidal are encouraged to continue individual therapy rather than participate in group therapy, at least until they are in a more stable condition. Briere (1996a) describes in greater detail guidelines for screening, for example, the distinction between suicidal thoughts (common in trauma survivors) versus major suicide risk, and between a drug addict and a client who occasionally uses drugs. In this regard, it should be determined whether such negative factors, as mediated by any specific strengths (e.g., good affect regulation capacities), are likely to interfere with each particular youth's individual response to group therapy. Potential obstacles for regular attendance, such as transportation and scheduling issues, are also discussed and a plan made so that group members can maintain regular attendance. This may involve, when possible, taxi vouchers or bus passes being given to group members who require them, and scheduling the group at the most optimal time to maximize regular attendance for all members. Clients who cannot commit to weekly attendance should be referred back to their individual therapist.

Assessment. Because assessment is a significant component of ITCT-A, it is also a part of the group therapy component. In clinic-based intervention, this does not require any new testing or evaluation, since, ideally, assessment already occurs in three-month increments. However, in school-based group interventions, where individual therapy may not be a component, we recommend using the TSCC-A (which has no sexual items, as often requested by school administrators and/or parents) in the initial intake interview, as well as at regular intervals and at the end of treatment to determine treatment effectiveness.

Matching on affect regulation capacity. Groups should ideally consist of clients with relatively equivalent abilities to tolerate emotional distress. When group members have been screened for similar affect regulation skills, the trauma disclosures and processing activities of any one group member are less likely to trigger another member into an excessive emotional or cognitive state—in other words, all members share generally equivalent therapeutic windows (see Chapter 14), such that undershooting or overshooting is less common.

Although affect regulation matching is generally a good idea, in some cases there will not be sufficient potential members available to sort them into such groups. As a result, the clinician may have to include clients of differing levels of emotional regulation capacity and thus may have to pay special attention to the possibility that some members may become overwhelmed if other members fully process their trauma. Unfortunately, this means that a given therapy group may be less helpful for some members than others; especially those whose capacities support the activation and processing of very distressing material, since they will necessarily have to be constrained to some extent in groups with individuals who have less ability to modulate strong emotional experiences (Briere, 1996a). In such situations, the best that the clinician may be able to do is to screen out those adolescents with especially poor affect regulation capacity. This will increase the likelihood that survivors will not be overwhelmed by other clients' emotional processing, and group members will have greater opportunities to discuss and respond to abuse memories without worrying about—and/or stigmatizing—those who might be especially overwhelmed by such material. Clients with especially poor affect regulation capacities, or especially powerful trauma memories, may need more time in individual therapy before they can participate in group therapy. Clients who are clinically depressed and at risk for suicidality also will benefit from a significant course of individual therapy prior to attending group therapy sessions.

Group Rules/Session Guidelines

Clients are informed during the screening interview, as well as in the first session, of the guidelines and rules of group therapy. These guidelines help to establish a predictable structure for the group and reinforce a sense of safety for group members.

• **Confidentiality.** In general, however, what is discussed in the group remains in the group. However, given that attendees generally are minors, they are also informed of the reporting responsibilities of the cotherapists in the event of suspected child abuse. If group members have concerns about the group discussion or process, they are encouraged to express these concerns in the group session. Members are also informed that group therapists will be conferring with their individual therapists. If the individual therapist is not at the same agency, a consent for release (exchange) of information will be signed by the holder of the privilege (e.g., parent, emancipated minor or young adult, social worker).

• **Time for each member in each session.** All group members are allowed a certain amount of uninterrupted time per session, including during "check-in" at the beginning of the group, to speak about their issues, concerns, or feelings. Group members are told that they are there to express their own feelings and that it is not their job to focus on changing others.

• **Mutual respect.** Differences of opinion or disagreements with other group members are expressed in a supportive, respectful manner rather than a confrontational, aggressive way. Members are encouraged to express how they feel without being intentionally hurtful toward others. Younger group members and/or residential treatment clients who may have previously exhibited physically aggressive behavior are informed that such behavior will not be tolerated, and timeouts will be given if such behavior occurs. If disrespectful, hurtful behavior toward others continues, the client will be asked to leave the group.

• **Attendance.** Group members are informed that they must arrive on time and stay for the full group session and, whenever possible, attend all scheduled sessions. If a member is not able to attend a session for a significant and unavoidable reason, he or she should inform the group cotherapists ahead of time. If a group member is not able to commit to regular weekly attendance, he or she should be referred back to his or her individual therapist. Members are also informed that if at any point they are considering dropping out of the group, they must discuss this within the group session before making a decision.

• **Outside contact.** Discussions between group members outside of group is not recommended. However, if this occurs, it is important to share this information at the next group session. Group members are encouraged to use the group to ask for help and to look to group members for support within group sessions, not outside of them. Under no circumstances are sexual relationships between members acceptable.

Gender Composition

It is suggested that all groups be comprised of adolescents of a single sex (i.e., separate groups for males and females), particularly when groups are focused on sexual victimization. This is because mixed-gender trauma groups tend to involve two challenges:

• Heterosexual members of such groups tend to respond to the presence of opposite-sex members with behaviors associated with sexual-romantic dynamics, including "showing off," flirting, or discussions of male-female differences in social contexts. Homosexual/gay or transgendered youth may evidence the same issues, but various factors (including the smaller ratio of such adolescents to their specifically heterosexual peers) typically reduce the prevalence or intensity of this issue. As a result, they are typically assigned to groups of their own (or chosen) gender. Sexual and romantic discussions and behaviors are a healthy part of adolescent development and socialization, regardless of the individual's gender or sexual orientation. They may, however, easily distract members from talking about, and processing, their traumatic pasts.

- Survivors of trauma generally often have less difficulty exploring their pasts when in the presence of same-sex group members. This is especially true of those with sexual abuse histories, who may experience greater shame or, in some cases, even triggered memories when disclosing in the presence of opposite-sex group members. In addition, clients may feel more comfortable addressing sexuality issues, sex-role orientation, and other gender-related issues in groups with members of their gender, although this is not always the case for gay or lesbian youth. The issue of transgendered youth may sometimes present further challenges, although this can be negotiated within the group. Often, as noted earlier, the transgendered adolescent will choose to attend sessions with members of his or her self-identified gender, as opposed to his or her biological one. In the context of environments where transgendered youth are sufficient in number, specific groups based on self-identified gender may be best. When a trauma-focused group is focused more on community violence or traumatic loss, especially with younger adolescents, it may be possible to include both genders in the same group. In MCAVIC's storefront/alternative school settings, for example, group therapists and attendees involved both genders.

Age Composition

Clinicians should consider limiting groups to members of specific age ranges, for example, 12- to 15-year-olds, 16- to 18-year-olds, or 19- to 21-year-olds. When possible, an age range of no more than three years is recommended. Screening interviews prior to group selection can facilitate the process of matching group members—as much as possible—in terms of developmental functioning, as this may vary considerably, even within a small age range.

Younger adolescents often differ from older ones in several respects: (1) they may be less mature emotionally and cognitively, such that they have different needs and capacities that affect how group treatment should occur; (2) it may be that exposure to the abuse/victimization stories of older adolescents will be too activating, and perhaps even traumatizing for younger ones; and

(3) younger members may be intimidated by the presence of older youth in the same group, leading to a decreased willingness to be vulnerable and open about trauma issues. Conversely, older group members often do better in groups of their peers, where they can openly discuss their concerns and issues and where they may feel more understood by other members.

Special Issues in ITCT-A Groups

It is sometimes helpful to conduct groups with individuals who have certain issues or experiences in common. Examples of such groups are those who share histories of specific traumas (e.g., sexual abuse, hate crimes, refugee experiences) or who are especially identified with certain stressors or lifestyles (e.g., substance-abusing adolescents, homeless youth, or those who identify themselves as gay, bisexual, or transgendered). It is sometimes preferable for group members who have experienced intrafamilial sexual abuse to not be mixed with group members who have experienced solely extrafamilial sexual abuse, especially if the incest occurred over a significant period of time. Race-specific groups are sometimes conducted, to the extent that members have experienced oppressive circumstances that require discussion and processing without dominant-race participants and/or where specific cultural issues are sufficiently salient (e.g., reservation concerns for Native American youth or refugee stress for Cambodian adolescents from immigrated families). In each of these cases, the issue is typically one of shared experience: adolescent survivors may feel most safe and most comfortable with other youths who have been through similar experiences, as opposed to group members who cannot relate to their specific concerns or may even represent a group who has done them harm.

In all cases, however, the therapist should consider the downside of homogenous groups, especially the possibility that opportunities for cross-cultural or cross-demographic discussions and rapprochements are missed. Culturally diverse groups can provide opportunities for members to discuss their individual cultural identities and beliefs, as well as explore their perceptions of other cultures and learn more about them. Discussion of these perceptions and assumptions can increase youths' awareness and understanding of other cultural groups and challenge biases that may have interfered with their relationships with others at school and in the community. Especially when gang membership or affiliation tends to be associated with specific cultural/ethnic backgrounds (e.g., Latino, African American, Anglo, Tonganese) and more prevalent in poverty-stricken communities, group therapy may offer an opportunity for adolescents to become less afraid and more open to cultural groups other than their own.

It also may be important to address in group the social and political context in which violence and abuse occurs. In their book on group treatment, Mendelsohn and colleagues (2011), for example, note that sexual assault and other forms of violence can serve to preserve and reinforce male social dominance. Because, like others, adolescents have been influenced by the society in which they live, they may hold sex-stereotypic beliefs and racist beliefs that may be explored and modified most effectively through group therapy. Challenges to these beliefs by peers in a safe, supportive environment can lead to healthier relationships, a sense of empowerment, and a broadening of choices and opportunities.

Group Leaders

In general, whenever possible, there should be two group leaders, both of the same gender as the group participants—especially if sexual abuse or assaults are being discussed in group sessions. Group work with trauma survivors is often quite intense, and it is usually not sufficient for only one clinician to be present. The cotherapist model allows the clinicians to "share the work": backing each other up when necessary but also providing two sets of eyes and ears so that subtle and/or important group dynamics are less likely to be missed.

When possible, the cotherapists also should share the same cultural background of at least some of the group members. For example, a group comprised of Latino/Latina and African American members may benefit from having a least one therapist who is Latino/Latina or African American. Paddison, Einbender, Maher, and Strain (1993), for example, note that "dyads of similar background are preferred so that a member does not feel like the 'only' one," referring to cultural background, marital status (for older adolescents), sexual orientation, and so forth.

In contrast to the economically driven practices of some agencies, we suggest that at least one group cotherapist be an experienced clinician who has led groups for trauma survivors in the past. Because group therapy for maltreated youth can be challenging, leadership of such groups should not be an entry-level job for newly trained or accredited therapists. It may be possible for one of the cotherapists to be a trainee or intern, or inexperienced staff therapist, if he or she has had some related trauma-focused therapy experience and as long as the other cotherapist is an experienced trauma therapist who is familiar with the ITCT-A treatment model. In the worst case, employing untrained therapists in group treatment, without an experienced cofacilitator, can result in negative outcomes for both group members and clinicians.

Group coleaders not only track the progress of the group members regarding trauma processing, skill building, and meeting their individual goals, but also monitor the ongoing process of the cotherapy relationship and leader interactions regarding group process. We recommend that coleaders meet prior to each session for planning and after each session for debriefing. Ideally, a supervisor or consultant who is not a coleader should meet with group leaders on a weekly basis.

Group Structure and Focus

Group treatment can be open or structured. Open or "drop-in" groups admit members at any time, often do not have a specific number of sessions planned, and typically do not address a single specific issue in any given session—whatever the group members wish to discuss, as long as it is trauma-related, is accepted. In "closed" or structured groups, the same members remain in the group for its life span, and the group tends to be more specifically content- or task-oriented, with specific activities and foci for each session. In either instance, the group should have no more than five to eight group members for optimal group participation and cohesion (Yalom & Leszcz, 2005).

Unfortunately, attrition is common with adolescent group members, and it is sometimes difficult to determine the number of youth who should initially be invited. It is our experience that fewer than five members can lead to undue emotional intensity for group members, and a too-large group (e.g., with over eight attendees) may interfere with cohesion and not allow enough time for all members to fully participate. For this reason, we recommend that initial recruitment, when possible, be more at the upper end of the number range (i.e., eight to ten) than the lower. Group sessions usually last one to one and a half hours, although some groups—for example, in residential or school settings—may be constrained to a lesser time period.

Open or "drop-in" groups. Open groups are likely to have less cohesion, since a variable number of members attend each session, but they can be, nonetheless, quite beneficial—especially in school settings such as alternative, "storefront" school campuses, or in residential or psychiatric hospital settings. At alternative school settings, for example, MCAVIC provided counseling services to high-risk, multiply traumatized students who had been removed from their regular schools due to behavior problems. Students often returned to their regular school campus in the midst of ITCT-A group sessions or were placed at the storefront site after group sessions had begun. In that instance, as with most open groups, there were opportunities for newer members to learn from older ones, who were familiar with the group process and could provide information and feedback.

Closed or structured groups. Structured group therapy usually consists of a specific series of content-related sessions and is closed to new members. Often, these groups meet for somewhere between eight and 16 sessions, although some agencies and clinicians offer longer (or, occasionally, shorter) session series. Given the particular immediacy for many trauma survivors, waiting lists—involving a significant lapse in time from initial screening interview to the onset of the first group session—are generally not recommended. Closed groups provide a greater opportunity for mutually supportive relationships to form between members, for greater cohesion among members to contribute to more in-depth exploration of trauma experiences, and for a greater sense of safety to contribute positively to group process. For this reason, we generally recommend a closed-group format whenever possible. See Briere (1996a) for a detailed discussion of open versus closed groups in the treatment of sexual abuse survivors, in particular.

Within-Session Structure

For both open and closed groups, it is important that group members have an opportunity to "check in" at the beginning of each session, providing comments on how they are currently feeling, events that have occurred in the previous week, and thoughts or feelings regarding the previous group session. During this initial 10 to 15 minutes of the session, clients are ideally provided with a simple snack (e.g., water or soft drinks, fruit, cheese, cookies), as most groups are typically held in the clinic setting after school or work, and school-based groups may be held during the students' lunch period. At the beginning of the session, possibly prior to the onset of the "work" part of the session, group members also may be led in a 10-minute focused-breathing, guided-imagery, or relaxation exercise (see Chapter 11).

During the group discussion and activity portion of the group, it is important that the coleaders ensure that all members have an opportunity to describe their experiences equally. The last 10 to 15 minutes of the session is devoted to the group members sharing their thoughts and feelings regarding what occurred in the group session. Group members also may discuss and provide input for the selection of topics to be discussed in the next session, within the constraints of whatever is already planned. The internal structure of each session also allows for closure and positive appraisal of the group process, so that clients can leave each group session feeling relatively calm and optimistic.

Termination Issues

In our experience, youth involved in ITCT-A groups often become quite attached to the group and the other group members. There may be a significant sense of group cohesion and identity—in some cases, the group may have become the most significant social and therapeutic experience the traumatized youth has encountered to date. For this reason, group leaders should be aware of the possibility of termination issues for some group members—necessitating regular reference to the short-term focus of the group, regular reminders of the number of sessions remaining, and some direct recognition of the understandable sadness that may arise upon termination of the group.

Postgroup Interactions

Especially in clinic-based groups, there may be a desire for members to maintain contact once the group has finished. There should be discussion during the final session about this, and group members should be supported in whatever decision they make. It is important that members discuss their expectations of such relationships, including their likely duration. In addition, it should be emphasized that such relationships should not replace group or individual therapy if more therapy is needed. Termination can be an especially complicated issue when group members are attending the same school or live in the same community, since it is likely that former group members will encounter one another, and relationships formed in group will be challenged by the absence of structure and different expectations of the postgroup context.

Final Assessment

Ideally, clients are assessed again at the termination of the groups described in this chapter, using the same measures applied at the beginning of the group—in most cases the TSCC or TSCC-A (the latter does not contain any sexual symptom questions and thus is used in school-based programs where there may be parental resistance to the use of such items), augmented, when possible, with a more generic test such as the CBCL or CDI. Based on postgroup assessment, it may be determined that a given youth is still symptomatic in one or more areas and therefore may need to continue individual therapy and/or another series of group sessions. In such cases, it is often important that the therapist reach out to caretakers or legal guardians to explain the need for additional treatment, so that the youth will be allowed to continue in individual therapy and, hopefully, will not be stigmatized for requiring additional intervention.

Examples of ITCT-A Groups

Presented in Appendix VII are two examples of structured ITCT-A groups: one for female sexual abuse survivors in a clinic setting and one for youth exposed to community violence and traumatic loss, conducted in a school setting. The reader may adapt one or both of these to match the specific needs of his or her client group. Although abuse-focused ITCT-A groups should generally follow this outline, the chronology, specific session topics, and number of sessions for a given topic can be adjusted according to the individual needs and level of functioning of the group members.

Conclusion

As noted earlier, we recommend that a course of individual therapy (ideally ITCT-A) precede and, in some cases occur concurrently with, group sessions. In many cases, use of the ATF-A during individual treatment will help the client and therapist to determine when (or whether) the client is ready to participate in group sessions. When accompanying individual treatment, group therapy can serve as an important adjunct, allowing further processing of trauma, increased affect regulation capacities, and enhanced self/identity functioning, as well as peer support that cannot occur in individual therapy.

Note

1. One exception to this general rule is the "posttherapy group," where all members have been in prior individual treatment, and screening suggests that each member is able to participate without negative effects.

20

ITCT-A Treatment Outcome Results

Cheryl Lanktree, Natacha Godbout,
and John Briere

T he findings presented in this chapter are a subset of a larger outcome
study (Lanktree et al., 2010) of 151 multiply traumatized children and
youth who received either ITCT-C or ITCT-A at the MCAVIC-USC Child
and Adolescent Program. The reader is referred to that larger study for more
details on the research methodology involved, as well as a discussion of the
broader context of doing research on socially marginalized, inner-city children and adolescents.

Methods

Data for this study came from a record review of 70 sequentially presenting
adolescent clients, ages 12 to 18, who received ITCT-A at MCAVIC-USC.
Upon approval from the Institutional Review Board of the Memorial Health
Services Research Council, data were collected on client demographics,
trauma history, and symptom scales. Months in therapy was indexed by time
from first to last available assessment data. Because different adolescents

remained in treatment for different periods of time, the total number of sessions varied from client to client.

Participants

Clients were referred by parents, other agencies, clinics, or hospitals or were identified and recruited through MCAVIC-USC's outreach activities in the public school system. All lived in Long Beach, California, or surrounding communities. In Long Beach, 78 percent of children and youth are ethnic/cultural minorities, and approximately one-third live below the poverty line (Long Beach Press-Telegram, 2001). To be admitted to the clinic, participants had to (a) report at least one traumatic event from which they suffered significant psychological symptoms and (b) read English at a level that permitted psychological testing.

Assessment

When possible, psychological testing was performed at intake, three-month intervals, and termination, and involved the administration of several psychological measures, including the TSCC. An additional test involved a parent or caretaker report (the CBCL) but was not always collected, given frequent parental nonparticipation. Because of significant missing data for the parent report measures, only the TSCC was used in this study. Although the TSCC is typically administered to children and youth ages 8 to 16, the manual allows for its use with 17-year-olds (Briere, 1996b). In the current study, it was administered to one 18-year-old youth as well.[1]

Clients' history of trauma exposure was determined at intake through use of the Core Clinical Characteristics forms, a structured series of items developed by the NCTSN and augmented by MCAVIC-USC staff to include additional traumatic stressors reported by the child, caretakers, or child welfare social workers. Traumas assessed were child sexual abuse, child physical abuse, witnessing domestic violence, community violence, traumatic loss of a family member or friend, medical trauma, and "other" traumatic events. In some cases, the adolescent disclosed additional traumas during the process of ongoing treatment, at which time these were added to the client's clinical record.

Absence of Comparison Group

Due to the severity and complexity of symptoms endorsed by MCAVIC-USC clients, the absence of other complex trauma treatment programs for adolescents in the Long Beach area, and SAMHSA's funding requirement for treatment development and testing, but not randomized control studies, it was not possible to include a waitlist or alternative treatment comparison group to evaluate treatment effects. As a result, the findings presented here should be seen as exploratory since improvement in symptomatology might be due, at least in part, to the mere passage of time, rather than a specific treatment effect. See, however, Lanktree et al. (2010) for a detailed discussion of this issue.

Results

Participants

The mean age of youth in this study was 13.91 years ($SD = 1.60$), 21.4 percent ($N = 15$) were male, and 78.6 percent ($N = 55$) were female. Race/ethnicity was 48.6 percent ($N = 34$) Hispanic, 21.4 percent ($N = 15$) black/African American, 15.7 percent ($N = 11$) white, and 14.3 percent ($N = 10$) Asian or other.

Most (91.4%) clients were in treatment for three to six months ($M = 6.86$ months, $SD = 4.74$ months, ranging from three to 24 months). Clients' last TSCC score, regardless of when treatment ended, was carried forward to the time of the longest treatment for any client. This procedure, Last Observation Carried Forward (LOCF), provides a conservative estimate of overall treatment effects and has been used in other child trauma treatment outcome studies (e.g., Cohen, Mannarino, & Knudsen, 2005).

Symptomatology as a Function of Demographics and Pre- Versus Post-Treatment Status

Within-subjects analyses of variance (ANOVAs) revealed no effects of sex, nor an interaction between sex and pre-post assessment period, on TSCC scale scores. However, as indicated in Table 20.1, clients' scores on each of the TSCC scales (Anxiety, Depression, Anger, Posttraumatic Stress, Dissociation, and Sexual Concerns) decreased significantly from pre- to post-treatment. Post-treatment status was most associated with reductions in posttraumatic stress (partial $\eta^2 = .27$) and least with reductions in sexual concerns (partial $\eta^2 = .10$). See Figure 20.1 for a graphical representation of treatment outcome. ANOVA with polynomial contrasts indicated that there was a linear (direct) relationship between number of months in treatment (3–5, 6–8, or 9 or more) and the amount of improvement in TSCC scores ($F[2, 148] = 3.90$, $p = .022$).

Table 20.1 TSCC Scale Scores at Pre- Versus Post-Treatment

TSCC scale	N	Pre-treatment		Post-treatment		F	p <	Partial eta2
		M	SD	M	SD			
Anxiety	70	8.37	5.90	4.19	4.02	20.63	.001	.23
Depression	70	8.71	6.54	4.99	5.03	14.79	.001	.18
Anger	70	8.73	6.95	5.54	4.96	11.44	.001	.14
Posttraumatic Stress	70	11.73	7.15	6.39	5.09	24.67	.001	.27
Dissociation	70	9.47	6.79	5.89	4.61	16.51	.001	.20
Sexual Concerns	66	4.80	4.85	2.83	3.54	7.19	.01	.10

Note: Within groups, controlling for age and gender.

Figure 20.1 Pre-Post Differences on TSCC Scales

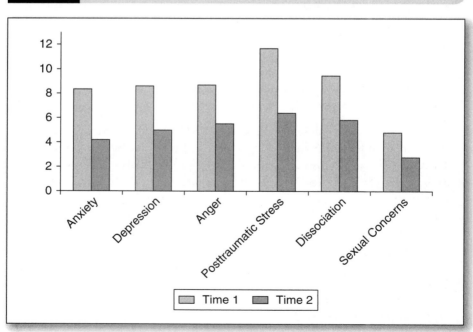

Discussion

This study provides support for the effectiveness of ITCT-A in a sample of 70 inner-city, multiply traumatized, socially marginalized adolescents. Although the absence of a control group limits definitive conclusions, exposure to the intervention approach described in this book was associated with substantial reductions in anxiety, depression, posttraumatic stress, anger, dissociation, and, to a lesser extent, sexual issues. Further, this decrease was dose dependent: the longer a youth was in therapy, the greater his or her improvement.

The finding that longer-term treatment was associated with the most symptom reduction is potentially important. It replicates other research indicating that some traumatized children may require more than the usual three or four months prescribed by most cognitive-behavioral approaches in order to achieve significant symptom remission. In a study by Lanktree and Briere (1995), for example, some symptoms (including sexual concerns) did not lessen significantly until six months of treatment. Such findings, including the current results, suggest that some children and adolescents, especially those with more severe and complex symptomatology, may be better served by treatment approaches such as ITCT-A that are extendable beyond the short term (Amaya-Jackson & DeRosa, 2007; Najavits, Sullivan, Schmitz, Weiss, & Lee, 2004).

Note

1. When this individual was removed from the sample and the data reanalyzed, there were no significant changes in the findings reported here.

21

Three Case Examples

Presented in this chapter are three examples of ITCT-A in the treatment of complex trauma. In each case, circumstances, symptomatology, and trauma histories have been combined across multiple individuals, and client demographics have been altered. As a result, these cases should be seen as examples of common complex trauma presentations, possible ITCT-A intervention approaches, and possible treatment outcomes. As noted in Chapter 20, treatment with ITCT-A was associated with substantial reductions in all symptom areas measured by the TSCC. However, the symptom improvements presented in the following cases are merely examples; some youth exhibit more improvement in response to ITCT-A than what is outlined here, and some respond less well or require more time in treatment.

Rose

Rose is a 17-year-old Asian American female, referred to an ITCT-A therapist by her school counselor following an incident of drunkenness and indirect suicidal threats at school. She has a long history of child maltreatment and attachment disruption. She was removed from her biological mother's care at age six, after she disclosed ongoing physical abuse, and child protective services found evidence of extreme neglect. Rose and a younger sister were adopted by a Caucasian couple when she was seven.

Her biological mother has a history of mental disorder, variously diagnosed with schizophrenia and bipolar affective disorder. She also has a long history of polysubstance abuse, and it is suspected that Rose was exposed to alcohol and other drugs in utero. Rose had inconsistently supervised visitations with her biological mother on a monthly basis until age 10, reporting later that these times were tumultuous and sometimes involved angry verbal tirades, physical abuse, and possibly sexually inappropriate behavior. Currently, contact with her biological mother is by phone only, due to the chaotic nature of their relationship and her mother's continuing abuse potential. During a recent visit with family members, Rose met her biological father for the first time since age three. Rose reports that she is well treated and cared for by her adoptive parents and that she loves them and feels loved in return. At intake, she reported wanting more connection to her biological family members. She feared the impact this will have on her adoptive family.

Rose has a history of ADHD, attributed to prenatal substance exposure, with associated problems in attention, concentration, and memory. She was in special classes through middle school but was returned to mainstream education in high school. At intake, she reported chronic depression, low self-esteem, weight problems, and interpersonal conflicts, as well as long-term abuse of cold medication, alcohol, and marijuana. She acknowledged that substance use is more likely to occur when in the presence of older male friends, which had recently led to several unprotected sexual encounters.

After psychometric assessment (TSCC and CBCL youth report) and the intake interview, Rose was rated as having a number of treatment targets on the ATF-A, as indicated in Column 1 that follows.

Assessment-Treatment Flowchart–Adolescent Version (ATF-A)

Priority ranking (circle one for each symptom):

1 = Not currently a problem: no treatment currently necessary

2 = Problematic, but not an immediate treatment priority: treat at lower intensity

3 = Problematic, a current treatment priority: treat at higher intensity

4 = Most problematic, requires immediate attention

(S) = Suspected, requires further investigation

Assessment Period

	Intake			
Date:	7/12/09	10/22/09	1/15/10	
Problem Area	Tx Priority	Tx Priority	Tx Priority	Tx Priority
1. Safety—environmental	1 2(3)4 (S)	(1)2 3 4 (S)	(1)2 3 4 (S)	1 2 3 4 (S)
2. Caretaker support issues	(1)2 3 4 (S)	(1)2 3 4 (S)	(1)2 3 4 (S)	1 2 3 4 (S)
3. Anxiety	1(2)3 4 (S)	1(2)3 4 (S)	1(2)3 4 (S)	1 2 3 4 (S)
4. Depression	1 2 3(4)(S)	1 2(3)4 (S)	1(2)3 4 (S)	1 2 3 4 (S)
5. Anger/aggression	(1)2 3 4 (S)	1(2)3 4 (S)	(1)2 3 4 (S)	1 2 3 4 (S)
6. Low self-esteem	1 2 3(4)(S)	1 2(3)4 (S)	1(2)3 4 (S)	1 2 3 4 (S)
7. Posttraumatic stress	(1)2 3 4 (S)	(1)2 3 4 (S)	(1)2 3 4 (S)	1 2 3 4 (S)
8. Attachment insecurity	1 2(3)4 (S)	1(2)3 4 (S)	1(2)3 4 (S)	1 2 3 4 (S)
9. Identity issues	1 2(3)4 (S)	1(2)3 4 (S)	1(2)3 4 (S)	1 2 3 4 (S)
10. Relationship problems	1 2(3)4 (S)	1(2)3 4 (S)	1 2(3)4 (S)	1 2 3 4 (S)
11. Suicidality	1 2(3)4 (S)	(1)2 3 4 (S)	(1)2 3 4 (S)	1 2 3 4 (S)
12. Safety—risky behaviors	1 2(3)4 (S)	1(2)3 4 (S)	(1)2 3 4 (S)	1 2 3 4 (S)
13. Dissociation	(1)2 3 4 (S)	(1)2 3 4 (S)	(1)2 3 4 (S)	1 2 3 4 (S)
14. Substance abuse	1 2 3(4)(S)	1 2 3(4)(S)	1 2(3)4 (S)	1 2 3 4 (S)
15. Grief	(1)2 3 4 (S)	(1)2 3 4 (S)	1 2(3)4 (S)	1 2 3 4 (S)
16. Sexual concerns and/or dysfunctional behaviors	1 2(3)4 (S)	(1)2 3 4 (S)	1(2)3 4 (S)	1 2 3 4 (S)
17. Self-mutilation	(1)2 3 4 (S)	(1)2 3 4 (S)	(1)2 3 4 (S)	1 2 3 4 (S)
18. Other: ADHD	1 2(3)4 (S)	1 2(3)4 (S)	1(2)3 4 (S)	1 2 3 4 (S)
19. Other: _____	1 2 3 4 (S)	1 2 3 4 (S)	1 2 3 4 (S)	1 2 3 4 (S)

After consulting the AFT-A and Problems-to-Components Grid, Rose's clinician began treatment with a focus on establishing a positive therapeutic relationship. Because Rose's primary abusive figure was her biological mother, she had significant initial problems forming a trusting relationship with her (female) therapist. However, over a period of months, and some difficult moments, Rose was increasingly able to be more open, and disclosive, in therapy and began to respond to the clinician as a benign, even helpful, person. During this process, she was able to address significant attachment issues associated with her biological mother, triggered by misinterpretations of the therapist's behavior. Her therapist also worked with Rose on safety issues, including suicidality, substance abuse, and ways she might reduce her sexual behavior, or at least make it safer in terms of disease and pregnancy risk. She taught Rose the breathing exercise described in Chapter 11, which Rose embraced almost immediately and applied often. Rose denied current suicidal ideation or past suicide attempts, in fact denying that she had threatened suicide at school. Although she was willing to problem-solve around sexual risk, she was adamant that her substance abuse was necessary for her ongoing functioning. Because her adoptive parents were supportive and empathic in their relationship with Rose, no caretaker or family therapy interventions were initiated at the beginning of treatment. However, they were periodically involved in collateral sessions and, ultimately, family therapy, focused primarily on reinforcing support and attachment connections and better communication between Rose and her parents about her history and current concerns.

Although formal exposure therapy was not included in Rose's early treatment, she spent considerable time in treatment recounting abuse experiences and "fights" she had experienced from her biological mother, although typically framing her maltreatment as deserved consequences for bad behavior. Similarly, she spent considerable time discussing conflicts and what appeared to be several coerced sexual experiences with peers while intoxicated. Per her abuse experiences, however, these were recounted as normal events or things she had precipitated. The clinician was supportive of these disclosures, and expressed caring and concern when appropriate, but did not ask Rose to process these events cognitively or emotionally. At the same time, however, she avoided expressing agreement with Rose about her having caused or deserved physical, sexual, or psychological maltreatment.

By Assessment Period 2 (12 weeks), Rose reported a reduction in sexual risk taking, generally by avoiding males that she had previously "partied" with, including gang members. This also reduced her experience of relational conflict, since she was no longer subject to the emotional chaos associated with this behavior. Although the therapist doubted that merely avoiding males was a solution for Rose, she was happy to see that Rose's current environment was physically safer. Rose also reported a decrease in depression and low self-esteem, seemingly due to her growing attachment to the therapist and an increased sense of hope for her future. She continued to deny any suicidal thoughts, plans, or impulses, nor did psychological testing indicate suicidality. Rose noted that she seemed a little more irritable with her adoptive mother and more likely to get mad over small things, ironically because this parental figure was a safer person than her original mother. This was normalized by the therapist as potential evidence that she was getting more in touch with her feelings because, "Actually, you've got things that you have a right to be mad about, even if it has more to do with your birth mother."

In the next three months, the clinician introduced the cognitive processing and trigger identification/intervention components. Rose began to explore her negative views of herself and their probable basis in her birth mother's psychological, emotional, and physical maltreatment of her. Early in this process, she both castigated and defended her biological mother to the therapist, although the clinician was not, in fact, criticizing Rose's mother—instead affording Rose the opportunity to "go back" and recall what had happened when she was young, how she interpreted it then, and what she thought about it now. During this cognitive reconsideration component, Rose frequently became emotionally upset, requiring grounding and reminders to do the breathing exercise. The trigger identification and intervention component of ITCT-A was initially difficult because Rose was unable to identify triggered emotional and cognitive responses as such, instead seeing them as logical reactions to the current environment or evidence that she was "schizo." Eventually, however, she began to embrace this component, especially in terms of the increased behavioral control it afforded her. She began a more healthy relationship with a boy she met at school, although this was associated with a greater awareness of being triggered in close relationships. When this relationship became more intimate, it also activated unprocessed sexual issues, which became problematic in her connection with this young man. Finally, at 22 weeks, Rose found out that her biological father had left the area, without saying goodbye to Rose and without information as to where he had gone. Rose surprised herself with how upset she became about this, although the experience provided her with an opportunity to process abandonment and loss issues in treatment.

As shown in Column 3, Rose continued to improve by the end of 24 weeks, with decreased ATF-A ratings on depression, anger, low self-esteem, risky behaviors, and, somewhat surprisingly (given her relative refusal to discuss this issue), substance abuse. As expected, she was rated higher on the ATF-A on grief, relationship problems, and sexual concerns.

Rose remains in therapy, and her therapist expects that she will require a number of additional sessions. She is now more directly undergoing titrated exposure, focused primarily on her physical abuse history and her responses to hearing that her biological father had gone away. Her substance abuse is still a significant problem, and the combination of her new relationship, loss of her biological father, and growing connection to her therapist appears to be stimulating more issues around attachment, betrayal, and abandonment. In addition, as she becomes less emotionally avoidant, and titrated exposure continues, she is verbalizing more distress about her life, past and present. However, Rose reports psychological and social improvement, overall. Further, her performance in school is on the upswing—including, according to her teacher, a seeming reduction in her ADHD-related symptoms.

Anthony

Anthony is a 13-year-old White male who was referred for therapy after disclosing sexual abuse (including repeated penetration) by an adult friend of the family from age five to eight. He lived with his mother from birth to until age 10, at which time she married, moved out of state, and left him with his maternal aunt and uncle. Although Anthony had visited his mother's sister and her husband in the past, he did not know them well, and they were not especially attached to him or his mother. This pattern of maternal abandonment was not new to Anthony; his mother reportedly was an alcoholic who frequently left her son in the care of neighbors, friends, or relative strangers. According to his aunt, Anthony's mother is now "clean and sober" but has had another child with her husband and does not want custody of Anthony. She continued to have regular phone calls with him, after which he usually became visibly distraught, experiencing flashbacks and, later, nightmares. Anthony had traveled to his mother's home several times each year but often returned home expressing anger toward her, particularly with regard to feeling ignored by her. The friend of the family admitted to the sexual abuse and is currently incarcerated. His aunt reported that their church had provided guidance and support during the years that she and her ailing husband had been parenting Anthony. Nevertheless, she admitted, they had trouble feeling close to Anthony, and they were regularly upset and perplexed by his behavior in school and at home.

Anthony presented at intake with sexual preoccupations and sexually reactive behavior. He reported flashbacks of oral copulation by the family friend and frequently masturbated in view of his aunt while watching television. On one occasion, he was seen at school attempting to fondle another boy his age—at which point he was placed on suspension for a week and threatened with expulsion. He had few friends and was prone to angry outbursts, sometimes involving striking out at others and breaking things. He reported chronic nightmares and ongoing insomnia.

At intake, Anthony's ATF-A indicated significant treatment targets in a number of areas, especially sexual concerns and behaviors, and posttraumatic stress. His ATF-A is presented here.

Assessment-Treatment Flowchart–Adolescent Version (ATF-A)

Priority ranking (circle one for each symptom):

1 = Not currently a problem: no treatment currently necessary

2 = Problematic, but not an immediate treatment priority: treat at lower intensity

3 = Problematic, a current treatment priority: treat at higher intensity

4 = Most problematic, requires immediate attention

(S) = Suspected, requires further investigation

Assessment Period

	Intake			
Date:	3/24/10	6/26/10	9/29/10	
Problem Area	Tx Priority	Tx Priority	Tx Priority	Tx Priority
1. Safety— environmental	①2 3 4 (S)	①2 3 4 (S)	①2 3 4 (S)	1 2 3 4 (S)
2. Caretaker support issues	1②3 4 (S)	1②3 4 (S)	①2 3 4 (S)	1 2 3 4 (S)
3. Anxiety	1 2③4 (S)	1②3 4 (S)	1②3 4 (S)	1 2 3 4 (S)
4. Depression	①2 3 4 (S)	①2 3 4 (S)	1②3 4 (S)	1 2 3 4 (S)
5. Anger/aggression	1 2③4 (S)	1②3 4 (S)	1②3 4 (S)	1 2 3 4 (S)
6. Low self-esteem	1 2③4 (S)	1②3 4 (S)	1②3 4 (S)	1 2 3 4 (S)
7. Posttraumatic stress	1 2 3④(S)	1 2③4 (S)	1②3 4 (S)	1 2 3 4 (S)

(Continued)

(Continued)

Problem Area	Intake			
Date:	3/24/10	6/26/10	9/29/10	
	Tx Priority	Tx Priority	Tx Priority	Tx Priority
8. Attachment insecurity	1 2 (3) 4 (S)	1 2 (3) 4 (S)	1 (2) 3 4 (S)	1 2 3 4 (S)
9. Identity issues	1 (2) 3 4 (S)	1 (2) 3 4 (S)	(1) 2 3 4 (S)	1 2 3 4 (S)
10. Relationship problems	1 2 (3) 4 (S)	1 (2) 3 4 (S)	1 (2) 3 4 (S)	1 2 3 4 (S)
11. Suicidality	(1) 2 3 4 (S)	(1) 2 3 4 (S)	(1) 2 3 4 (S)	1 2 3 4 (S)
12. Safety—risky behaviors	1 (2) 3 4 (S)	(1) 2 3 4 (S)	(1) 2 3 4 (S)	1 2 3 4 (S)
13. Dissociation	1 (2) 3 4 (S)	(1) 2 3 4 (S)	(1) 2 3 4 (S)	1 2 3 4 (S)
14. Substance abuse	(1) 2 3 4 (S)	(1) 2 3 4 (S)	(1) 2 3 4 (S)	1 2 3 4 (S)
15. Grief	(1) 2 3 4 (S)	(1) 2 3 4 (S)	(1) 2 3 4 (S)	(1) 2 3 4 (S)
16. Sexual concerns and/or dysfunctional behaviors	1 2 3 (4) (S)	1 2 3 (4) (S)	1 (2) 3 4 (S)	1 2 3 4 (S)
17. Self-mutilation	(1) 2 3 4 (S)	(1) 2 3 4 (S)	(1) 2 3 4 (S)	1 2 3 4 (S)
18. Other: _____	1 2 3 4 (S)	1 2 3 4 (S)	1 2 3 4 (S)	1 2 3 4 (S)
19. Other: _____	1 2 3 4 (S)	1 2 3 4 (S)	1 2 3 4 (S)	1 2 3 4 (S)

The first three months of ITCT-A included weekly individual therapy sessions focusing primarily on safety, building a therapeutic relationship, and increasing Anthony's affect regulation skills through grounding, breathing exercises, and increased involvement in sports and art activities (painting and drawing). His aunt and uncle attended weekly collateral sessions and a parenting support group, where they received psychoeducation regarding the impacts of sexual abuse, and learned more positive and supportive parenting strategies. These included ways to reinforce Anthony's appropriate behavior and expression of emotions and methods whereby they and Anthony could become interpersonally closer and foster greater attachment.

Over time, Anthony's caretakers were able to implement more consistent behavioral consequences that were positive in nature, such as rewarding his improved behavior with privileges, an allowance, and praise. More generally, they were increasingly able to support his verbalizations and feelings about the abuse, which allowed more processing on his part, increased self-esteem, and less shame.

Given Anthony's attachment issues and affect regulation problems, it was deemed especially important that he feel as safe and supported as possible in therapy before directly processing traumatic material. Fortunately, Anthony was able to share interests in sports and music with his male therapist and became increasingly engaged with him over time. As he became more involved in therapy and with the therapist, he began to express improved self-esteem. As his aunt noted, "He's really happy with [the therapist]. It's like he has a new father, or a brother."

As Anthony seemed to settle into therapy, the therapist introduced him to the Trigger Grid and devoted the first 15 minutes or so of each session to identifying his triggers, determining how he could know he was being triggered, and figuring out what he could do when this occurred. Eventually, Anthony was able to identify a number of triggers (e.g., men [especially their mouths and hands], interpersonal closeness with male peers, sexual stimuli in the environment, fantasies, and his own developmentally appropriate sexual feelings). He and his therapist also engaged in cognitive reconsideration, wherein Anthony described in significant detail his thoughts and assumptions about why he was abused and what it meant about him. Particularly at issue was the fact that the family friend "picked" Anthony over other children in the extended family and neighborhood and that, on occasion, he felt special and wanted in this man's eyes—a stark contrast to how he believed others (especially his mother) saw him at the time. The clinician supported Anthony's exploration of these issues, not telling him what he should think but, rather, asking questions (per Chapter 12) that stimulated him to fully consider what actually had occurred and why it happened, from the perspective of a now-older boy who was no longer under coercion. During this process, the clinician regularly expressed support for Anthony and praise at his ability to come up with new, less self-blaming hypotheses regarding his sexual abuse and, later, his mother's abandonment of him. Occasionally, the therapist's visible caring for Anthony triggered Anthony's memories of sexual abuse and fears of abandonment. However, the therapist normalized these phenomena—without directly discussing them and thus inadvertently shaming him—and Anthony became less triggered over time.

After three months of therapy, Anthony's behavior at school and at home had improved. He reported fewer nightmares and flashbacks of his sexual abuse and having fewer intrusive memories of abandonment by his mother. He continued to express anger regarding his traumatic experiences, but he was able to continue engaging in the breathing exercises, trigger identification through the Trigger Grid, cognitive processing, and affect regulation activities that he had learned in therapy.

As treatment continued, Anthony began to more directly process his abuse and abandonment experiences. This included writing about the sexual abuse using the *Written Homework About My Trauma* exercise presented in Appendix V, writing (but not sending) letters to both his sexual abuser and his mother, and ongoing conversations with his therapist about what had happened, and what he felt and thought, generally in the manner outlined in Chapter 12. When this exposure work became especially challenging, he was coached to use the grounding and breathing exercises that he had learned earlier, as well as, when at home, to play a CD of a guided, calming meditation narrated in his therapist's voice.

In family therapy, Anthony and his aunt and uncle focused on safety (primarily ways in which they could be more engaged and protective of him, as well as keeping him out of situations where he might be triggered and act out) and communication of feelings between family members—especially his aunt and uncle's growing caring for—and attunement to—Anthony. Role-plays, board games, and a family genogram were also part of family treatment, allowing Anthony to express his feelings and gain greater trust of, and connection to, his caretakers and for them to communicate positive feelings to him. These activities also facilitated discussion of the intergenerational transmission of trauma and related feelings, including his aunt and uncle's own experiences of emotional and physical abuse. With his aunt and uncle's support, Anthony was able to problem-solve ways to maintain a relationship with his mother, but to do it more on his terms. Most obviously, this meant that he no longer visited her in person but, instead, used the telephone to have regular, but limited, conversations with her. He also learned how to terminate these calls when his mother became abusive and to reach out to his aunt and uncle, afterward, when upset by what she had said.

Over time, Anthony's social world began to expand. He became more involved in afterschool programs and began having more contact with a few, close friends—including having them over to his house to play video games and watch movies. Therapist-prescribed family outings became less of a chore and more enjoyable, as was his increased contact with extended family members. The effect of these activities was to increase Anthony's self-confidence and to help him view himself as "normal" and in normal relationships with others.

Anthony's sexual preoccupations and excessive masturbation did not decrease in the first three or four months of ITCT-A, as is often the case (e.g., Lanktree & Briere, 1995), although he was able to avoid inappropriate sexual behaviors with others, and he no longer masturbated in the presence of his aunt or uncle. At the six-month assessment point, however—as he became increasingly able to identify feelings and triggers that contributed to sexual acting out, and as his work on processing the sexual abuse began to have an impact—Anthony's scores on the CSBI and the TSCC Sexual Concerns scale were significantly lower, and the clinician was able to rate him lower in this problem area on the ATF-A. Gradually, over a number of months, he was able to create an increasingly more coherent and non-self-blaming narrative of his sexual abuse, as well as the neglect and abandonment he suffered when living with his mother. This was apparent in the time lines he created in therapy (see Chapter 12), as well as the drawings and collages he made, which slowly changed from anger, despair, and self-hatred to more matter-of-fact and less-angry depictions of what he had undergone, with themes of self-acceptance and entitlement to protection.

By the end of therapy, Anthony was able to discuss with his family more specific experiences of sexual abuse and explore with them issues related to normal sexual development—including the notion that not all of his sexual responses and feelings were abuse related. Especially helpful, in this regard, was a book provided by the therapist, *It's Perfectly Normal* (Harris, 1996), which they read together in family sessions. This recommended resource, an illustrated book designed for youths, includes information about all aspects of sexual development, sexuality, sexual orientation, and sexual abuse.

The ATF-A completed after six months of treatment revealed that Anthony had experienced significant reductions in most symptom areas, albeit with some problematic sexual concerns (occasional intrusive memories of his abuse) but no dysfunctional sexual behavior. Although individual therapy continued for another month, to further address trauma memories, as well as to deal with termination issues, family communication and support had improved sufficiently that no further family therapy sessions were needed.

Alicia

Alicia is a 19-year-old Hispanic female, referred for ITCT-A after discharge from a psychiatric hospital, where she had been treated for a suicide attempt. She was born in Nicaragua but has been living in the United States since age seven. Her mother and father separated when she was six. Her father was physically and verbally abusive toward her mother and dismissive of Alicia. Alicia reports that she was molested at ages five and six by two of her father's friends and believes that her father had direct knowledge of these events, "But he didn't do nothing." She currently lives with her mother and has had no contact with her father for several years. She reports that her relationship with her mother is "OK," although her mother appeared somewhat disengaged from her during intake and collateral sessions and had generally failed to intervene in Alicia's self-endangering behaviors. When Alicia was 14, she was in a one-year abusive relationship with a 19-year-old male. She reports that he hit and sexually assaulted her throughout their relationship. Following a particularly violent beating, Alicia sought protection from older, male gang members in her community. She remained affiliated with this gang for the next three years, a time she mostly describes positively, although she notes having been "jumped" by male members on several occasions. She has tattoos of this gang on her left upper arm.

At intake, Alicia reported that she had been depressed since she was 11, when she started thinking of herself as different from other girls. This was also when she made the first of four suicide attempts. Since age 11, she has been hospitalized three times for depression, suicidality, and self-mutilation. Hospital records also report prior risky behaviors, including her gang affiliation, excessive drinking, drug abuse (methamphetamine and marijuana), several episodes of bingeing and purging, and short-lived sexual relationships with multiple partners, some of whom were abusive toward her. She has been in juvenile detention or, later, jail four times since age 15, twice for drug possession, once for prostitution, and once for assault. Treatment records indicate that Alicia was avoidant and guarded with staff during hospital admissions and in fact, was labeled as "electively mute" on one occasion. When seen by an ITCT-A therapist at age 18, however, she was considerably more verbal and forthcoming.

Presented below is her ATF-A at intake and at three, six, and nine months.

Assessment-Treatment Flowchart–Adolescent Version (ATF-A)

Priority ranking (circle one for each symptom):

1 = Not currently a problem: no treatment currently necessary

2 = Problematic, but not an immediate treatment priority: treat at lower intensity

3 = Problematic, a current treatment priority: treat at higher intensity

4 = Most problematic, requires immediate attention

(S) = Suspected, requires further investigation

Assessment Period

	Intake			
Date:	2/2/10	5/1/10	8/4/10	11/6/10
Problem Area	Tx Priority	Tx Priority	Tx Priority	Tx Priority
1. Safety— environmental	1 2 ③ 4 (S)	1 2 ③ 4 (S)	1 ② 3 4 (S)	1 ② 3 4 (S)
2. Caretaker support issues	1 2 3 ④ (S)	1 2 ③ 4 (S)	1 ② 3 4 (S)	1 ② 3 4 (S)
3. Anxiety	1 ② 3 4 (S)	1 ② 3 4 (S)	1 ② 3 4 (S)	① 2 3 4 (S)
4. Depression	1 2 3 ④ (S)	1 2 ③ 4 (S)	1 2 ③ 4 (S)	1 ② 3 4 (S)
5. Anger/aggression	1 2 ③ 4 (S)	1 ② 3 4 (S)	1 2 ③ 4 (S)	1 2 ③ 4 (S)
6. Low self-esteem	1 2 ③ 4 (S)	1 2 ③ 4 (S)	1 ② 3 4 (S)	1 ② 3 4 (S)
7. Posttraumatic stress	1 2 3 ④ (S)	1 2 ③ 4 (S)	1 ② 3 4 (S)	① 2 3 4 (S)
8. Attachment insecurity	1 2 ③ 4 (S)	1 2 ③ 4 (S)	1 ② 3 4 (S)	1 ② 3 4 (S)
9. Identity issues	1 ② 3 4 (S)	1 ② 3 4 (S)	1 2 ③ 4 (S)	1 ② 3 4 (S)
10. Relationship problems	1 2 ③ 4 (S)	1 2 ③ 4 (S)	1 ② 3 4 (S)	1 ② 3 4 (S)
11. Suicidality	1 2 3 ④ (S)	1 2 ③ 4 (S)	1 ② 3 4 (S)	① 2 3 4 (S)
12. Safety—risky behaviors	1 2 3 ④ (S)	1 2 ③ 4 (S)	1 ② 3 4 (S)	1 ② 3 4 (S)
13. Dissociation	1 ② 3 4 (S)	1 ② 3 4 (S)	① 2 3 4 (S)	① 2 3 4 (S)
14. Substance abuse	1 2 3 ④ (S)	1 2 ③ 4 (S)	1 2 ③ 4 (S)	1 ② 3 4 (S)
15. Grief	① 2 3 4 (S)	① 2 3 4 (S)	① 2 3 4 (S)	① 2 3 4 (S)
16. Sexual concerns and/or dysfunctional behaviors	1 2 ③ 4 (S)	1 2 ③ 4 (S)	1 ② 3 4 (S)	1 ② 3 4 (S)
17. Self-mutilation	1 2 3 ④ (S)	1 2 ③ 4 (S)	1 ② 3 4 (S)	① 2 3 4 (S)
18. Other: Bingeing/ purging	1 ② 3 4 (S)	① 2 3 4 (S)	① 2 3 4 (S)	① 2 3 4 (S)
19. Other: _____	1 2 3 4 (S)	1 2 3 4 (S)	1 2 3 4 (S)	1 2 3 4 (S)

Alicia's response to ITCT-A was quite positive, especially in comparison to the rocky therapeutic course documented in her psychiatric records. She appeared to bond quickly with her therapist, who also was of Hispanic heritage, a female, and well-conversant with the issues of gang-involved adolescents. Initial therapeutic targets, as suggested by her ATF-A and PCG, were to engage and strengthen the therapeutic relationship, increase safety (in the environment, as well as from self-endangering or risky behaviors), reduce depressive and suicidal symptoms, and increase caretaker support. Although Alicia denied significant posttraumatic stress in the intake interview, psychological testing suggested a diagnosis of PTSD. In light of her other, even more pressing problems, and the usual requirement that the client be relatively stable before exposure therapy can occur (Chapters 11 and 14), her therapist assumed that processing of trauma memories should be delayed until later in treatment. However, Alicia displayed a relative eagerness to discuss (and report to authorities) her sexual abuse, as well as the battering and rapes that she experienced from her ex-boyfriend. For this reason, the titrated exposure and cognitive processing (especially trigger identification and intervention) components of ITCT-A occurred within the first month of treatment, albeit in the context of ongoing support, stabilization, and concrete attempts to increase safety. Alicia was also evaluated by a trauma-informed psychiatrist, who determined that psychiatric hospitalization was not warranted but that antidepressant medication was. Alicia refused medication, however, reportedly given her negative experiences with previous psychiatric treatment.

Alicia's mother, with some initial reluctance, was involved in collateral treatment, both group and individual. Given the severity of Alicia's presenting issues, family therapy was not initiated early in treatment, although it was planned for a future point. It soon became apparent that Alicia's mother cared about her daughter, and was invested in her well-being, but was unable to connect with her sufficiently—or notice her current difficulties—due to her own history of childhood trauma and associated attachment problems. This meant that the primary targets of collateral treatment for her mother were to (a) become more aware of her daughter as someone needing her care and attention and (b) learn how to increase the mother-daughter attachment bond through greater expressed attunement and positive regard. This work was partially successful, in that Alicia's mother did become more involved in her daughter's life and became more visibly supportive. However, her own difficulties were significant, including an avoidant attachment style, considerable denial and dissociation, and unprocessed (and unexpressed) resentment that her daughter was getting therapeutic attention, when she, as a child, had not. Despite these issues and concerns, Alicia's mother refused to enter her own psychotherapy.

In part due to the emotional and cognitive processing components of ITCT-A, Alicia relatively quickly was able to link her substance abuse, risky sexual behavior, and self-endangerment to low self-esteem, internally directed anger, and the need to avoid memories and feelings. She also became more aware of the extent to which her mother was disengaged and nonprotective and the impacts this had on her feelings of self-worth. As might be expected after only three months of therapy, these insights—and even her partial desensitization of some trauma memories—did not translate into profound changes in her behavior. Nevertheless, at Assessment Point 2, her ATF-A indicated some improvement in suicidality, self-mutilation, and involvement in risky behavior, as well as reduced depression, anger, and posttraumatic stress.

Fortunately, Alicia made additional progress over the next six months, as she continued to process her trauma history and attachment issues, learn new coping strategies, and reduce her reliance on substance abuse and tension-reduction behaviors as a way to manage emotional distress. An important component of her continuing recovery was her mother's increasing connection to her, including her greater awareness of her daughter's needs and entitlements. Alicia did have to confront, however, her mother's ultimate limitations in this regard, as well as her understandable frustration and anger at this fact. Alicia terminated therapy after nine months, although both she and her therapist agreed that further treatment might be helpful at some point.

22

Summary

This book briefly summarizes a structured but open-ended therapy for traumatized adolescents and young adults. A central notion in this approach is that treatment for complex posttraumatic outcomes must be, itself, potentially complex. Effective intervention almost always requires customization, not only in response to the youth's particular psychological circumstance—his or her symptoms, problems, and behaviors—but also to the social and cultural matrix in which he or she is embedded. This is especially true when the sociocultural context involves marginalization and danger. Treating psychological symptoms, alone, in a chronically endangered young person is as likely to be unsuccessful as solely providing social advocacy for a youth with major psychological difficulties.

We also suggest that, for many multiply traumatized youth, the type and intensity of psychological treatment must reflect an accurate appraisal of his or her ability to "handle" the effects of any given intervention. Most significantly, the high stress load, environmental challenges, and reduced affect regulation capacities of many young complex-trauma survivors require the clinician to titrate treatment: providing neither too little nor too much therapeutic exposure or cognitive material, so that the client is neither undertreated nor overwhelmed. This means that although one youth might tolerate, and rapidly respond to, a classic cognitive-behavioral approach, another might require months of stabilization, safety interventions, and affect regulation training before even beginning to undertake such a process. Although we recognize current economic and professional pressures to provide short-term interventions to those with psychological difficulties, many of our most injured children and youth suffer too much, and in too many ways, to expect that they will respond to treatment in a matter of weeks or even, in some cases, months.

We end with a plea for greater social support of programs and agencies that work with traumatized youth. Millions of young people in North America have been abused, neglected, and otherwise traumatized, a substantial proportion of whom also live with poverty, discrimination, and diminished social resources. These children and youth do not disappear after such maltreatment: As they age, they fill our clinics, psychiatric hospitals, emergency rooms, and, perhaps most unfortunately, our jails. Yet, funding for effective treatment, child welfare, and child protection is declining in our society, not increasing (see, for example, the 2010 report by the Center on Budget and Policy Priorities: http://www.cbpp.org/cms/index.cfm?fa=view &id=1214). In recent years, a number of public mental health clinics, trauma-focused or otherwise, have closed—or had their services curtailed—for lack of funding. In fact, in some instances, the case histories typified at the end of this book have a different ending: one in which young clients were engaged in helpful treatment at the hands of dedicated practitioners, only to have their therapy abruptly ended as clinics are shuttered and therapists laid off.

On a less dire note, a relatively recent federal effort, the National Child Traumatic Stress Network, was created by Congress to help address the dearth of mental health services for traumatized children and youth. As of November 2009, this network, funded or previously funded by the Substance Abuse and Mental Health Administration, U.S. Department of Health and Human Services, is comprised of over 60 academic and community service centers. This initiative has contributed to the well-being of many thousands of traumatized young people and is an excellent example of what society can do when inspired. Clearly, however, the problem is much larger than any individual governmental project can address, as most traumatized youth in North America go untreated. Further, such funding initiatives are vulnerable to political dynamics, including future defunding of "nonessential" governmental entities, especially at times of economic challenge. Ultimately, the therapies outlined in this and other volumes can only work if there is widespread recognition of the need for such interventions and a national will to prioritize the well-being of our children.

Appendix I

Initial Trauma Review

Adolescent/Young Adult Version (ITR-A)

T his semistructured interview allows the clinician to cover the primary forms of trauma potentially experienced by adolescents (i.e., those between the ages of 12 and 21). The clinician may wish to paraphrase these questions in order to make them "fit" better into the session. However, (1) try to use the behavioral descriptors (don't just ask about "abuse" or "rape"), and (2) only ask as many questions at a given time period as is tolerated by the adolescent. Remaining questions can be asked at later points within the first few sessions. The question *How old were you the first time?* usually indicates whether or not the trauma was a form of child abuse. The questions *When this happened, did you ever feel very afraid, horrified, or helpless?* and *Did you ever think you might be injured or killed?* indicate whether the trauma meets Criterion A2 for DSM-IV PTSD or ASD.

1. [Childhood physical abuse] "Has a parent or another adult who was in charge of you ever hurt or punished you in a way that left a bruise, cut, scratches, or made you bleed?"

   ☐ Yes
   ☐ No

   If yes,

   "How old were you the first time?" _____
   "How old were you the last time?" _____

(also available at johnbriere.com)

195

"When this happened, did you ever feel very afraid, horrified, or helpless?"

☐ Yes
☐ No

"Did you ever think you might be injured or killed?"

☐ Yes
☐ No

2. **[Sexual abuse]** "Has anyone who was five or more years older than you ever done something sexual with you or to you?"

☐ Yes
☐ No

If yes,

"How old were you the first time?" _____

"How old were you the last time?" _____

"When this happened, did you ever feel very afraid, horrified, or helpless?" [*NOTE: For sexual abuse only, this part is not necessary for PTSD Criterion A*]

☐ Yes
☐ No

"Did you ever think you might be injured or killed?" [*NOTE: For sexual abuse only, this part is not necessary for PTSD Criterion A*]

☐ Yes
☐ No

3. **[Peer sexual assault]** "Has anyone who was less than five years older than you ever done something sexual to you that you didn't want or that happened when you couldn't defend yourself (for example, when you were intoxicated or asleep)?"

☐ Yes
☐ No

If yes,

"How old were you the first time?" _____

"How old were you the last time?" _____

"When this happened, did you ever feel very afraid, horrified, or helpless?"

☐ Yes
☐ No

"Did you ever think you might be injured or killed?"

☐ Yes
☐ No

4. [Disaster] "Have you ever been involved in a serious fire, earthquake, flood, or other disaster?"

☐ Yes
☐ No

If yes,

"How old were you the first time?" _____

"How old were you the last time?" _____

"When this happened, did you ever feel very afraid, horrified, or helpless?"

☐ Yes
☐ No

"Did you ever think you might be injured or killed?"

☐ Yes
☐ No

5. [Motor vehicle accident] "Have you ever been involved in a serious automobile accident?"

☐ Yes
☐ No

If yes,

"How old were you the first time?" _____

"How old were you the last time?" _____

"When this happened, did you ever feel very afraid, horrified, or helpless?"

☐ Yes
☐ No

"Did you ever think you might be injured or killed?"

☐ Yes
☐ No

6. [Partner abuse] "Have you ever been slapped, hit, beaten, or hurt in some other way by someone you were dating or who you were in a sexual or romantic relationship with?"

☐ Yes
☐ No

If yes,

"How old were you the first time?" _____

"How old were you the last time?" _____

"When this happened, did you ever feel very afraid, horrified, or helpless?"

☐ Yes
☐ No

"Did you ever think you might be injured or killed?"

☐ Yes
☐ No

7. **[Nonintimate peer assault]** "Have you ever been physically attacked, assaulted, stabbed, or shot at by someone who wasn't a parent, date, or sexual partner?"

☐ Yes
☐ No

If yes,

"How old were you the first time?" _____

"How old were you the last time?" _____

"When this happened, did you ever feel very afraid, horrified, or helpless?"

☐ Yes
☐ No

"Did you ever think you might be injured or killed?"

☐ Yes
☐ No

8. **[Torture—if the adolescent is an immigrant from another country]** "In the country where you used to live, were you ever tortured by the government or by people against the government?"

☐ Yes
☐ No

If yes,

"How old were you the first time?" _____

"How old were you the last time?" _____

"When this happened, did you ever feel very afraid, horrified, or helpless?"

☐ Yes
☐ No

"Did you ever think you might be injured or killed?"

☐ Yes
☐ No

9. **[Police trauma]** "Have you ever been hit, beaten, assaulted, or shot by the police or other law enforcement officials?"

☐ Yes
☐ No

If yes,

"How old were you the first time?" _____

"How old were you the last time?" _____

"When this happened, did you ever feel very afraid, horrified, or helpless?"

☐ Yes
☐ No

"Did you ever think you might be injured or killed?"

☐ Yes
☐ No

10. **[Medical trauma]** "Have you ever been in the hospital because you were very sick or very hurt?"

☐ Yes
☐ No

If yes,

"How old were you the first time?" _____

"How old were you the last time?" _____

"When this happened, did you ever feel very afraid, horrified, or helpless?"

☐ Yes
☐ No

"Did you ever think you might die?"

☐ Yes
☐ No

11. **[Witnessing trauma]** "Have you ever seen someone else get killed, badly hurt, or sexually assaulted?"

    ☐ Yes
    ☐ No

    If yes,

    "How old were you the first time?" _____

    "How old were you the last time?" _____

    "When this happened, did you ever feel very afraid, horrified, or helpless?"

    ☐ Yes
    ☐ No

    "Did you ever think you might be injured or killed?" [NOTE: *Not required for PTSD Criterion A*]

    ☐ Yes
    ☐ No

12. **[Other trauma]** "Has any other very bad or upsetting thing ever happened to you?"

    ☐ Yes
    ☐ No

    If yes, what was it? (If more than one, pick the worst other thing that happened)

    _____

    _____

    "How old were you the first time it happened?" _____

    "How old were you the last time it happened?" _____

    "When this happened, did you ever feel very afraid, horrified, or helpless?"

    ☐ Yes
    ☐ No

    "Did you ever think you might be injured or killed?"

    ☐ Yes
    ☐ No

Appendix II

ITCT-A Assessment Locator

ATF-A Item	Assessment (Tests applicable only for relevant age ranges)
1. Safety—environmental	Adolescent self-report in session (A-S), parent/caretaker report in session (C-R)
2. Caretaker support issues	A-S, C-R, and clinical impressions during parent interview
3. Anxiety	A-S, C-R, CBCL, BASC-2, PAI-A, MMPI-A, TSCC, TSSA, TSI, TSI-2
4. Depression	A-S, C-R, CBCL, CDI, BDI-II, BASC-2, TSCC, TSSA, TSI, TSI-2
5. Anger/aggression	A-S, C-R, BASC-2 (parent report), CBCL, PAI-A, TSCC, TSSA, TSI, TSI-2
6. Low self-esteem	A-S, C-R, BASC-2, TSCS
7. Posttraumatic stress	A-S, C-R, PAI-A, MMPI-A, TSCC, TSSA, TSI, TSI-2, DAPS, UPID
8. Attachment insecurity	A-S, C-R, BASC-2, TSI-2, TSSA
9. Identity issues	A-S, C-R, IASC, TSI, TSI-2
10. Relationship problems	A-S, C-R, BASC-2, CBCL, TSSA
11. Suicidality	A-S, C-R, TSCC, PAI-A, TSI-2, TSSA, DAPS, SIQ

(Continued)

(Continued)

ATF-A Item	Assessment (Tests applicable only for relevant age ranges)
12. Safety—risky behaviors	A-S, C-R, TSCC, BASC-2, TSI, TSI-2
13. Dissociation	A-S, C-R, TSCC, TSSA, DAPS, TSI, TSI-2
14. Substance abuse	A-S, C-R, BASC-2, PAI-A, TSI, TSI-2, DAPS
15. Grief	A-S, C-R
16. Sexual concerns and/or dysfunctional behaviors	A-S, C-R, TSCC, TSSA, TSI, TSI-2
17. Self-mutilation	A-S, C-R

Appendix III

Assessment-Treatment Flowchart

Adolescent/Young Adult Version (ATF-A)

Client Name: _____

Priority ranking (circle one for each symptom):

   1 = Not currently a problem: no treatment currently necessary

   2 = Problematic, but not an immediate treatment priority: treat at lower intensity

   3 = Problematic, a current treatment priority: treat at higher intensity

   4 = Most problematic, requires immediate attention

   (S) = Suspected, requires further investigation

Assessment Period: _____

	Intake			
Date	_____	_____	_____	_____
Problem Area	Tx Priority	Tx Priority	Tx Priority	Tx Priority
1. Safety—environmental	1 2 3 4 (S)	1 2 3 4 (S)	1 2 3 4 (S)	1 2 3 4 (S)
2. Caretaker support issues	1 2 3 4 (S)	1 2 3 4 (S)	1 2 3 4 (S)	1 2 3 4 (S)

(Continued)

(Continued)

Problem Area	Intake			
Date	____	____	____	____
Problem Area	Tx Priority	Tx Priority	Tx Priority	Tx Priority
3. Anxiety	1 2 3 4 (S)	1 2 3 4 (S)	1 2 3 4 (S)	1 2 3 4 (S)
4. Depression	1 2 3 4 (S)	1 2 3 4 (S)	1 2 3 4 (S)	1 2 3 4 (S)
5. Anger/aggression	1 2 3 4 (S)	1 2 3 4 (S)	1 2 3 4 (S)	1 2 3 4 (S)
6. Low self-esteem	1 2 3 4 (S)	1 2 3 4 (S)	1 2 3 4 (S)	1 2 3 4 (S)
7. Posttraumatic stress	1 2 3 4 (S)	1 2 3 4 (S)	1 2 3 4 (S)	1 2 3 4 (S)
8. Attachment insecurity	1 2 3 4 (S)	1 2 3 4 (S)	1 2 3 4 (S)	1 2 3 4 (S)
9. Identity issues	1 2 3 4 (S)	1 2 3 4 (S)	1 2 3 4 (S)	1 2 3 4 (S)
10. Relationship problems	1 2 3 4 (S)	1 2 3 4 (S)	1 2 3 4 (S)	1 2 3 4 (S)
11. Suicidality	1 2 3 4 (S)	1 2 3 4 (S)	1 2 3 4 (S)	1 2 3 4 (S)
12. Safety—risky behaviors	1 2 3 4 (S)	1 2 3 4 (S)	1 2 3 4 (S)	1 2 3 4 (S)
13. Dissociation	1 2 3 4 (S)	1 2 3 4 (S)	1 2 3 4 (S)	1 2 3 4 (S)
14. Substance abuse	1 2 3 4 (S)	1 2 3 4 (S)	1 2 3 4 (S)	1 2 3 4 (S)
15. Grief	1 2 3 4 (S)	1 2 3 4 (S)	1 2 3 4 (S)	1 2 3 4 (S)
16. Sexual concerns and/or dysfunctional behaviors	1 2 3 4 (S)	1 2 3 4 (S)	1 2 3 4 (S)	1 2 3 4 (S)
17. Self-mutilation	1 2 3 4 (S)	1 2 3 4 (S)	1 2 3 4 (S)	1 2 3 4 (S)
18. Other: ____	1 2 3 4 (S)	1 2 3 4 (S)	1 2 3 4 (S)	1 2 3 4 (S)
19. Other: ____	1 2 3 4 (S)	1 2 3 4 (S)	1 2 3 4 (S)	1 2 3 4 (S)

Appendix IV

Problems-to-Components Grid (PCG)

	Problem (from ATF-A)	Treatment component that may be useful (in approximate order of importance)
1	Safety—environmental	Safety training, system interventions, psychoeucation
2	Caretaker support issues	Family therapy, intervention with caretakers
3	Anxiety	Distress reduction/affect regulation training, titrated exposure, cognitive processing, medication
4	Depression	Cognitive processing, relational processing, relationship building and support, group therapy, medication
5	Anger/aggression	Distress reduction/affect regulation training, trigger identification/intervention, cognitive processing
6	Low self-esteem	Cognitive processing, relational processing, group therapy, relationship building and support
7	Posttraumatic stress	Distress reduction/affect regulation training, titrated exposure, cognitive processing, psychoeducation, relationship building and support, trigger identification/intervention, medication

(Continued)

(Continued)

	Problem (from ATF-A)	Treatment component that may be useful (in approximate order of importance)
8	**Attachment insecurity**	Relationship building and support, relational processing, group therapy, family therapy
9	**Identity issues**	Relationship building and support, relational processing, group therapy
10	**Relationship problems**	Relationship building and support, relational processing, cognitive processing, group therapy
11	**Suicidality**	Safety training, distress reduction/affect regulation training, cognitive processing, systems intervention
12	**Safety—risky behaviors and tension-reduction behaviors**	Psychoeducation, safety training, cognitive processing, titrated exposure, trigger identification/intervention, distress reduction/affect regulation training
13	**Dissociation**	Distress reduction/affect regulation training, affect regulation training, emotional processing, trigger identification/intervention
14	**Substance abuse**	Trigger identification/intervention, distress reduction/affect regulation training, titrated exposure
15	**Grief**	Cognitive processing, relationship building and support, psychoeducation, titrated exposure
16	**Sexual concerns and/or dysfunctional behaviors**	Distress reduction/affect regulation training, psychoeducation, safety training, cognitive processing, titrated exposure, trigger identification/intervention
17	**Self-mutilation**	Distress reduction/affect regulation training, trigger identification/intervention, cognitive processing, titrated exposure

Appendix V

Written Homework About My Trauma

This homework has to do with the trauma that you and your therapist agreed that you should write about. There might be a lot of traumas in your life, so, remember, this is just about the trauma that you and your therapist picked this time. After each question, write an answer in as much detail as you can, in the amount of space you have. When you are done, save this homework, and bring it to your next session so that you and your therapist can read it together. You don't have to answer all these questions at the same time. You can put it down and then start on it again later. If it is too upsetting to finish, you can stop and talk to your therapist about it in your next session.

1. What happened to you?

_____

_____

_____

_____

(also available at johnbriere.com)

207

2. What were your feelings when it was happening?

3. What was the worst feeling after it happened?

4. What did you think when it was happening?

208

5. What did you think after it was over?

6. What did you do after it happened?

7. What was the worst thing about what happened?

8. Is there anything about what happened that has made you stronger or better or smarter?

Appendix VI

What Triggers Me? (The Trigger Grid)

What Is a Trigger?

_____

Times I Have Been Triggered

1. _____

2. _____

3. _____

(also available at johnbriere.com)

4. _____

5. _____

6. _____

7. _____

8. _____

9. _____

10. _____

What Kinds of Things Trigger Me? (What Are My Triggers?)

1. _____

2. _____

3. _____

4. _____

5. _____

6. _____

7. _____

8. _____

9. _____

10. _____

What Happened After I Got Triggered?

Trigger #	What I Thought After This Trigger	What I Felt After This Trigger	What I Did After This Trigger
1			
2			
3			
4			

(Continued)

213

(Continued)

Trigger #	What I Thought After This Trigger	What I Felt After This Trigger	What I Did After This Trigger
5			
6			
7			
8			
9			
10			

How I Know I've Been Triggered

1. _____

2. _____

3. _____

4. _____

What I Could Do So That I Wouldn't Get Triggered

1. _____

_____

_____

2. _____

_____

3. _____

_____

_____

_____

5. _____

_____

4.

5.

6.

7.

8.

217

What I Could Do After I Get Triggered That Would Make It Better and I Wouldn't Get So Upset or Mad

1. _____

_____

_____

2. _____

_____

9. _____

_____

10. _____

_____

3.

4.

5.

6.

219

7.

8.

9.

10.

Appendix VII

Outlines for Two ITCT-A Therapy Groups

As described in Chapter 19, ITCT-A therapy groups can be adapted for different settings and to meet the specific needs of different trauma survivors. Presented here are outlines for two such groups: one for sexual abuse survivors in an outpatient clinic and one for traumatized adolescents in a school setting. In both cases, although specific topics and activities are presented, the general principles of trauma-focused group therapy outlined in Chapter 19 should be adhered to.

ITCT-A Group for Adolescent Female Sexual Abuse Survivors

This group intervention for sexually abused younger adolescents, aged 12 to 15, was initially developed by Hernandez and Watkins (2007), and further expanded here. Prerequisites for participation in this 12-week group were recent and/or current ITCT-A individual therapy, ability and commitment to attend all weekly sessions, interest in further processing traumatic experiences, and sufficient affect regulation skills to cope with the possibility of being triggered by others in group sessions.

- Screening

Once referrals are received, prospective members are interviewed and, if accepted into the group, asked to complete relevant pregroup assessment measures, such as the TSCC.

- **Session 1: Introduction to the Group**

Topics and activities: Introductions, overview of the group, confidentiality, and rapport/trust building. Group leaders note that all of the girls are in the group because they have been sexually abused but generally do not expand further during the first session. In some cases, especially when individual therapy has occurred or is continuing through the course of the group sessions, group members may wish to share briefly in this initial session what sexual abuse experiences they have had. This can reduce anxiety associated with having to disclose their traumatic experiences. Rules of confidentiality are reviewed, since some of the girls may attend school together or associate with each other in other contexts. They are asked not to talk about the group outside of the group, although this cannot always be prevented. If outside communication occurs between group members, it is important that they discuss these contacts within the group setting. No sexual relationships between group members are permitted. Although this might seem unlikely for this age group, externalized sexual behavior is not especially uncommon among younger sexual abuse survivors.

In order to reduce anxiety associated with introductions, group members interview each other, in pairs, and then share with the group what that member told her about herself. Group members may also draw self-portraits representing how they feel at the start of group therapy. These self-portraits are kept by the cotherapists and then are compared with self-portraits completed at the end of group therapy. In addition, group members may wish to write personal goals they hope to accomplish with their participation in the group. These are kept by cotherapists, but a copy is returned to the group member so that they can refer to them and revise as needed as they proceed through the group sessions.

- **Session 2: Learning About Sexual Abuse**

Topics and activities: Psychoeducation regarding common reactions to sexual abuse. Members are presented with psychoeducation about the thoughts and feelings often experienced by sexual abuse survivors. Group members are asked to share symptoms that they have observed in themselves and in other sexual abuse survivors. Materials relevant to their trauma experiences, especially child sexual abuse and peer sexual assault, may be distributed and discussed. Materials must be age-appropriate and reviewed by the cotherapists prior to distribution. For example, excerpts from *Don't Give It Away!* (Vanzant, 1999),

My Body, Myself—The What's Happening to My Body Book for Girls (Madaras & Madaras, 2000) and, for male groups, the *What's Happening to My Body Book for Boys* (Madaras & Madaras, 2007) may be used. Sometimes clients also will want to share the names of books or movies relevant to sexual abuse, such as *I Know Why the Caged Bird Sings* (Angelou, 1969) and *Push* (Sapphire, 1996), made into the movie *Precious*.

- **Session 3: Learning About and Expressing Feelings Related to the Trauma**

Topics and activities: Activities to explore and express feelings, especially how clients felt before, during, and after the abuse, and upon disclosure, if relevant. Clients who are more reticent about directly expressing their feelings verbally can be invited to write a letter to the perpetrator or person who did not protect her (with explicit instructions not to send it, at least at that time), write a poem about her feelings, or simply list, on paper, the feelings she had before, during, and after the abuse ended or was disclosed (as for many trauma survivors, the disclosure may be delayed until well after the abuse ended). Group members may choose to use an art activity such as Color-Your-Life (O'Connor, 1983), using different colors in an abstract fashion to depict feelings about the abuse.

- **Session 4: Specific Exploration of Trauma-Related Perceptions**

Topics and activities: Collage or art depicting how they believe others see them, how they view themselves "on the inside," and their feelings about how they were affected by the abuse. For example, group members have made collages with pictures and words depicting the alcoholism of their perpetrator; unseeing, disbelieving, and unprotective family members; other related abuse (physical abuse, domestic violence, community violence); the perpetrator, represented symbolically (e.g., by male in black-and- white-striped prison garb, as a devil or other threatening figure); and other symbols of their trauma and the impacts on them. This tends to be a session where clients focus on visual expression of their experiences, through art, which can then lead to exploration of their trauma narrative and deeper emotional processing. Group members also may create a box with drawings, photos, and words glued on the outside to depict how they believe others see them. Then, in the same fashion, they can draw and/or glue photos and words on the inside of the box to depict how they perceive themselves.

- **Session 5: Specific Exploration of Traumatic Events Experienced**

Topics and activities: Writing a narrative of their abuse history. Generally, per Chapter 12, group members write about their trauma exposure and then read it to the group. Another approach is the "hat game," involving all group members and coleaders writing questions concerning sexual abuse experiences, which are then placed in a container or hat. Each group member draws a question and answers it, after which all other group members also answer the question. If a group member declines to answer, he or she is not pressured to do so but is asked to express the feelings he or she is having and why it is difficult to answer the question. This process often helps the recalcitrant group member to address the question in some manner and, sometimes, to disclose more specific details regarding their experiences and feelings. Especially for less verbal group members, this can be the beginning of the development of a more detailed trauma narrative.

- **Session 6: Specific Exploration of Trauma (Continued)**

Topics and activities: Sharing trauma narratives with the group, per Session 5. This session can begin with a meditation or relaxation period, whereby group members focus on their breath and pay attention to their thoughts (see Chapter 11 for the specific exercise). As they further share their narratives and related feelings, the courage of each member and of others in the group is emphasized. The cotherapists typically invite all group members, before the session ends, to mention something positive that they noticed about each other in the processing of their trauma narrative. As this is also the midpoint of the group, and may involve new trauma-related material, the group therapists may debrief with clients' individual therapists (with completed consent for information, if needed). Group members are also encouraged to evaluate their progress in the group and how they are working toward meeting their goal(s).

- **Session 7: Addressing Thoughts and Feelings About Sex and Sexuality**

Topics and activities: Group members use their narrative to help them talk about sexuality and to integrate their experiences into their lives. It is common during this session for group members to share feelings of being coerced by peers to have sex, difficulties they may have in enjoying consensual sexual experiences with partners, sexual identity issues, and other concerns related to difficulties with intimacy. Older adolescents sometimes disclose that they have increased flashbacks and nightmares when they are engaged in a sexual relationship, even with a partner with whom they feel safe. Psychoeducation materials normalizing sexual feelings and sexual development, describing safer sexual behaviors, and covering other related topics are often helpful at this point.

- Session 8: Begin Exploring Problem Solving

Topics and activities: This session relates in particular to affect regulation and affect tolerance. A general discussion is facilitated about whether there are things survivors can do to improve their lives, decrease the likelihood of further victimization, and get through times when their feelings are triggered. It may be helpful during this session for group members to work on their trigger grids (Chapter 13), as they identify situations that activate memories and feelings, and discuss what they can do to take care of themselves at such times. Group members may also identify those whom they can turn to for support and how they can expand their repertoire of coping skills outside the group (e.g., physical activity, art, music, reading, journal writing, etc.).

- **Session 9: Learning About Boundaries and Safety**

Topics and activities: Developing a specific safety plan regarding the possibility of future abuse or other relational trauma. Adolescents often benefit from discussing potential dangerous situations in their lives that might result in additional physical and sexual assaults. This may also include who they identify as safe versus unsafe in their families, as well as those who can help to keep them safe, such as supportive peers, coaches, teachers, neighbors, etc. Because so much of abuse and neglect occurs within attachment relationships and family systems, this can also be a session wherein group members explore, through family genograms (Chapter 17), how risks to safety, and boundary violations, have occurred intergenerationally within their family. They can then identify ways to change these patterns and be safer in the future.

- **Session 10: Focusing on Self-Esteem**

Topics and activities: Exploring and identifying a client's positive qualities. This session involves discussion of potentially "positive" outcomes of experiencing abuse (e.g., how it has made them stronger, the idea that "If I got through that, I can deal with this. . . .").

Leaders of groups where self-esteem issues are especially paramount may choose to adjust the sequence of session topics, so that this session occurs at an earlier stage. It is often a helpful strategy to include an activity at the beginning and/or end of this session, wherein group members share their perceptions of positive attributes of the other group members. It is especially important that no one be overlooked during this activity.

An example of an activity to increase self-esteem and feelings of being accepted by others, as well as increasing compassion for—and appreciation of—one another, is the "balloon game." This activity is particularly helpful for younger group members and those who are less verbal. Each group member writes one supportive message for each of the other group members, along with one self-care message for themselves, on a piece of paper. Group members fold and insert the piece of paper into a deflated balloon, blow it up, and toss it around the room. Each member then takes one balloon (not their own) and pops it. They then read aloud the messages and discuss any feelings associated with these messages.

- **Session 11: Building Positive Coping Strategies for Painful Memories**

Topics and activities: Learning to avoid being triggered and, if it can't be avoided, what can be done to cope with triggered states (both what they identified on the trigger grid described in Chapter 13 and Appendix VI, as well as additional options they have come up with since completing the grid). In addition to trigger identification and discussion, group members also discuss how to handle relationships so that they can be safe and how to avoid being revictimized in general. Depending on the level of affect regulation capacities in the group, members will sometimes benefit from this session being conducted earlier in the sequence, so that they can be better prepared to do trauma processing later on. If group members are having particular difficulty with this material, cotherapists and group members may wish to extend this topic to more than one session.

- **Session 12: Termination Group**

Topics and activities: Overview/recap of the group. In the last group meeting, members make individual disclosures about what they gained from the group. Members may also create a self-portrait to be compared with the one they created in the first session, review their goals and what they have accomplished or gained from being in the group, as well as review any other material representing their progress in the group, such as music, journal writing, artwork, etc. Group members are encouraged to describe their goals for the future. It is also important that all group members share in a celebration during this session, which typically involves special food brought from home or that the coleaders have provided. At this time, clients can complete post-group measures, such as the TSCC.

If the leaders and the group members so desire, the group may be extended for another four sessions. In such cases, additional topics may include sex roles, stereotypes, and gender issues (using collages, role-plays, and exploration of non-gender-stereotypic behaviors), as well as more on family relationships, including exploration of primary-attachment relationships, caretaking failures and disappointments, role models, and those who did provide nurturance.

School-Based Group for Traumatic Loss/Community Violence

Often, adolescents in school settings with complex trauma exposure and symptoms are not clinically referred, because they have not been identified as traumatized. In other cases, parents or guardians are not amenable to their treatment in a clinical setting, but will consent to school-based group sessions. The following is a general group session outline for younger adolescents (aged 12–14 years) attending middle school who have experienced traumatic loss (e.g., of a parent or close friend) and community violence (e.g., witnessing shootings). The first version of this model was developed at MCAVIC by Karianne Chen, M.S., M.F.T. and Kathleen Watkins, Ph.D., with earlier contributions from other MCAVIC therapists who provided school-based interventions. This model has been further expanded here to include additional components. A version of this model has also been used in an alternative education setting (Neale & Aguila, 2004) with more emphasis on behavior management in the classroom, crisis intervention, acute problem solving, reducing at-risk behavior in the community, and expanding choices. Clients in this environment were fairly guarded and less likely to disclose the full nature of their trauma exposures.

This model is aimed toward younger adolescents because it is difficult to coordinate a weekly school-based group for older youth (i.e., those attending high school)—primarily due to the constraints of academic schedules and difficulties removing students from academic classes. However, this model can be applied to older adolescents in programs where there is a specific focus on assisting troubled youth, for example, residential treatment-oriented schools or day treatment programs that include an academic component.

It is not unusual for youth attending school-based groups to disclose new, or additional, child abuse and neglect experiences, thereby necessitating reports to child protection agencies. For this reason, any school-based intervention like ITCT-A should have a built-in procedure for dealing with child maltreatment reporting, as well as, when possible, an option to refer especially traumatized children to individual therapy.

Presented here is the ITCT-A model for school-based intervention. As was true of the previous group model, the specific topics and activities—as well as the order in which they are applied—may vary according to the specific needs of the youth involved.

- **Screening**

Once referrals are received, prospective members are interviewed and, if accepted into the group, asked to complete relevant pregroup assessment measures, such as the TSCC-A or CBCL.

- **Session 1: Introduction to the Group**

Topics and activities: Introductions, overview of the group, group rules and guidelines that are posted at each group, confidentiality, rapport/trust building, and creating a safe therapeutic environment. Clients are asked to make a brief statement about why they are attending the group (e.g., "I saw a cousin get shot" or "I told my teacher that my dad hits me"). Cotherapists introduce the use of a behavioral chart (this is not always needed for older adolescents) to monitor each member's positive behaviors and means for reinforcement (e.g., stars or stickers for behaviors, then a pizza party for the group when their goal is reached).

Because the group is held at a school site, confidentiality is discussed, including the limits of confidentiality when there is a need to report suspected child abuse or danger to self or others. Group members are instructed to not discuss what is shared in group sessions outside of group. To build cohesiveness, members agree on a group name and make a banner that is posted at each session. Adolescents interview each other in pairs (per the sexual abuse group) and then describe to the other members what they learned about the group member he or she interviewed. Self-portraits are completed and discussed in terms of the client's self-perceptions and feelings regarding participating in the group. Group members describe and/or write their goals for participating in the group. Icebreakers to help build trust and rapport among group members may be used, such as a board game, art therapy, or physical activity such as role-playing a favorite place, animal, or person/hero.

- **Session 2: Building Cohesion and Trust**

Topics and activities: Activities related to identity development, safety in the group, and increasing connection and comfort with other group members.

Group members share briefly why they are in the group and typically participate in activities such as drawings, collages, and/or writing exercises as well as role-plays to facilitate self-expression and reinforce a sense of safety and boundaries. These activities are focused on describing who they are and their interests, likes, and dislikes. Group members each share at least one positive impression about all other group members. Group and individual goals are discussed further and revised as needed.

- **Session 3: Identifying Feelings and Emotions**

Topics and activities: Activities related to identifying and processing feelings associated with traumatic experience(s). Group members typically have not had an opportunity to explore and express their feelings in a supportive environment. They are encouraged to identify their feelings, including those associated with the traumatic experience(s), and explore how they are, in fact, normal reactions to an abnormal/distressing situation (e.g., witnessing community violence, experiencing a traumatic loss). Members connect feelings to their traumatic experiences using games (e.g., Ungame), art (e.g., self-portraits), and writing exercises (e.g., letter to the person they lost, a description of how they felt before the loss versus after). Group members may also role-play distressing situations so they can act out how they express and/or manage feelings. This session begins the process of learning more adaptive ways to express and manage feelings.

- **Session 4: Learning About Trauma and Loss**

Topics and activities: Psychoeducation regarding different types of trauma and their impacts, focusing primarily on community violence and traumatic loss. Information is provided by cotherapists regarding common trauma experiences in the locale where the members live, and trauma-related reactions such as posttraumatic stress, anxiety, depression and sadness, anger, and dissociation that group members might be experiencing. Members are encouraged to begin discussing their past and current reactions to their traumatic experiences. As the majority of group members are likely to have experienced a traumatic loss that may also be related to community violence, they are encouraged to discuss how the commonly acknowledged stages of grief—denial, anger, bargaining, depression, and acceptance—relate to them.

- **Session 5: Anger Management/Affect Regulation**

Topics and activities: Psychoeducation and activities that help group members to identify when they may feel triggered and how to cope with triggered feelings. Since group members attending school-based group sessions typically have not had a course of individual therapy, it is important that they develop affect regulation skills before engaging in cognitive or emotional processing of their actual trauma experiences. Group members identify ways that they get triggered and react (using the trigger grid presented in Appendix VI) and engage in role-plays that help them to understand the perspective of others and explore alternative ways of responding. Group members may also create collages, write, or engage in art activities that address these questions: What makes them angry? How does their behavior affect others? How can they respond differently so that there are no negative consequences? In one store-front group, members viewed videos of admired professional athletes behaving aggressively toward others while playing a sport. Members then discussed the negative consequences for these role models and alternative ways they might have dealt with their anger. Group cotherapists instruct group members in affect regulation skills such as relaxation exercises, breath training, and/or introduce them to meditation (see Chapter 11). This session may be repeated an additional time if group members appear to require further focus on affect regulation skills.

- **Session 6: Specific Exploration of Trauma Events**

Topics and activities: Creating a trauma narrative through drawings, writing, collages, and other group activities. Group members create collages or drawings that relate to their traumatic experiences. Members may also use the "hat game" (see Session 5 in the previous group outline), using questions about traumatic experiences written by group members and coleaders that are then placed in a hat or container. As previously described, each group member draws a question that he or she responds to, with the other members then taking turns answering the question (e.g., "Where were you when your friend/loved one died?"). This intervention has been especially effective with groups in which members are processing more violent, or intrusive, experiences and are having difficulty directly verbalizing them. Group members also may write a letter to the perpetrator or person who did not protect them or support them. Younger group members may also use a board game such as the Ungame to facilitate discussion of specific experiences and feelings.

- **Session 7: Further Processing of the Trauma Narrative**

Topics and activities: Group members further process their trauma narrative per Session 6. Group members add more details to their narrative, including how they are reminded of their traumas, the worst moments of the trauma, and trauma-related symptoms and feelings. Members also may honor the memory of their lost loved one through a poem, drawing, song, or letter. Throughout this and the previous session, group members are encouraged to describe their current feelings when describing what happened to them.

- **Session 8: Cognitive Processing**

Topics and activities: Group members describe cognitions associated with trauma experiences and provide feedback to each other. Group members identify negative beliefs and cognitions related to their trauma narrative. Discussion is focused on cognitive reframing/reconsideration (see Chapter 12), exploring beliefs and distortions about the trauma, and addressing feelings of self-blame, guilt, fears, and powerlessness. Group members provide supportive feedback to each other and, in some groups, engage in role-plays to enact situations associated with distorted cognitive beliefs (e.g., witnessing a friend being shot in a drive-by shooting and realizing that they could not have prevented their friend's death).

- **Session 9: Staying Safe and Recognizing Positive Aspects of Their Lives. [Note: If there are immediate safety issues for group members, this session may be scheduled earlier in the sequence of sessions.]**

Topics and activities: Group members explore ways that they can be safe, including expanding positive coping skills. Some group members may have lost family members or close friends to violence, so they will need to explore ways that they are and can continue to be safe. Group members discuss how they can build a safety repertoire—expanding coping skills and their support systems and developing a safety plan (see Chapter 9). Members may role-play unsafe situations and problem-solve ways to seek help. They may explore ways in which they can prevent further traumatic experiences, by identifying risky situations and dangerous environments and discussing ways to avoid risk of trauma (e.g., avoid a particular neighborhood, prevent risk of gang-related involvement by engaging in an after-school sport or other extracurricular activity).

- **Session 10: Building Self-Esteem and Social Skills**

Topics and activities: Group members participate in activities focused on improving self-perceptions, self-capacities, and a greater sense of empowerment. This session focuses on group members becoming more self-aware and mindful through meditation exercises (see Chapter 11) and "checking in on" their internal states. They may share with each other their responses to statements such as "I am good at . . . ," "I can help others by . . . ," and/or create a collage depicting "I am . . . ," thereby incorporating self-awareness and meaning that has been developed from prior trauma processing. They may also review their trauma narrative in the context of strengths gained, and skills learned, from the trauma. More severely traumatized adolescents often have difficulty forming relationships with others and feeling empathy for others' experiences. As members are able to process their traumatic experiences, feel supported by others, and gain more positive self-identities, they are likely to be more emotionally available to others, have greater empathy, and be able to form stronger relationships, thereby increasing their self-esteem. Group members are encouraged to increase their relatedness with others by listening to other group members share their self-perceptions and by verbalizing positive qualities they observe in each other.

- **Session 11: Caring for Others and Positive Coping**

Topics and activities: Group members explore further ways to increase their relatedness to others and positive coping strategies. Discussion and activities focus on increasing their ability to empathize with others, manage their own reactions, and recognize the gains that they have made. This session is particularly focused on relational aspects of their coping and may also connect to work they are doing (or have done) in individual and/or, occasionally, family therapy. Group members also explore through discussion their current family and peer relationships. Group members may role-play common challenging situations so that they can generate more options for positive coping.

- **Session 12: Making Plans for the Future and Celebration**

Topics and activities: In this session, members review what they have gained in participating in the group and discuss their goals for the future. Group members share stories, journals, artwork, and music reflecting what they have learned about themselves through the group. In some groups, the therapists may keep a folder of each member's artwork, writing exercises, collages, etc., until the last session, when they take their folders home. Group members discuss the extent to which they have been able to process their trauma experiences and related feelings and any changes in self-esteem, coping ability, sense of empowerment, or safety that they have experienced. Members review their initial goals for the group and whether they achieved them, and offer supportive feedback to each other. They discuss plans and goals for the future. To celebrate the group and the work accomplished, members usually choose to share a pizza or cake and ice cream, or they bring a favorite dish to the final session. Group members complete postgroup assessment measures and self-portraits at this final session.

References

Abney, V. D. (2002). Cultural competency in the field of child maltreatment. In J. E. B. Myers, L. Berliner, J. Briere, C. T. Hendrix, T. Reid, & C. Jenny (Eds.), *The APSAC handbook on child maltreatment* (2nd ed.). Newbury Park, CA: Sage.

Achenbach, T. M. (2002). *Achenbach System of Empirically Based Assessment (ASEBA)*. Burlington, VT: Research Center for Children, Youth, & Families.

Allen, J. G. (2001). *Traumatic relationships and serious mental disorders*. Chichester, England: Wiley.

Amaya-Jackson, L., & DeRosa, R. (2007). Treatment considerations for clinicians in applying evidence-based practice to complex presentations in child trauma. *Journal of Traumatic Stress, 20*, 379–390.

American Psychiatric Association. (2000). *Diagnostic and statistical manual of mental disorders* (4th ed.). Washington, DC: Author.

Angelou, M. (1969). *I know why the caged bird sings*. New York: Bantam.

Baldwin, M. W., Fehr, B., Keedian, E., Seidel, M., & Thompson, D. W. (1993). An exploration of the relational schemata underlying attachment styles: Self-report and lexical decision approaches. *Personality and Social Psychology Bulletin, 19*, 746–754.

Bassuk, E. L., & Donelan, B. (2003). Social deprivation. In B. L. Green, M. J. Friedman, J. T. V. M. De Jong, S. D. Solomon, T. M. Keane, J. A. Fairbank, et al. (Eds.), *Trauma interventions in war and peace: Prevention, practice, and policy* (pp. 33–55). New York: Kluwer/Plenum.

Bateman, A., & Fonagy, P. (2004). *Psychotherapy for borderline personality disorder: Mentalization-based treatment*. New York: Oxford University Press.

Berliner, L. (2005). The results of randomized clinical trials move the field forward. *Child Abuse and Neglect, 29*, 103–105.

Berman, A. L., Jobes, D. A., & Silverman, M. M. (2006). *Adolescent suicide: Assessment and intervention* (2nd ed.). Washington, DC: American Psychological Association.

Berthold, S. M. (2000). War traumas and community violence: Psychological, behavioral, and academic outcomes among Khmer refugee adolescents. *Journal of Multicultural Social Work, 8*, 15–46.

Biegel, G. M. (2009). *The stress reduction workbook for teens.* Oakland, CA: Instant Help Books.

Blaustein, M. E., & Kinniburgh, K. M. (2010). *Treating traumatic stress in children & adolescents: How to foster resilience through attachment, self-regulation, and competence.* New York: Guilford.

Bowlby, J. (1988). *A secure base: Parent-child attachment and healthy human development.* New York: Basic Books.

Breslau, N., Davis, G. C., & Andreski, P. (1991). Traumatic events and post-traumatic stress disorder in an urban population of young adults. *Archives of General Psychiatry, 48,* 216–222.

Breslau, N., Wilcox, H. C., Storr, C. L., Lucia, V. C., & Anthony, J. C. (2004). Trauma exposure and posttraumatic stress disorder: A study of youths in urban America. *Journal of Urban Health, 81,* 530–544.

Briere, J. (1992). *Child abuse trauma: Theory and treatment of the lasting effects.* Newbury Park, CA: Sage.

Briere, J. (1995). *Trauma Symptom Inventory (TSI).* Odessa, FL: Psychological Assessment Resources.

Briere, J. (1996a). *Therapy for adults molested as children* (2nd ed.). New York: Springer.

Briere, J. (1996b). *Trauma Symptom Checklist for Children (TSCC).* Odessa, FL: Psychological Assessment Resources.

Briere, J. (2000). *Inventory of Altered Self Capacities (IASC).* Odessa, FL: Psychological Assessment Resources.

Briere, J. (2001). Evaluating treatment outcome. In M. Winterstein & S. R. Scribner (Eds.), *Mental health care for child crime victims: Standards of care task force guidelines* (pp. 10/1–10/6). Sacramento: California Victims Compensation and Government Claims Board, Victims of Crime Program, State of California.

Briere, J. (2002). Treating adult survivors of severe childhood abuse and neglect: Further development of an integrative model. In J. E. B. Myers, L. Berliner, J. Briere, C. T. Hendrix, T. Reid, & C. Jenny (Eds.), *The APSAC handbook on child maltreatment* (2nd ed., pp. 175–202). Newbury Park, CA: Sage.

Briere, J. (2003). Integrating HIV/AIDS prevention activities into psychotherapy for child sexual abuse survivors. In L. Koenig, A. O'Leary, L. Doll, & W. Pequenat (Eds.), *From child sexual abuse to adult sexual risk: Trauma, revictimization, and intervention* (pp. 219–232). Washington, DC: American Psychological Association.

Briere, J. (2004). *Psychological assessment of adult posttraumatic states: Phenomenology, diagnosis, and measurement* (2nd ed.). Washington, DC: American Psychological Association.

Briere, J. (2007). *Trauma Symptom Review for Adolescents.* Unpublished psychological test.

Briere, J. (2011). *Trauma Symptom Inventory-2 (TSI-2).* Odessa, FL: Psychological Assessment Resources.

Briere, J. (in press). Compassion and mindfulness in psychotherapy for trauma survivors. In C. K. Germer & R. D. Siegel (Eds.), *Compassion and wisdom in psychotherapy.* New York: Guilford.

Briere, J. (in progress). *Trauma symptom scales for adolescents.* Unpublished psychological test.

Briere, J., & Gil, E. (1988). Self-mutilation in clinical and general population samples: Prevalence, correlates, and functions. *American Journal of Orthopsychiatry, 68,* 609–620.

Briere, J., Hodges, M., & Godbout, N. (2010). Traumatic stress, affect dysregulation, and dysfunctional avoidance: A structural equation model. *Journal of Traumatic Stress, 23,* 767–774.

Briere, J., & Rickards, S. (2007). Self-awareness, affect regulation, and relatedness: Differential sequels of childhood versus adult victimization experiences. *Journal of Nervous and Mental Disease, 195,* 497–503.

Briere, J., & Scott, C. (2006). *Principles of trauma therapy: A guide to symptoms, evaluation, and treatment.* Thousand Oaks, CA: Sage.

Briere, J., & Scott, C. (in press). *Principles of Trauma Therapy, 2nd edition.* Thousand Oaks, CA: Sage.

Briere, J., Scott, C., & Weathers, F. W. (2005). Peritraumatic and persistent dissociation in the presumed etiology of PTSD. *American Journal of Psychiatry, 162,* 2295–2301.

Briere, J., & Spinazzola, J. (2005). Phenomenology and psychological assessment of complex posttraumatic states. *Journal of Traumatic Stress, 18,* 401–412.

Briere, J., & Spinazzola, J. (2009). Standardized assessment of complex posttraumatic disturbance in childhood, adolescence, and adulthood. In C. Courtois & J. Ford (Eds.), *Complex traumatic stress disorders: An evidence-based clinician's guide.* New York: Guilford.

Bryant, R. A., & Harvey, A. G. (2000). *Acute stress disorder: A handbook of theory, assessment, and treatment.* Washington, DC: American Psychological Association.

Bryant-Davis, T. (2005). *Thriving in the wake of trauma: A multicultural guide.* Westport, CT: Praeger.

Butcher, J. N., Williams, C. L., Graham, J. R., Archer, R. P., Tellegen, A., Ben-Porath, Y. S., et al. (1992). *MMPI-A (Minnesota Multiphasic Personality Inventory–Adolescent): Manual for administration, scoring, and interpretation.* Minneapolis: University of Minnesota Press.

Byerly, C. M. (1985). *The mother's book: How to survive the incest of your child.* Dubuque, IA: Kendall/Hunt.

Byng-Hall, J. (1999). Family and couple therapy: Toward greater security. In J. Cassidy & P. R. Shaver (Eds.), *Handbook of attachment: Theory, research and clinical applications* (pp. 625–645). New York: Guilford.

Carter, R. T. (2007). Racism and psychological and emotional injury: Recognizing and assessing race-based traumatic stress. *Counseling Psychologist, 35,* 13–105.

Center on Budget and Policy Priorities. (2010). *An update on state budget cuts.* Retrieved from http://www.cbpp.org/cms/index.cfm?fa=view&id=1214.

Chen, A., Keith, V., Airriess, C., Li, W., & Leong, K. J. (2007). Economic vulnerability, discrimination, and Hurricane Katrina: Health among black Katrina survivors in eastern New Orleans. *Journal of the American Psychiatric Nurses Association, 13,* 257–266.

Classen, C. C., Palesh, O. G., & Aggarwal, R. (2005). Sexual revictimization: A review of the empirical literature. *Trauma, Violence, and Abuse: A Review Journal, 6,* 103–129.

Cloitre, M., Cohen, L. R., & Koenen, K. C. (2006). *Treating survivors of childhood abuse: Psychotherapy for the interrupted life.* New York: Guilford.

Cloitre, M., Koenen, K. C., Cohen, L. R., & Han, H. (2002). Skills training in affective and interpersonal regulation followed by exposure: A phase-based treatment for PTSD related to childhood abuse. *Journal of Consulting and Clinical Psychology, 70,* 1067–1074.

Cloitre, M., Stovall-McClough, K. C., Miranda, R., & Chemtob, C. M. (2004). Therapeutic alliance, negative mood regulation, and treatment outcome in child abuse-related posttraumatic stress disorder. *Journal of Consulting and Clinical Psychology, 72,* 411–416.

Cloitre, M., Stovall-McClough, K. C., Nooner, K., Zorba, P., Cherry, S., Jackson, C. L., et al. (2010). Treatment for PTSD related to childhood abuse: A randomized controlled trial. *American Journal of Psychiatry, 167,* 915–924.

Cochrane, S. V. (2005). Evidence-based assessment with men. *Journal of Clinical Psychology, 61,* 646–666.

Cohen, J. A., Berliner, L., & March, J. E. (2000). Guidelines for treatment of PTSD: Treatment of children and adolescents. *Journal of Traumatic Stress, 13,* 566–568.

Cohen, J. A., Deblinger, E., Mannarino, A. P., & De Arellano, M. A. (2001). The importance of culture in treating abused and neglected children: An empirical review. *Child Maltreatment, 6,* 148–157.

Cohen, J. A., Mannarino, A., & Knudsen, K. (2005). Treating sexually abused children: One year follow-up of a randomized controlled trial. *Child Abuse & Neglect, 29,* 135–145.

Cole, P. M., & Putnam, F. W. (1992). Effect of incest on self and social functioning: A developmental psychopathology perspective. *Journal of Consulting and Clinical Psychology, 60,* 174–184.

Cook, A., Spinazzola, J., Ford, J., Lanktree, C., Blaustein, M., Cloitre, M., et al. (2005). Complex trauma in children and adolescents. *Psychiatric Annals, 35,* 390–398.

Courtois, C., & Ford, J. (Eds.). (2009). *Treating complex traumatic stress disorders: An evidence based guide.* New York: Guilford.

Cummings, S., & Monti, D. J. (Eds.). (1993). *Gangs: The origins and impact of contemporary youth gangs in the United States.* Albany: State University of New York Press.

Dalenberg, C. J. (2000). *Countertransference and the treatment of trauma.* Washington, DC: American Psychological Association.

DeRosa, R., & Pelcovitz, D. (2008). Group treatment for chronically traumatized adolescents: Igniting SPARCS of change. In D. Brom, R. Pat-Horenczuk, & J. D. Ford (Eds.), *Treating traumatized children: Risk, resilience, and recovery* (pp. 225–239). London: Routledge.

Dionne, R., Davis, B., Sheeber, L., & Madrigal, L. (2009). Initial evaluation of a cultural approach to implementation of evidence-based parenting interventions in American Indian communities. *Journal of Community Psychology, 37,* 911–921.

Elliott, D. M. (1994). Impaired object relationships in professional women molested as children. *Psychotherapy, 31,* 79–86.

Elliott, D. M., & Briere, J. (1994). Forensic sexual abuse evaluations of older children: Disclosures and symptomatology. *Behavioral Sciences and the Law, 12,* 261–277.

Exner, J. E., Jr. (1974). *The Rorschach: A comprehensive system* (Vol. 1). New York: John Wiley.

Farley, M. (Ed.). (2003). *Prostitution, trafficking, and traumatic stress.* New York: Haworth Maltreatment & Trauma Press.

Fisher, B. S., Cullen, F. T., & Turner, M. G. (2000). *The sexual victimization of college women.* Washington, DC: Bureau of Justice Statistics and National Institute of Justice, U.S. Department of Justice.

Foa, E. B., & Kozak, M. J. (1986). Emotional processing of fear: Exposure to corrective information. *Psychological Bulletin, 99,* 20–35.

Foa, E. B., Molnar, C., & Cashman, L. (1995). Changes in rape narrative during exposure therapy for posttraumatic stress disorder. *Journal of Traumatic Stress, 8,* 675–690.

Foa, E. B., & Rothbaum, B. O. (1998). *Treating the trauma of rape: Cognitive-behavioral therapy for PTSD.* New York: Guilford.

Fontes, L. A. (2005). *Child abuse and culture: Working with diverse families.* New York: Guilford.

Ford, J. D. (2007). Trauma, posttraumatic stress disorder, and ethnoracial minorities: Toward diversity and cultural competence in principles and practices. *Clinical Psychology: Science and Practice, 15,* 62–67.

Friedrich, W. N. (1990). *Psychotherapy of sexually abused children and their families.* New York: W. W. Norton.

Friedrich, W. N. (2002). *Psychological assessment of sexually abused children and their families.* Thousand Oaks, CA: Sage.

Germer, C. K., Siegel, R. D., & Fulton, P. R. (Eds.). (2005). *Mindfulness and psychotherapy.* New York: Guilford.

Giaconia, R. M., Reinherz, H. Z., Silverman, A. B., Pakiz, B., Frost, A. K., & Cohen, E. (1995). Traumas and posttraumatic stress disorder in a community population of older adolescents. *Journal of the American Academy of Child and Adolescent Psychiatry, 34,* 1369–1380.

Gil, E. (1996). *Treating abused adolescents.* New York: Guilford.

Gil, E. (2006). *Helping abused and traumatized children: Integrating directive and non-directive approaches.* New York: Guilford.

Gil, E., & Drewes, A. (Eds.). (2005). *Cultural issues in play therapy.* New York: Guilford.

Gilbert, P. (2009). Introducing compassion-focused therapy. *Advances in Psychiatric Treatment, 15,* 199–208.

Goodman, T. A. (2005). Working with children: Beginner's mind. In C. K. Germer, R. D. Siegel, & P. R. Fulton (Eds.), *Mindfulness and psychotherapy* (pp. 197–219). New York: Guilford.

Greenland, S. K. (2010). *The mindful child: How to help your kid manage stress and become happier, kinder, and more compassionate.* New York: Free Press.

Habib, M. (2009, April). *Structured Psychotherapy for Adolescents Responding to Chronic Stress (SPARCS).* In C. Lanktree (Chair), *Treatment of complex trauma: Multiple approaches, practical applications, and cultural adaptations.* Pre-Meeting Institute conducted at the All-Network Conference of the National Child Traumatic Stress Network, Orlando, FL.

Habib, M., Labruna, V., & Newman, J. (in preparation). Implementation of a manually guided group treatment: A phenomenological approach to treating traumatized adolescents in residential settings. *Journal of Child and Adolescent Trauma.*

Harris, R. H. (1996). *It's perfectly normal: Changing bodies, growing up, sex, and sexual health.* Somerville, MA: Candlewick.

Herman, J. L. (1992). Complex PTSD: A syndrome in survivors of prolonged and repeated trauma. *Journal of Traumatic Stress, 5,* 377–392.

Herman, J. L., Perry, C., van der Kolk, B. A. (1989). Childhood trauma in borderline personality disorder. *American Journal of Psychiatry, 146,* 490–494.

Hernandez, S., & Watkins, K. (2007). *Group therapy for sexually abused female adolescents.* Unpublished manuscript.

Hughes, D. A. (2007). *Attachment-focused family therapy.* New York: W. W. Norton.

Huppert, F. A., & Johnson, D. M. (2010). A controlled trial of mindfulness training in schools: The importance of practice for an impact on well-being. *The Journal of Positive Psychology, 5,* 264–274.

Janoff-Bulman, B. (1992). *Shattered assumptions: Towards a new psychology of trauma.* New York: Free Press.

Jones, R. T., Hadder, J. M., Carvajal, F., Chapman, S., & Alexander, A. (2006). Conducting research in diverse, minority, and marginalized communities. In F. Norris, S. Galea, M. J. Friedman, & P. Watson (Eds.), *Methods for disaster mental health research* (pp. 265–277). New York: Guilford.

Jordan, C. E., Nietzel, M. T., Walker, R., & Logan, T. K. (2004). *Intimate partner violence: Clinical and practice issues for mental health professionals.* New York: Springer.

Karver, M. S., Shirk, S., Handelsman, J., Fields, S., Gudmundsen, G., McMakin, D., et al. (2008). Relationship processes in youth psychotherapy: Measuring alliance, alliance-building behaviors, and client involvement. *Journal of Emotional and Behavioral Disorders, 16*(1), 15–28.

Kessler, R. C., Sonnega, A., Bromet, E., Hughes, M., & Nelson, C. B. (1995). Posttraumatic stress disorder in the National Comorbidity Survey. *Archives of General Psychiatry, 52,* 1048–1060.

Koenig, L., O'Leary, A., Doll, L., & Pequenat, W. (Eds.). (2003). *From child sexual abuse to adult sexual risk: Trauma, revictimization, and intervention.* Washington, DC: American Psychological Association.

Kovacs, M. (1992). *Children Depression Inventory (CDI) manual.* Toronto, ON: Multi-Health Systems.

Lambert, M. J., & Barley, D. E. (2001). Research summary on the therapeutic relationship and psychotherapy outcome. *Psychotherapy, 38,* 357–361.

Lanktree, C. B. (2008, August). *Cultural adaptations to complex trauma treatment with children and adolescents.* Paper presented at the annual meeting of the American Psychological Association, Boston, MA.

Lanktree, C. B., & Briere, J. (1995). Outcome of therapy for sexually abused children: A repeated measures study. *Child Abuse & Neglect, 19,* 1145–1155.

Lanktree, C. B., & Briere, J. (2008a). Assessment—Psychometric—Child. In G. Reyes, J. Elhai, & J. Ford (Eds.), *Encyclopedia of psychological trauma* (pp. 58–62). New York: Wiley.

Lanktree, C. B., & Briere, J. (2008b). Integrative Treatment of Complex Trauma for Children (ITCT-C): A guide for the treatment of multiply traumatized children aged eight to twelve years. Unpublished treatment manual. Long Beach, CA: MCAVIC-USC Child and Adolescent Trauma Program, National Child Traumatic Stress Network.

Lanktree, C. B., Briere, J., Godbout, N., Hodges, M., Chen, K., Trimm, L., et al. (2010). *Treating multi-traumatized, socially-marginalized children: Results of a naturalistic treatment outcome study.* Unpublished manuscript, University of Southern California.

Lanktree, C. B., Gilbert, A. M., Briere, J., Taylor, N., Chen, K., Maida, C. A., et al. (2008). Multi-informant assessment of maltreated children: Convergent and discriminant validity of the TSCC and TSCYC. *Child Abuse & Neglect, 32,* 621–625.

Linehan, M. M. (1993). *Cognitive-behavioral treatment of borderline personality disorder.* New York: Guilford.

Madaras, L., & Madaras. A. (2000). *My body, myself—The what's happening to my body book for girls.* New York: Newmarket Press.

Madaras, L., & Madaras, A. (2007). *My body, myself—The what's happening to my body book for boys.* New York: Newmarket Press.

Macbeth, B. L., Sugar, J. A., & Pataki, C. S. (2009, May). *Incidence of trauma exposure in a child psychiatric outpatient setting.* Poster presentation at the annual meeting of the Association for Psychological Science, San Francisco, CA.

Marsella, A. J., Friedman, M. J., Gerrity, E. T., & Scurfield, R. M. (Eds.). (1996). *Ethnocultural aspects of posttraumatic stress disorder: Issues, research, and clinical applications.* Washington, DC: American Psychological Association.

Martin, D. J., Garske, J. P., & Davis, M. K. (2000). Relation of the therapeutic alliance with outcome and other variables: A meta-analytic review. *Journal of Consulting and Clinical Psychology, 68,* 438–450.

McArthur, D. S., & Roberts, G. E. (1982). *Roberts Apperception Test for Children manual.* Los Angeles: Western Psychological Services.

McGoldrick, M., Gerson, R., & Schellenberger, S. (1999). *Genograms: Assessment and intervention* (2nd ed.). New York: W. W. Norton.

McGoldrick, M., Giordano, J., & Pierce, J. K. (Eds.). (1996). *Ethnicity & family therapy* (2nd ed.). New York: Guilford.

McKay, M. M., Lynn, C. J., & Bannon, W. M. (2005). Understanding inner city child mental health need and trauma exposure: Implications for preparing urban service providers. *American Journal of Orthopsychiatry, 75*, 201–210.

Mendelsohn, M., Herman, J., Schatzow, E., Coco, M., Kallivayalil, C., & Levitan, J. (2011). *The trauma recovery group: A practice guide.* New York: Guilford.

Molnar, B. E., Shade, S. B., Kral, A. H., Booth, R. E., & Watters, J. K. (1998). Suicidal behavior and sexual/physical abuse among street youth. *Child Abuse and Neglect, 22*, 213–222.

Morey, L. C. (2008). *Personality assessment inventory–adolescent (PAI-A).* Lutz, FL: Psychological Assessment Resources.

Myers, J. E. B. (2002). The legal system and child protection. In J. E. B. Myers, L. Berliner, J. Briere, C. T. Hendrix, C. Jenny, & T. Reid (Eds.), *The APSAC handbook on child maltreatment* (pp. 305–325). Thousand Oaks, CA: Sage.

Myers, J. E. B., Berliner, L., Briere, J., Hendrix, C. T., Reid, T., & Jenny, C. (Eds.). (2002). *The APSAC handbook on child maltreatment* (2nd ed.). Thousand Oaks, CA: Sage.

Nader, K. (2007). *Understanding and assessing trauma in children and adolescents: Measures, methods, and youth in context.* New York: Rutledge.

Najavits, L. M. (2002). *Seeking safety: A treatment manual for PTSD and substance abuse.* New York: Guilford.

Najavits, L. M., Sullivan, T. P., Schmitz, M., Weiss, R. D., & Lee, C. S. N. (2004). Treatment utilization of women with PTSD and substance dependence. *American Journal of Addictions, 13*, 215–224.

Neal, S., & Aguila, J. C. (2004). *Intensive, short-term, trauma-focused behavioral interventions for at-risk traumatized youth.* Workshop presented at the 12th Annual Colloquium of the American Professional Society on Abuse of Children, Hollywood, CA.

O'Connor, K. (1983). The color-your-life technique. In C. E. Schaefer & K. J. O'Connor (Eds.), *Handbook of play therapy, volume two: Advances and innovations.* New York: John Wiley.

Ouimette, P., & Brown, P. J. (2003). *Trauma and substance abuse: Causes, consequences, and treatment of comorbid disorders.* Washington, DC: American Psychological Association.

Paddison, P. L., Einbender, R. G., Maher, E., & Strain, J. J. (1993). Group treatment with incest survivors. In P. L. Paddison (Ed.), *Treatment of adult survivors of incest* (pp. 35–54). Washington, DC: American Psychiatric Press.

Pearce, J. W., & Pezzot-Pearce, T. D. (2007). *Psychotherapy of abused and neglected children.* New York: Guilford.

Pearlman, L. A., & Courtois, C. A. (2005). Clinical applications of the attachment framework: Relational treatment of complex trauma. *Journal of Traumatic Stress, 18*, 449–459.

Pennebaker, J. W. (1993). Putting stress into words: Health, linguistic, and therapeutic implications. *Behaviour Research and Therapy, 31,* 539–548.

Perez, M. C., & Fortuna, L. (2005). Psychosocial stressors, psychiatric diagnoses and utilization of mental health services. *Journal of Immigrant and Refugee Services, 3,*107–124.

Pitman, R. K, Altman, B., Greenwald, E., Longpre, R. E., Macklin, M. L., Poiré, R. E., et al. (1991). Psychiatric complications during flooding therapy for posttraumatic stress disorder. *Journal of Clinical Psychiatry, 52,* 17–20.

Polusny, M. A., Rosenthal, M. Z., Aban, I., & Follette, V. M. (2004). Experiential avoidance as a mediator of the effects of adolescent sexual victimization on negative adult outcomes. *Violence and Victims, 19,* 109–120.

Putnam, F. (2003). Ten-year research update review: Child sexual abuse. *Journal of the American Academy of Child and Adolescent Psychiatry, 43,* 269–278.

Pynoos, R., Rodriguez, N., Steinberg, A., Stuber, M., & Frederick, C. (1998). *The UCLA PTSD Index for DSM IV.* Los Angeles: UCLA Trauma Psychiatry Program.

Pynoos, R. S., Steinberg, A. M., & Piacentini, J. C. (1999). A developmental psychopathology model of childhood traumatic stress and intersection with anxiety disorders. *Biological Psychiatry, 46,* 1542–1554.

Rayburn, N. R., Wenzel, S. L., Elliott, M. N., Hambarsoomians, K., Marshall, G. N., & Tucker, J. S. (2005). Trauma, depression, coping, and mental health service seeking among impoverished women. *Journal of Consulting and Clinical Psychology, 73,* 667–677.

Renzetti, C. M., & Curran, D. J. (2002). *Women, men, and society* (5th ed.). Boston: Allyn & Bacon.

Resick, P. A., & Schnicke, M. K. (1993). *Cognitive processing therapy for rape victims: A treatment manual.* Newbury Park, CA: Sage.

Reynolds, C. R., & Kamphaus, R. W. (2006). *Behavior assessment system for children* (2nd ed.). New York: Pearson.

Reynolds, W. M. (1988). *Suicide ideation questionnaire professional manual.* Odessa, FL: Psychological Assessment Resources.

Rimm, D. C., & Masters, J. C. (1979). *Behavior therapy: Techniques and empirical findings.* New York: Academic Press.

Roid, G. H., & Fitts, W. H. (1994). *Tennessee Self-Concept Scale* [Rev. manual]. Los Angeles: Western Psychological Services.

Runtz, M., & Briere, J. (1986). Adolescent "acting out" and childhood history of sexual abuse. *Journal of Interpersonal Violence, 1,* 326–333.

Saltzman, A., & Goldin, P. (2008). Mindfulness based stress reduction for school-age children. In S. C. Hayes & L. A. Greco (Eds.), *Acceptance and mindfulness interventions for children, adolescents, and families* (pp. 139–161). Oakland, CA: New Harbinger.

Saltzman, W. R., Babayon, M., Lester, P., Beardslee, W., & Pynoos, R. S. (2008). Family-based treatments for child traumatic stress: A review and current innovations. In D. Brom, R. Pat-Horenczyk, & J. D. Ford (Eds.), *Treating traumatized children: Risk, resilience, and recovery* (pp. 240–254). London: Routledge.

Sapphire. (1996). *Push*. New York: Vintage Contemporaries/Vintage Books.

Saxe, G. N., Ellis, B. H., & Kaplow, J. B. (2007). *Collaborative treatment of traumatized children and teens: The trauma systems therapy approach*. New York: Guilford.

Schneir, A., Stefanidis, N., Mounier, C., Ballin, D., Gailey, D., Carmichael, H., et al. (2007). Trauma among homeless youth. *Culture and Trauma Brief*. Washington DC: National Child Traumatic Stress Network. (http://www.nctsnet.org/nctsn_assets/pdfs/culture_and_trauma_brief_v2n1_HomelessYouth.pdf)

Schore, A. N. (2003). *Affect dysregulation and disorders of the self*. New York: W. W. Norton.

Schwab-Stone, M., Ayers, T., Kasprow, W., Voyce, C., Barone, C., Shriver, T., et al. (1995). No safe haven: A study of violence exposure in an urban community. *Journal of the American Academy of Child and Adolescent Psychiatry, 34,* 1343–1352.

Semple, R. J., & Lee, J. (in press). *Mindfulness-based cognitive therapy for anxious children: A manual for treating childhood anxiety*. Oakland, CA: New Harbinger.

Siegel, D. J. (1999). *The developing mind: Toward a neurobiology of interpersonal experience*. New York: Guilford.

Singer, M. I., Anglin, T. M., Song, L. Y., & Lunghofer, L. (1995). Adolescents' exposure to violence and associated symptoms of psychological trauma. *Journal of the American Medical Association, 273,* 477–482.

Smikle, C. B., Satin, A. J., Dellinger, C. L., & Hankins, G. D. (1995). Physical and sexual abuse. A middle-class concern? *Journal of Reproductive Medicine, 40,* 347–350.

Stamatakos, M., & Campo, J. V. (2010). Psychopharmacologic treatment of traumatized youth. *Current Opinion in Pediatrics, 22,* 599–604.

Stern, D. N. (2000). *The interpersonal world of the infant: A view from psychoanalysis & developmental psychology*. New York: Basic Books.

Study estimates 1/3 of state families living in poverty. (2001, July 25). *Long Beach Press-Telegram*, p. A1.

Sugar, J. A., & Ford, J. D., (accepted with revisions). Peritraumatic dissociation and posttraumatic stress disorder in psychiatrically impaired youth. *Journal of Traumatic Stress*.

Taylor, S. (2003). Outcome predictors for three PTSD treatments: Exposure therapy, EMDR, and relaxation training. *Journal of Cognitive Psychotherapy, 17,* 149–161.

Teasdale, J. D., Segal, Z. V., & Williams, M. G. (1995). How does cognitive therapy prevent depressive relapse and why should attentional control (mindfulness training) help? *Behaviour Research and Therapy, 33,* 25–39.

Thompson, S. J., McManus, H., & Voss, T. (2006). Posttraumatic stress disorder and substance abuse among youth who are homeless: Treatment issues and implications. *Brief Treatment and Crisis Intervention, 6,* 206–217.

Tiet, Q. Q., Finney, J. W., & Moos, R. H. (2006). Recent sexual abuse, physical abuse, and suicide attempts among male veterans seeking psychiatric treatment. *Psychiatric Services, 57,* 107–113.

van der Kolk, B. A. (2005). Developmental trauma disorder: Toward a rational diagnosis for children with complex trauma histories. *Psychiatric Annals, 35,* 401–408.

van der Kolk, B. A., Roth, S. H., Pelcovitz, D., Sunday, S., & Spinazzola, J. (2005). Disorders of extreme stress: The empirical foundation of a complex adaptation to trauma. *Journal of Traumatic Stress, 18,* 389–399.

Vanzant, I. (1999). *Don't give it away!* New York: Fireside.

Walsh, R. (1988). Two Asian psychologies and their implications for Western psychotherapists. *American Journal of Psychotherapy, 42,* 543–560.

Webber, M. (1991). *Street kids: The tragedy of Canada's runaways.* Toronto, ON: University of Toronto Press.

Widom, C., & Kuhns, J. (1996). Childhood victimization and subsequent risk for promiscuity, prostitution, and teenage pregnancy: A prospective study. *American Journal of Public Health, 86,* 1607–1612.

Yalom, I. D., & Leszcz, M. (2005). *The theory and practice of group psychotherapy* (5th ed.). New York: Basic Books.

Yates, G. L., MacKenzie, R., Pennbridge, J., & Cohen, E. (1988). A risk profile comparison of runaway and non-runaway youth. *American Journal of Public Health, 75,* 820–821.

Yates, G. L., Mackenzie, R. G., Pennbridge, J., & Swofford, A. (1991). A risk profile comparison of homeless youth involved in prostitution and homeless youth not involved. *Journal of Adolescent Health, 12,* 545–548.

Yehuda, R. (2004). Risk and resilience in posttraumatic stress disorder. *Journal of Clinical Psychiatry, Suppl 1,* 29–36.

Young, B. H., Ruzek, J. I., & Ford, J. D. (1999). Cognitive-behavioral group treatment for disaster-related PTSD. In B. H. Young & D. D. Blake (Eds.), *Group treatments for post-traumatic stress disorder* (pp. 149–200). Philadelphia: Brunner/Mazel.

Zlotnick, C., Donaldson, D., Spirito, A., & Pearlstein, T. (1997). Affect regulation and suicide attempts in adolescent inpatients. *Journal of the American Academy of Child & Adolescent Psychiatry, 36,* 793–798.

Index

Pages followed by f, t, or n indicate a figure, table, or note respectively.

About the Authors

John N. Briere, Ph.D., is an associate professor of psychiatry and psychology at the Keck School of Medicine, University of Southern California, and director of the Psychological Trauma Program at LAC+USC Medical Center. He is a past president of the International Society for Traumatic Stress Studies and recipient of the Outstanding Contributions to the Science of Trauma Psychology Award from the American Psychological Association. Designated as a "Highly Cited Researcher" by the Institute for Scientific Information, he is the author or coauthor of a number of books, articles, chapters, and psychological tests in the areas of trauma, child abuse, and interpersonal violence. His website is www.johnbriere.com.

Cheryl B. Lanktree, Ph.D., is a licensed clinical psychologist in private practice and a clinical associate professor of psychiatry and the behavioral sciences at the Keck School of Medicine, University of Southern California. She was the principal investigator for the federally funded program that piloted the treatment model described in this book. Dr. Lanktree has published various papers and chapters, as well as two treatment manuals, on the assessment and treatment of trauma in children and adolescents. The developer of Integrative Treatment of Complex Trauma (ITCT), she provides workshops and trainings nationally and internationally. Her website is www.cblanktree.com.